# ROTHERHAM

## at War and Peace
### Life in the Area from 1914–1945

## MARGARET DRINKALL

The History Press

First published 2011

The History Press
The Mill, Brimscombe Port
Stroud, Gloucestershire, GL5 2QG
www.thehistorypress.co.uk

ISBN 978 0 7524 6295 0

Typesetting and origination by The History Press
Printed in Great Britain

# CONTENTS

# FOREWORD

**M**argaret Drinkall has delved into the archives of the *Rotherham Advertiser* to underpin her research into the years 1914–1945; years which challenged the ingenuity, courage and stoicism of the community.

Combining anecdotal accounts and the narrative from the *Advertiser* of the day, ensures that the passage of time is not allowed to diminish the real pain and suffering of the period, and the legacy of deprivation which lingered long after the last bullet had been fired.

The author draws heavily on testimonies that vividly recall the hardship, bravery, patriotism and determination of the Rotherham community. Photographs of prisoners of war, as well as of soldiers and seaman listed as killed in action or missing, brought home the sacrifices being endured. An interview with prisoner seaman George Beal in the *Advertiser* in November 1918, revealed that being a POW was much harsher than the sanitised celluloid versions later featured on the big screen in such popular films as *Escape to Victory, The Great Escape, Stalag 17* and *Colditz*.

Returning First World War soldiers and seamen had been promised 'a land fit for heroes', but instead found overcrowding, unemployment and housing shortages, with up to three families living in the same house. The inter-war years were not without hardship either, with strikes, riots, the rise of Bolshevism and a real fear of revolution. However, the *Advertiser* reported that the first Remembrance Day in 1919 was 'soul warming', as traffic stopped and 'men took off their hats and every person stood perfectly rigid and even the children and horses remained unmoving.' The drums of war were beating through the 1930s, and on 3 September 1939 Prime Minister Neville Chamberlain declared that Britain was at war with Germany.

Unlike the First World War, where the only aerial threat came from the occasional, but notoriously unreliable, zeppelin, the 1939–45 conflict brought the very real danger of gas and air attacks and, as a result, the children of Rotherham were evacuated from the congested urban areas to rural Wentworth, Thurcroft, Ravenfield, Hooton Roberts, Aston, Anston, Woodsetts, Harthill and Thorpe Salvin. Adding to the logistical difficulties, hundreds of children from the Greater London area were sent to the town. Rationing was introduced and women were called on, not only to work in the fields raising crops, but to take the place of their husbands – who had been called up to fight – in munitions factories and the steelworks, while trying to maintain a semblance of home and family life.

Throughout, the people of Rotherham relied on the *Advertiser* to provide details on how the war was progressing, though more and more the reports had to be censored to avoid giving sensitive information to the enemy. For the same reason, little was printed about industries for fear of attracting bombing raids.

Margaret Drinkall has set out in harrowing and graphic detail the reality of the two world wars, contrasting the individual experiences with the national picture, and chronicling the uneasy years of peace, which brought their own challenges and tales of hardship. Those who lived through the difficult times between 1914 and 1945 will find echoes of their past, while the post-war generations will find this a fascinating and insightful account of the traumatic thirty-one years which helped fashion the Rotherham of today.

Doug Melloy, Editor, *Rotherham Advertiser*, 2011

# ACKNOWLEDGEMENTS

In July 1922, the local newspaper the *Rotherham Advertiser* requested that the people of Rotherham should remember the impact that the First World War had on the town and the changes which had been made throughout those years. They recommended that:

> ...it be placed on record how the town was transformed by its army battalions, the recruitment drives which took place, the massive loss of life, food shortages, queues and rationing, how women were performing men's work and the zeppelin raids. Cannot the Corporation set about the task of producing such a book?

Although the Corporation was unable to produce such a book at the time, this book is my own small attempt to try to redress that balance. I have also extended it to cover the Second World War, as well as the interwar period. This book is not intended to concentrate on the many battles which took place during the war years, as other historians have more than adequately covered such matters. My intention is to cover the impact that the years 1914–45 had on the people of Rotherham.

During this period we see, as never before, mechanised warfare bringing the battlefields closer to home. Men fighting at the front were for the first time aware that their families were at risk of bombing raids at home. During the war period air raids and blackouts became the norm, and the fear engendered by this type of warfare was felt in the town. Advances in technical warfare were progressed quickly to combat enemy superiority. Aircraft, which were originally developed to attack the zeppelins, were later responsible for taking war into the air. In the Second World War, tanks replaced cavalry horses and through both wars Rotherham saw the rise of munitions manufacture.

War destroys families, and the most important impact would be felt by the townspeople themselves, waiting to hear news of loved ones away fighting. From the research completed for this book, I have discovered that soldiers generally experienced real camaraderie in their daily trials risking life and limb; but this was coupled with the fear and expectation that life could be extinguished in a second. This gave rise to British 'Tommy' closeness amongst comrades, who were truly brothers in arms.

I have extensively referred to the *Rotherham Advertiser* within this book, as it is a very powerful resource for anyone wishing to know more about the town for the last 170 years. The *Advertiser* was a prominent voice during this time, calling for a war memorial to be erected in the town as early as October 1916. They also asked the authorities to establish a Remembrance Day for the 1 July 1916, when the 'big push' had claimed millions of lives, stating that, 'this day will go down in history for the numbers of Rotherham men that died'. There are many reports of soldiers having the newspaper sent out to them and some described reading the *Advertiser* in the trenches as well as when in sunnier climes. Often it was the only way for soldiers to find out about other battles that were being fought elsewhere. One can imagine the way the paper would also have brought back to them the sights of the town and a touch of home whilst among those terrible conditions.

All the photographs in this book are used with the kind permission of the *Rotherham Advertiser* or the Rotherham Archives and Local Studies Department. Without their advice and help this book could not have been written. The only exception is the photograph of the Kilnhurst colliery disaster, which the *Sheffield Telegraph* has given me permission to reproduce here.

Inevitably, the newspaper contained many reports from parents of the young men who were reported missing while fighting in the war. Tragically, amongst the pictures of the men winning medals are the young men and women who were reported dead or injured. We are indeed fortunate that we have these precious records, as when the paper shortage was announced in February 1916 many local newspapers went out of circulation for the rest of the war. The *Advertiser* carried on to the end though. When the announcement of the end of the hostilities was pinned up in the window of the *Advertiser* offices in Henry Street, for all to see, it was reported that people were constantly coming into the building to ask if it was true, to ensure that the news was accurate and not a prank. Thankfully the *Rotherham Advertiser* continues today. Indeed, for the jubilee edition in January 1918 it was noted that it was one of the few newspapers to be collected by the British Museum Library, and that all the back copies were bound and kept there. It would be interesting to find out if these copies are still in existence.

During the war years Rotherham was a town of contrasts. On the one hand you had the industrial expansion, and the consequential financial growth, caused by the munitions works, whilst on the other there were still signs of poverty, overcrowding and ill health. By contrast, the interwar period was one of conflict and dispute. Men returning from the battlefield expected to see improvements, but they were to be disappointed. However, lessons were learnt during these years and the gradual improvements in housing and health are testament to this. Better facilities and care, particularly for mothers and babies, led to the development of a Welfare State which is today second to none.

The production of any book is a team effort and, once again, my thanks go to Cate Ludlow and other individuals at The History Press, particularly the sterling efforts of Anna O'Loughlin who carefully edited the book and made sense of my ramblings. My thanks, as always, go to my family for their support and friends for their encouragement. But perhaps most of all my grateful thanks go to the countless men and women who gave their lives so that we in Rotherham, and in the neighbouring towns, might live in peace.

> They shall not grow old, as we that are left grow old:
> Age shall not weary them, nor the years condemn.
> At the going down of the sun and in the morning
> We will remember them.
>
> Laurence Binyon, from 'For the Fallen'

# PART 1

# THE FIRST WORLD WAR

## 1

# RECRUITMENT AND MOBILIZATION

Judging by the columns of the *Rotherham Advertiser*, at the beginning of 1914 not many people thought that a terrible war, which would last for four years, was about to take place before the end of the year. The war, which was to become known as the Great War, would, before its end, involve thousands of local men sacrificing their lives for King and Country. The year started quietly enough and the main news items in the early months of that year included the opening of the Cinema House on Doncastergate. The paper advertised 'continuous performances', where the population of the town could watch films such as *The Tower of Terror*, *Jewels of Sacrifice*, *The Multimillionaire Caprice* and finally, the hint of what was to come, *Jack the Conscript*. Going to the cinema was a popular activity, and the cheap seats ensured that there was usually very large attendance. These cinemas showed a variety of films and provided a sanctuary where, for a few pennies, people could avoid the worries and concerns of daily life.

On 23 March 1914, it was announced that the band of the York and Lancaster Regiment would play at the bandstand of Clifton Park at the weekends. This battalion included many local men who, in a few short months, would be fighting for their lives. Clifton Park had been open to the public since 1891, when it had been bought by the council. It became, and remains, a popular place for visitors.

In the same edition of the newspaper there was a report of a new billiard saloon, boasting nine full-size tables, opening in the Empire Buildings on the High Street on 9 April. There was little mention of the gathering war clouds, apart from top politicians and eminent men of the country making proclamations about the war and reassuring people that a peaceful settlement would soon be found. There is little doubt, however, that the populace of Rotherham would have been speculating about whether the war would take place. Hidden away on page 16 in the *Advertiser* of 9 May, was a statement from the Archbishop of Canterbury speaking for the (long-winded) British Council of Associate Councils of Churches in the British and German Empires for Fostering Friendly Relations. One of the speakers, Revd Dr Latimer of Berlin, expressed 'gratification that the misunderstandings between Britain and Germany had been cleared away' and claimed that 'the German people had genuine regard for the British'. Dr Spicker, president of the council in Germany, said that 'the armaments in Germany were not intended as a menace to Great Britain but as protection for their own commerce and possessions'. Judging by the writings of the time, there seemed to be a surreal quality to life in the town as powerlessly they watched events unfold.

As we have seen, matters went on much as before. Since 1902, following the Boer War, the English children had celebrated Empire Day at their schools and no one saw any reason to change the arrangements, which took place on 24 May 1914. The day was renowned for encouraging young people of the town to understand that Britain was part of a larger Empire and that it depended on them to show their patriotism for King and Country. To celebrate Empire Day, schools held parades and celebrations to this end. Young people would deliver patriotic addresses to the teachers and assembled audiences, patriotic songs were sung and little Union Jack flags were waved. One such celebration was held at Doncaster Road School, where it was reported that, 'Miss Doris Eaglestone led the parade dressed as Britannia joined by other children dressed in national costume of the colonies of the Empire which supported her.'

There was also a report that, on 6 June, a proposal for mixed bathing at the swimming baths had been turned down by the Rotherham Town Council, as it was felt that it would lead to 'the decline of maidenly modesty'. These trivial incidents do not give the impression that many people in the town were only too aware that war was just a few weeks away.

Empire Day at Thornhill Council School.

Only in the section devoted to national news did the newspaper reflect the uneasy balance of what was at first termed the 'War in Europe'. The news revealed that France was growing uneasy over the loss of territory to Germany, and other countries were concerned by Germany's growing unification. But as we now know, it took a Bosnian Serb to ignite the flame with the assassination of Archduke Franz Ferdinand of Austria. The events that were to follow have been well documented and therefore do not concern us here. Suffice it to say that last-minute hopes of peace were still being held on 1 August, when the *Advertiser* ran a piece stating that Britain was 'still balanced between war and peace'. The day before, the Press Association had re-assuredly stated:

> ...there are no marked developments in the European situation directly to affect this country. In diplomatic and official worlds London seems slightly more optimistic.

However, by 4 August the world was in no doubt about what was happening; Britain had declared war on Germany. There was also a determination that the people of the town of Rotherham would rise to the occasion, as events would prove. The Watch Committee was authorised to engage a sufficient number of special constables to deal with any emergency that arose. In the coming months, more special constables were appointed as increasing numbers of regular police constables chose to enlist.

The patriotism of the people of Rotherham was evident when the Mayor echoed this sentiment on the day after war had been declared. There was a meeting held in the council chamber of the Town Hall on Wednesday 5 August, when the Mayor, Alderman P. Bancroft Coward, spoke of the state of affairs as 'a most serious and momentous time for King and Country.' He continued, 'I urge citizens to stand firm beneath the British flag, determined with brave stout hearts to make any sacrifice to resist the enemy. God save the King.'

The newspaper indicated the concerns of the town with the blunt headline, 'War Cloud Bursts'. It reported that the people of Rotherham gathered in the streets and were talking about the implications of war, but there was apparently no panic – just 'a determination to see the business through to the end'.

Just prior to the outbreak of war, on the weekend of the August Bank Holiday, the people of the town had gathered in crowds to send off the Rotherham detachment of the Territorial branch of the 5th Battalion of the York and Lancaster Regiment, who were leaving on a special train for their annual camp in Whitby. The Territorials was a battalion of men who usually had other jobs, for example as bricklayers, carpenters, steel men and miners, and who would train as soldiers in their spare time. Initially the men of the Territorial Army were seen by a few citizens as a bit of a joke, and comments had been made about them not being 'regular soldiers'. However, events would show that they were a force of men who fought bravely and won special regard from their battle comrades, as well as the people of the town. Huge crowds gathered at the railway station to send them off to Whitby. Little did these men know that their training would be cut short and that they would find themselves fighting for their lives in France within days of their return. Following the declaration of war, these Territorials were immediately called back and it was said that 'never were they greeted with such enthusiasm'. The recall of these Territorials was, for many people, the first intimation that the global situation had become extremely grave and that the nation's honour, greatness and even independence had

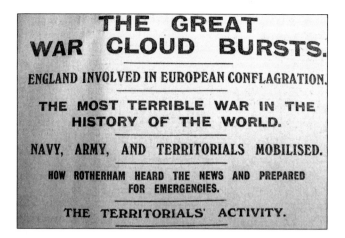

# THE GREAT WAR CLOUD BURSTS.

## ENGLAND INVOLVED IN EUROPEAN CONFLAGRATION.

## THE MOST TERRIBLE WAR IN THE HISTORY OF THE WORLD.

## NAVY, ARMY, AND TERRITORIALS MOBILISED.

### HOW ROTHERHAM HEARD THE NEWS AND PREPARED FOR EMERGENCIES.

### THE TERRITORIALS' ACTIVITY.

'The Great War Cloud Bursts.' Rotherham was at war.

been threatened. There is no doubt that the relatives of the Territorial soldiers treasured these last few days, which were for many the last ever days with their loved ones.

On 10 August, the Territorials received the news of their mobilisation and it was speedily arranged for them to have a ceremonial send off from the local dignitaries of Rotherham. It had been decided that the regimental colours would be left in the parish church, for safekeeping, until the end of the war. The emotional service had been arranged at very short notice and there had been no room left inside the church for the ordinary people. After the service, the soldiers marched from the Drill Hall, down Doncaster Road, along the High Street and onto Main Street to congregate at the fair ground in front of the Central Railway Station. The reporter from the *Advertiser* described 'a sea of faces' and 'acres of flag waving'. The Mayor made a statement to the men of Rotherham expressing his pleasure in giving this send off:

> It is with a sense of admiration that I survey this fine body of men prepared to face difficulties and duty for the safety of the King and Country. You take away the best and heartiest wishes of the people of the town and we will take very good care of those left behind. I grant you a speedy and safe return home.

The speech was delivered to great cheers for the Mayor, three cheers for the King and then a chorus of voices singing the national anthem. By quarter to twelve the first consignment of soldiers were pulling out of the station to destinations unknown. Pitiful scenes had been enacted at the railway station as wives and mothers kissed their loved ones goodbye, with the cry 'God be with you till we meet again.' The reality was that many of these men would never return home. Thankfully, this emotional send off had been filmed. It was advertised as 'animated photographs' when the film was shown at the High Street Picture Palace in May of the following year. It was reported that, 'The pictures were so clear that officers and men were easily recognizable and they portrayed scenes of incidents without parallel in our local and national history.' So popular was this film that crowds of people had attended the cinema and, as a consequence, its running was extended by a week. We can only imagine the reactions of

York and
Lancaster
Territorials
off to their
annual
camp at
Whitby.

the audience watching these dramatic events. Some viewers may have already lost their loved
ones and would have experienced the terrible anguish of seeing them once more on film.

The Territorials may have been seen as a bit of a joke to some, but in just a few months the
*Advertiser* was reporting on their brave conduct in the fighting. The paper was not allowed to
state where they were fighting, as it had been forbidden to report such things by the military
authorities, but they stated that the Territorials 'were fighting close to the front line'. One of
the soldiers wrote to the editor about the pride he felt as part of the Territorials, despite them
being 'the men who some Rotherham people thought would never go to war and whom they
sometimes rudely ridiculed when they saw them in their Saturday afternoon dress parades.'

The bravery and courage of the Territorials was highly praised in October 1917 by
Brigadier General R.L. Abercorn DSO (Distinguished Service Order). It was very unusual to
single out one battalion from the others, but he obviously felt that the regiment deserved high
commendation. He wrote, 'This battalion stands out above all others,' and addressing the men
he told them:

> You were given an object in the operation and went far beyond it and you held the
> ground after taking it. You did so under great hardship in the darkness and wet when
> you advanced over very difficult ground...I hope that men in the York's and Lancaster
> Regiment will remember that I live at Grantham and will call on me. I will do anything
> I can for the men of this Regiment.

This was very high praise indeed!

Letters from the front line were regularly printed in the columns of the *Advertiser*, informing
the populace at large, as well as the lads on the front line, on any issues that affected them at
home and at war. The military authorities had quickly seen that news from home was essential
for troop morale and ensured that free letters and postcards were distributed to the soldiers and
sailors to send news home. In Rotherham, Major Phillips VC announced to the parents and

**A Unique Film.**

There is something unique about the animated photographs, which are being shown this week at the High Street Picture Palace, of the departure for the Front of the 5th Battalion York and Lancaster Regiment (Rotherham's Territorials). The photography is wonderfully good, and the picture is so clear that officers and men can easily be recognised. To Rotherham people the film has an interest which no other film could possibly have. It pourtrays an incident, or rather a series of incidents, without parallel in our local or national history, and it is not surprising that there has been a big demand on the part of the local public to see the picture, which is to be shown for the last time to-night.

Animated photographs were shown at High Street Picture Palace.

relatives of the soldiers of the Territorial Army that anyone wanting to send a letter or parcel to their relatives at the front was requested to 'take them to the Drill Hall before ten o'clock' to be delivered. Recent archaeological evidence from the trenches indicates that the contents of these parcels might have included such delicacies as shaving equipment, toffees, tobacco and toothpaste. As we will see, the delivery of the local newspaper added to the communal spirit of the soldiers and sailors, who wanted to keep in touch with their hometowns.

The ordinary people of the town would have had no idea of what trench warfare was like, and a letter describing it was shared with the editor of the *Advertiser*. This letter was from a Captain C.V. Monier Williams of the Territorials, written to his parents in Rotherham, in May 1915. It was one of the first which described the trenches:

> Since I last wrote we have been sending parties of officers and NCOs down the trenches for 24 hours at a time for instructions. I went down on Tuesday night. We were taken in a motor bus to within five miles of the firing line and then walked in the dusk to Battalion Headquarters and from there our party was split up and we went into various trenches. Things in this part of the line were very quiet and only desultory firing was going on, but it was quite enough to make things interesting and a good many bullets were flying about. It gave me my first experience of being shot at. We walked about in front of the trenches and watched sappers dig a new trench and then walked along the old trench. These are very wide and very safe with comfortable sandbagged shelters with roofs of corrugated iron an earth that seems impregnable. About 200 yards away were similar trenches for the Germans. The ground in between covered in barbed wire entanglements. I left the trenches and went back to the Battalion HQ which are in a ruined farm and we had a good dinner and I examined the telegraphic equipment.

These trenches were to become home for some of the men serving on the front line. You will notice that in Captain Monier Williams' letter there is no mention of the flooding of the trenches, which is what most people remember from the films of the First World War. That is until December 1915, when a letter was received from 'four Rotherham lads', who were more realistic about the trenches and provided details that had not been heard before. The letter stated, 'We were waist deep in water in the trenches and were only supplied with waders, which came up to our waists.' They also wrote, 'If the people of Rotherham could see us they would think us as very curious creatures.'

The Drill Hall, where parcels and letters were left for the men on the front line.

In an effort to combat the waterlogged trenches caused by the clay soil, which retained water, upside down 'A' frames were built into the trenches and duckboards placed on them. In order to bring the war home to the people of Rotherham, it seems that in November 1916 large crowds were invited to see a model dugout which was built in Clifton Park. It was supposed to be 'superior to anything the Huns have yet devised'. The Clifton Park dugout was described as being big enough to accommodate a large family and deep enough to be safe from zeppelin bombs. The sides of the dugout were supported by wooden supports rather than by sand bags as in the dugouts on the front line.

The call to arms had now increased in the recruiting campaigns for the men of Rotherham, Barnsley, Doncaster and Sheffield. The West Riding Brigade marched through the streets of the town encouraging men to enlist. The following month, elaborate preparations were made in the town for another grand spectacle on Saturday 30 March. This was to mark the visit of a detachment of the York and Lancaster Regiment, at that time quartered in Pontefract Barracks. A drum and fife band of the 2nd Battalion was brought over from Limerick and they paraded in the streets of the town, recruiting men to enlist under the command of Major A.E. Ashton. These recruiting campaigns were very successful, and their momentum only intensified with the outbreak of war.

Many Yorkshire towns would have had recruitment offices and they would be supplemented by mobile recruitment endeavours, which the *Advertiser* would publicise. On Monday, 24 August 1914 it was announced that enough men of Rotherham were needed to make up two new battalions for the York and Lancaster Regiment and for what was now styled Lord Kitchener's New Army. The number of men required was 440 and the recruitment campaign would last for a week. Only five days later it was recorded that 236 men had enlisted for the new battalion. Some inter-town rivalry was promoted when it was announced that 100 men from Dinnington had also been recruited. The Dinnington colliery employers were anxious to support the workmen. The colliery manager announced that they would give each man who enlisted a bonus of £2. That would have been a lot of money in those days and no doubt was taken up with great enthusiasm. Now, with the impact of the beginning of the hostilities, the recruitment campaign did not let up. On 5 September more stirring addresses were made in

The trenches during the First World War.

College Square to packed crowds in front of the Court House. Before the speeches, bands had been playing patriotic tunes. Once again the Mayor addressed the crowds, asking people to remember the propaganda about the Germans' treatment of women and children, which was now being avidly read. He urged for 'the young men of the town to remember the traditions of the town and the regiments they were asked to join. Remember the horrors the Germans were responsible for. If France is to be beaten then England must follow.'

The famous recruiting poster of Lord Kitchener that was most widely recognised was the one where he points directly at the viewer with the words 'Your Country Needs You'. No doubt this poster would have been displayed in the streets of the town, but the *Advertiser* had its own recruiting adverts. In October of 1914, the newspaper was showing an advert with Britannia repeating Kitchener's request to a crowd of men, against a background of an industrial town, urging them to make that day the 'great day of decision'. These early adverts were slightly subtler, whilst still pounding the message home just as forcefully. In December 1914 there was an illustration of a soldier with his army rifle, standing at ease as 'A soldier of the King's Regiment at the Front covering themselves with Glory'. This was to encourage the reader 'to enlist today'.

A military parade on College Street.

Rotherham Archives & Local Studies Service. photo 8009

By September 1915, the war had been raging for a year and it seems that local men were less inclined to enlist. That month Captain Hallowes of Doncaster was recruiting another battalion for the 150th (Rotherham) Heavy Battery Royal Garrison Artillery, and the members of Rotherham Recruiting Committee were asked to raise a brigade of 240 men. Applicants were requested to be of good physique with a minimum height of 5ft 8ins. In this instance it was mentioned that 'It would be a fine opportunity for pals to become associated with a battery unit which they would have cause to be proud.' Heavy losses, which were now more apparent, made this campaign less successful and it was announced in December that many more men were still needed for this new regiment. Despite being a reduced regiment, the new battery was not allowed to rest on its laurels and within a fortnight these men were in France. News of the battery, now fighting at the front, was heard in July 1916 in a letter from Lieutenant Colonel Haywood of the Royal Engineers:

> ...yesterday I saw the battalion passing, which had guns and wagons with the Rotherham coat of arms on and which being a local man I recognised. They looked like any other soldiers, rather travel stained, but cheery and they were certainly a well-set up body of men.

He reported that the local boys had honoured their hometown by giving their shell-proofed dugouts such names as 'Rotherham House', 'Lindum House', 'College Inn' and 'Turf Tavern', the latter two being well-known local public houses of the town.

The day of 1 July 1916 will be remembered for the 'big push' and the first battle at the Somme when thousands and thousands of men were sent over the parapets of their trenches to a certain death. It had been decided by the British military authorities that the Somme was the place to open up the offensive on the Western Front. The strategy was to pound the German troops with non-stop bombs and send troops into 'No Man's Land', hoping that the enemy would be overcome and the war would be brought to an end. Of course, we know now that this was a mistake that would cost the lives of thousands of men. When it was revealed that numerous Rotherham men were reported as missing, and presumed dead following this battle, the *Advertiser* reporter noted:

> Can we forget those lusty lunged young fellows who in the early days of the war trooped in their hundreds to the recruiting office at Rotherham singing and shouting as they came? They are the same men who on the morning of July 1st jumped over the parapet of their trenches and 'roaring like lions' swept on to the German fortifications.

As the war years rolled by, we see that these recruiting campaigns were not attracting such enthusiastic responses as they had been. Part of the reason for this could have been that the munitions factories were encouraging men to stay in the town and work in a reserved occupation. The fact that young men were not enlisting and were remaining in Rotherham did not escape the notice of one famous man. He wrote a letter to the gentlemen and magistrates of the town, asking why people were failing to enlist, seemingly wanting to work and earn money whilst thousands of Rotherham men were being killed at the front. He wrote:

War Office

July 15th 1915

Sir,

I wish to express to you personally and to those who have helped you in your recruitment work my very best thanks for the energy that has been displayed by you in the matter of recruiting.

I would ask you to take an early opportunity of urging all able-bodied men in your neighbourhood to come forward and enlist so they may be trained as soldiers to take part in the war and help to keep our forces in the field at maximum strength.

I shall be glad to hear of any reason that may be given to you by young and suitable men not availing themselves of the opportunity to see service in the field where they are so much wanted.

I am sir,
    Your obedient servant
    Kitchener

This was a problem nationally as the number of enlisted men all over the country was falling. The increased use of propaganda turned the First World War into a moral crusade with men fighting for the honour of Britain. The large numbers of men enlisting in the early days of the war showed that the men of Rotherham were prepared to do their bit for King and Country, but the hundreds of pictures of dead, missing and wounded soldiers must have impacted on their patriotic inclinations. Nevertheless, the people of the town readily gave money for good causes, and gave more practical help to victims of the German atrocities that came to the town.

The call up campaign in the *Advertiser*, October 1914.

# 2

# EARLY CASUALTIES OF THE WAR

In August 1914 the Germans had decided on a plan to attack France by invading Belgium. When the Belgians rejected this plan, the Germans invaded anyway and the atrocities they inflicted on the inhabitants forced a terrified population to leave. Other countries offered to take some of the many Belgian refugees who were now fleeing from their homes. Britain was one of the countries that offered asylum to any Belgian people arriving at its shores. Leaving their homes and most of their possessions, these refugees fled with nothing more, in some cases, than the clothing on their backs. It was estimated that there were hundreds of thousands of refugees coming to England and Rotherham had agreed to have fifty of them. However, in the end many more than this were welcomed to the town. The first to arrive, a single family, came to Rotherham in September of 1914. The father's name was Frans de Roeck and he arrived with his wife and their baby on Sunday 6 September. Unlike some of the other refugees, Frans did have a relative in the town and it was reported that he was to stay with his brother Mr F. de Roeck, a well-known corn and seed merchant of Frederick Street. A reporter was dispatched to the house of his brother to interview him. He was described as a 'well set up young man' who had been unable to fight for his country due to ill health. Despite this, the reporter stated that 'he had gained the respect of every true Britisher'.

He also spoke of the atrocities that he had witnessed when the Germans had first captured his hometown. In one incident all the prisoners of a captured town were made to lie facedown on the floor. The Germans went along the lines of the prisoners and shot every third man, releasing the others. Thankfully Frans escaped with his life after this terrifying ordeal. He and his family were asked to attend a welcome meeting in College Square two days later, with other refugees, and were impressed by the enthusiasm and warmth of the Rotherham people towards them. The group was presented with a picture of the exiled King of the Belgians to great applause from the large numbers of people who had turned out to welcome them. The townspeople ensured that all the refugees were treated well whilst they remained in this country.

A further group of refugees arrived the following month. These were nineteen in number and included five married couples, one little girl and two babies aged six months and six weeks. On arrival they were taken in one of the Corporation's motorbuses to Thrybergh Country Park, where the members of the Rotherham and District Golf Club had agreed that they could be accommodated. Beds were made up for them in the large hall at the golf club until better arrangements could be made. Speaking in Flemish, one of the refugees thanked the people of the town for their welcome, stating, 'I say in the name of my family and my friends "Long Live England" and "England for Ever".' His speech resulted in resounding cheers from the townspeople.

The cost of all the refugees in the town was going to be substantial and the *Advertiser* took up this matter by asking people to help the refugees by subscribing 6*d* a month, or 1½*d* a week, towards their upkeep. It asked that people submit their names and addresses at the *Advertiser* offices, to then be forwarded to the proper authorities. Shortly afterwards, a Refugee Committee was appointed to deal with the subscriptions and any issues arising for the Belgian families. The following week the list of these subscribers were printed in the newspaper.

Another group of wounded refugee soldiers were due to arrive at Rawmarsh the following Saturday, 31 October 1914. When these soldiers arrived they were taken to the hospital. It was reported that they were not badly wounded and were expected to recover but, once again, that they were in dire need of socks, shirts, suits, brushes and combs, pipes, tobacco, jam, eggs, fruit and soap. In fact anything that could be spared. Later groups of refugees were temporarily installed at Eastwood House and in the rear part of Clifton House until they could be found more suitable accommodation. Every effort to help them feel 'at home' was made; such were the warm feelings towards the refugees that a firm of local opticians – Messrs Leadbetter and Peters of the Imperial Buildings, High Street, Rotherham – offered free eye tests and spectacles to them. To make sure the offer was understood, the advert repeated the offer in Flemish. Fundraising schemes were organised and subscriptions were gathered to ensure that their stay would be comfortable.

By December 1918, at the end of the war, the Belgian refugees were finally repatriated back to their homeland. By this time they had made good friends with the townspeople and great sadness was felt when they left. Of course, they had no idea about what they were returning back to. Their homes would probably not be standing and their only possessions

Belgian refugees arriving in Rotherham in October 1914.

Belgian refugees at
Oakwood Hall

were those they took back with them from Rotherham. After four years staying in the town, it was not just the language they had learnt, but also something of the culture of Rotherham people. A reporter at the time said, '[They] are now so Anglicised that one cannot distinguish them from the natives.'

Their treatment in this country had been reciprocated by their kindness to the British prisoners of war in Belgium. A prisoner, who had been in Belgium when he was captured, spoke highly of 'the treatment we received at the hands of the local people who would readily share crusts of bread with British prisoners and who were strongly punished by the Germans for doing so'. On the day they left Rotherham, to show their gratitude for their treatment, the people of the town received an illuminated address given to them from the Belgian refugees:

> We are all very grateful to you for the kindness you have shown us during the past four years and allow us to show our appreciation by presenting you with this small gift. You may rest assured we will never forget you and the trouble you have taken on our behalf. It is with deep regret that we must part from you and your great friendship.

The Belgians were readily accepted into the town, but it was a different treatment for enemy aliens residing in this country. In August 1914, the 'Alien Act' came into force, interning all Germans who were capable of military service if they were unable to produce papers of nationalisation. They had to report their presence to the local police station and would then be liable to be deported from Britain.

From the very early days at the beginning of the war, people of the town sent out the *Advertiser* to the men fighting at the front. Many of the soldiers spent large amounts of time waiting. These periods provided an opportunity to read the newspaper and catch up on activities that were happening in their hometown. Parcels and letters from their families in Rotherham were now regularly reaching the troops serving out in France. In one of the letters printed on 17 October 1914, Private Frederick Clarke of the 2nd Battalion of the Cold

Stream Guards thanked his mother, Mrs Clarke of 39 Fitzwilliam Road, for sending out the newspaper. He wrote, 'I am so glad that you sent me the *Advertiser*. I can take it with me tonight into the trenches and read it tomorrow. We have warm times occasionally as the Germans keep bombing us.'

The image of a young man reading the local newspaper whilst the carnage of war is all around him – probably imagining the people and places of the town and no doubt wishing to be home – is profoundly moving. Another Rotherham soldier, Private G. Andrews of the same battalion, who lived on Henley Grove Road, Masbrough, wrote a letter to his aunt, asking her to send him some clothing, which he listed, and the *Advertiser*. He also wrote:

> I am writing this whilst in the trenches and bullets are flying about wholesale, so I am trusting to God to be able to post it. I passed some dreadful sights this morning. German dead were scattered all over the place. I hope the war will soon be over and that we may have a jolly Christmas.

The conviction that the war would be over by Christmas was a wish that most people in the town, and the country at large, were hoping for. Indeed, many of the people who signed up did so in the hope that if they didn't hurry and enlist then their chance would soon be gone. No one expected the war to last for four long years. Private William Cawton of 27 Armer Street, Masbrough, with the King's Own Yorkshire Light Infantry, wrote home to let his mother know that he had been injured in his hand in October 1914, but stated, 'We are giving the Germans it and no mistake. I think it will soon be over and I shall be home to my Christmas dinner.'

The columns of the newspaper now regularly showed pictures and stories of the men fighting in the war. The lists of men are too numerous to produce here, but they serve as a reminder of what was happening to the local lads, and some are very touching. The war was

**READING THE "ADVERTISER" IN THE TRENCHES.**

Private Fred Clarke, of the 2nd Battalion Coldstream Guards, has again written home to his mother, Mrs. Clarke, of 39, Fitzwilliam road, Rotherham. He is still safe, though, as he says, they get a hot time of it. In the course of his letter he writes: "I am glad you sent me the 'Advertiser' as well as the others. I can take them with me to-night into the trenches and read them to-morrow. We have been in the trenches on and off for three weeks, and it gets monotonous. We have warm times occasionally, for the Germans keep shelling us. We have had several men killed and wounded with bits of shells, though more than half their shells do no damage, as they do not burst. We always give them a yell and a cheer when their dummy shells come."

The above letter was written on October 5th.

Reading the *Advertiser* in the trenches.

only twenty-four hours old when news was reported of the very first Rotherham victim of the First World War. He was Ernest Jubb, the son of Henry Jubb, a coppersmith employed by J. Youle & Company of Millgate. He was a sailor with the HMS *Amphion* on the 5 August 1914, when a mine had hit the ship at 6.30 a.m. Most of its crew was having breakfast when the incident occurred. The men who had been rescued could only look on with horror as the ship, still under momentum, was struck by a second mine just a half an hour later and sunk within fifteen minutes of the second explosion. Ernest had lived with his parents at Clifton Grove and had attended Wellgate School, leaving at the age of fourteen. His family, hearing the report, had contacted the Admiralty. The sad news was confirmed on the morning of Monday 10 August.

Letters were a regular feature in the newspaper. They were a way of keeping in touch with families, raising issues of concern and celebrating successful battles. One early letter was printed in the paper on 9 September 1914, its aim to offer some kind of hope to a worried family. It was reported that Mr F.W. Stephenson, a well-known Rotherham tradesman, had two sons serving in the war and was getting concerned when he hadn't heard from his younger son Oliver, a private with the 1st Battalion Cold Stream Guards. Another soldier, Private C.W. Carr, stationed with the 3rd Battalion of the same regiment, saw the letter and wrote to Mr Stephenson explaining the reasons why his son may have been unable to write. He pointed out that one reason might be due to delays in the post. He explained that many troops go missing after a big battle, when battalions get disorganised and the troops get scattered. As an example he said that after one battle, involving 1,200 men, there were only 88 names answered at the first roll call. The following day, after more troops had returned to their regiment, the roll call went up to 1,084 troops present. He reminded him that 'if anything had happened to [his] son [he] would have had a telegraph,' and advised Mr Stephenson not to give up hope.

It became the patriotic custom in the *Advertiser* to print pictures of very large families whose sons were all serving at the front, and many of these families are listed. In March of 1915 a widow was reported as having six of her sons and grandsons serving in France. They were reported to be the sons of George Norburn, who had recently died and who had been described as 'one of the old brigade'. His sons were listed as Sam, aged 42, who had been twenty-one years in the regular forces and was due to return home just before the outbreak of war; George, aged 38; Fred, aged 30; Henry Victor, aged 27; Ernest, aged 21; Percy, aged 19 and his grandson Charles, aged 19. In July 1916, the *Advertiser* showed the pictures of another family – this one of seven soldiers all belonging to one family and all involved in the war. They were the sons and sons-in-law of Mr Harry Woodhouse of 51 Orchard Street, Masbrough, 'who [were] serving or [had] served at the front'. These large families were lauded as being very patriotic, but one cannot help but wonder at how many of them survived and the sadness suffered by the parents losing multiple members of their families to the war effort.

Printed early for Christmas on Thursday, 24 December 1914, the *Advertiser* published whole pages of pictures of young men who had been killed in the fighting, with the heading:

Upholding the Honour of Britain, Rotherham and District Men amidst Shot and Shell. Toll for the Brave – The Brave that are No More.

Underneath the title on this particular day there were ninety-three pictures of Rotherham men who had given their lives in the five short months of the war. As the conflict went

Seven soldiers from the same family.

on the lists became longer, and added to these were the men who had been wounded or gone missing. By 1916, regular columns in the paper were from families asking for news of missing men. This intensified after the 'big push' of 1 July 1916, when, heartbreakingly, too many were found to be dead. On 30 September it was reported that the body of a missing soldier, Signaller Horace Keyworth, had been found. Horace had lived at 197 Kimberworth Road and had not been heard from since the 'big push'. A letter had been written from a comrade, Private H.A. Winders, after seeing the piece in the *Advertiser* asking for information. He wrote to Horace's parents informing them of their son's death:

> I am writing to tell you how extraordinarily sorry all your dear sons' comrades were to hear the sad news which was brought to us today. His body was found and buried by a Christian chaplain of His Majesties Forces in the field a few days ago, so you will see that he had a Christian burial. He was well known and well loved by every man in his battalion. The Corp and all the signallers to whose section Horace was attached speak of their great regret. Horace was one of the most cheerful and best men in the Regiment. He did not seem to know what fear was and his death is a great loss to us. I sincerely hope that you will look to God above to give you strength to bear the terrible news.

One week later, information was requested about Private C.A. Locke of the King's Own Yorkshire Light Infantry, who was also last heard of on 1 July. He had resided in Maltby until two years prior to the war, when he enlisted. The newspaper reported that his mother, Mrs Locke, would thankfully receive any information about him. In the same edition another soldier, Lance Corporal W. Lindley of the same regiment, was officially reported as missing since 1 July, and it stated that his father and sisters at 38 Holmes Lane, Rotherham 'would be grateful for any information respecting him.' The family asked that 'if this should meet the eye of any of his comrades who could give news of him, the family would be glad to hear from them.' Some families did not receive any definite news of their relative's death, leaving them without any form of closure. One family had to wait for fourteen years before their son's body turned up. On 8 February 1930, a French peasant found a battered disc with human remains on the Somme battlefields. The remains were identified as those of Private J.H. Cooper of the 1/5th York and Lancaster Regiment. His mother lived at 136 Nottingham Street, where she received a letter from the Earl of Lucan, who told her:

> We are told that the regiment was attacked on July 7$^{th}$ 1916 in front of Thiepval, north of the town of Albert. One of the soldiers told me that they had got into the second German line but had to give up the ground as the Prussian Guard who were against us called for re-enforcements and we could not hold it...After questioning every reliable witness we could find we had to reluctantly give up all hope of hearing any more about the fate of your son.

Then, after nearly fourteen years, Mrs Cooper received a letter informing her that it had been possible to finally identify the burial place of her son:

> The body of an unknown soldier was found in the vicinity of Hamel and in order to secure the reverent maintenance of the grave in perpetuity the remains were reverently and carefully reburied in Sarre Road Cemetery No 2 Beaumont Hamel, plot 29 Row J grave 12. When the remains were being removed the disc was found bearing Private Cooper's name and regiment particulars.

Private Cooper was one of the lucky ones; many more families never found the body of their sons and were left without hope for many years. These heartbreaking stories just give a tiny glimmer of the anguish suffered by the hundreds, if not thousands, of parents of the town who had no other choice but to wait for any news about their sons. The *Advertiser* stated, 'July 1$^{st}$ 1916 will be a blood red letter day for the Rotherham district as well as a day of glorious deeds.' The *Advertiser* was to campaign successfully for this day to be remembered at the end of the war, and castigated the military authorities for the fact that no mention was made of the day 'when millions of British soldiers went to their graves'. Thankfully, sometimes there was good news from soldiers who had been captured and whose family sent out the *Advertiser* to the place of their captivity. Private Walter De Ville of the York and Lancaster Regiment answered an advert in the newspaper requesting information. He wrote to the *Advertiser* saying that he had been wounded and was in the hands of the Germans. He also gave his home address, which was 32 Osberton Street, Dalton.

Using the columns of the newspaper families were able to keep in touch. This must have been the closest they could feel during the Christmas period, an especially poignant time of year when families should have been together. The fact that the war was not over for Christmas, as people had been led to believe, only made the sorrow greater.

# 3

# THE FIRST CHRISTMAS, RIOTS AND SHIRKERS

In December 1914 it looked like Christmas was being cancelled when it was announced that The Santa Claus League had postponed the distribution of toys that year. They stated that this was due to the prosperity of the working classes. Apparently their 'philanthropic needs were being transferred to other areas'. How much comfort this was to widows of large numbers of children is not stated, but it seems that in the event they were not forgotten. During November 1914 it was announced that America had sent gifts, including warm clothing and toys, for the children of Rotherham. These gifts had been received because of a scheme instigated by the American newspapers. It was announced that the gifts were to be sent over to England on the American ship *Jason*, which was expected to land in Devonport that same week. The scheme was originally meant for the orphans of the town's servicemen, but the response had been so good that many more gifts were available, providing for the poorer families of the town as well. The *Advertiser* requested that in order to qualify for these, the names of the children of non-commissioned officers and men usually resident or those on active service, be sent to the office of the local representative based at St George's Hall, 'no later than the 2$^{nd}$ December [of that] year'.

Not only was Christmas almost cancelled but it was announced that Bonfire Night would have to go uncelebrated also. The Chief Constable E. Weatherhogg stated that:

In accordance with the instructions from the Home Office no bonfires will be lit to celebrate Bonfire Night this year. In the interests of the Nation, no illuminations of any description are to be allowed while we are at war and that no bonfires or powerful exploding rockets emitting bright lights must be in evidence. On 5$^{th}$ November 1915 at 8pm, instead of celebrating Bonfire Night, a memorial service will be held at the Parish Church for all the men belonging to the town who have fallen in the service of their King and Country.

The *Advertiser* reported that many enlisted men's families were expected to attend the service, which would include the sounding of the 'Last Post' by buglers of the 3/5th Battalion of the York and Lancaster Regiment. It was announced that a choir would sing the hymn 'Oh God Our Help

St George's Hall, where toys from America were distributed to Rotherham's children in December 1914.

St. George's Hall.

in Ages Past', as it was 'the hymn sung by soldiers before going over the parapet of the trenches to reach the German lines'. As hundreds of families were already in mourning for their dear ones who would never return from the battlefield, the service would be particularly poignant.

But that Christmas the soldiers made the best of it as much as they could. Gunner W. Oxley of the 28th Battalion of the Royal Field Artillery wrote to his parents at 57 College Road, in December 1914, to tell them that the French people were very good to the British soldiers and had invited them into their houses to celebrate Christmas with them. He tried to cheer his parents by repeating the fallacy that the war was nearly finished and that it would not be long before he was home with them again. He wrote, 'You would laugh to see our troops sitting in the trenches where there are a lot of jokes dropped and we sing Christmas Carols.' Nevertheless, that same year the grocers of the town ensured that the boys at the front would not be forgotten. In December 1914, the Grocers Federation of the United Kingdom announced that they had developed a scheme to ensure that every soldier serving at the front line would receive a present that year. It was reported that Rotherham customers would see an attractive looking collection box on shop counters, and that they were encouraged to contribute at least one penny to ensure that a present could be delivered. The description of the gift was as follows: 'A small tin of toffees and a slip of paper extending Christmas greetings and the donor's heartiest thanks for the magnificent defence, which has held up the enemy for so long.' The size of these tins was suitable to fit in the soldier's pockets and would bear a picture of the King against the background of the Union Jack. On most Christmases the troops received presents from the Royal Family of cards and toffees and it was clear that the town of Rotherham was not going to forget its men at the front.

Christmas gifts from the soldiers and sailors on the front line were, of necessity, homemade and very individual. Many of the soldiers had access to postcards; some beautiful ones were made of silk and were sent home to offer comfort to relatives in the town. One present from a soldier in France, which he sent to his wife, was touching in the extreme. Private E. Torr of the York and Lancaster Regiment, of 44 Rawmarsh Road, sent a very unusual present that year; a poem attached to a piece of khaki material. It read:

> To the one I love
> In the Land of the Free
> Please accept this gift from me
> It is neither parcel
> Present or priceless packet
> But a piece of khaki
> From the front of my jacket

I am certain that this was one of the most emotional presents Mrs Torr would have received that year. The patriotic fervour was echoed by the *Advertiser*, which carried a Christmas message in 1916, on behalf of the families and relatives of the town, to the soldiers and sailors involved in the war effort:

FIGHT ON TILL THE PEACE OF BETHLEHEM FILLS THE WORLD.

The paper also reported on their families, printing, '[They] are full of thoughts of you all...we pray you may be guarded and guided by God...we wish we could see you home again beside the Christmas fires, your great work done and peace once more proclaimed.' These stirring messages must have warmed the hearts of the lads still under fire.

Much has been written about the first Christmas ceasefire, when it was said that German and British soldiers played football together – an incident that the military authorities ensured would never happen again. But it was these little episodes of receiving and sending messages from loved ones that would have mattered deeply to the men at the front and their families in Rotherham.

The *Advertiser* now included regular letters from soldiers. They were often sent primarily to the editor but eventually were seen by the town at large. Young men, receiving the paper from relatives at home, could see what the reaction to the letters had been. One of the earliest correspondents, a corporal in the Irish Guards named Peter Sheridan, appeared several times in its columns. He stated that he was fighting in France and that having witnessed first hand the patriotism and bravery of his comrades, that 'it [would] be a disgrace to every man of military age and fitness who cannot show at least a medal when the war is over.' This suggestion, which was taken seriously by the military authorities at the end of the war, ensured that all who had participated in it was given a medal. This was followed up on 22 December 1914 by an anonymous letter from 'A Rotherham Lad doing his Duty', which focussed on a theme returned to by Peter later, so it is probable that it was from him. It seems that he was particularly incensed by the reports of the local football matches in Rotherham and the large numbers of spectators at these matches, which were reported week after week. He said that the recent English League had boasted 334,000 people 'with nothing to do but watch 22 men kicking a football around'. If they wanted excitement, he offered that they should 'come round here, where our boys are doing their bit and take a turn at dodging bullets, shells and shrapnel.' He pointed out that, as a bonus, there was no entrance fee to pay.

Peter was one of the few lucky ones who managed to be sent home for Christmas in 1914. It seems that not only did the soldiers receive tins of toffees, but also gifts from the readers of the *Advertiser*. He sent a letter to the editor on his return to the trenches when he found the Christmas presents awaiting him. He wrote:

> Just a line to let you know that I am in the pink of condition and to say how pleased I was to receive your parcel. It came here whilst I was at home on leave. The muffler was especially welcome and the cigarette and paper were most acceptable. Will you let the people of Rotherham and Parkgate know how grateful I am to them. If the King of England had come home he could not have been better received than I was. You treated me like a gentleman. Hoping that you have a happy New Year, I remain yours truly. Peter Sheridan

Once again, he repeatedly thanked the people of the town for 'looking after Tommy over here', saying, 'if God spares me to come home after the war I will have an interesting diary which I will show the people in your district exactly what Tommy has gone through here.' It is to be hoped that he returned home safely.

The theme of football crowds was referred to again in October 1915 by 'some Rotherham lads in the trenches'. They spoke about the enthusiasm of the fighting soldiers and said it was like the men were going to watch Rotherham Town or County teams play football in the final for the league. They spoke of regret that they had no mouth organs to accompany singing and asked for any 'kind lady' to send one or two mouth organs or old melodeons out to them. They ended by writing, 'By the way we keep letting those Germans have some shot and shell.'

Some Rotherham people would send cards showing the picturesque parts of the town to their relatives at the front line. Sometimes, during heavy bombing, these possessions were lost until the next battalion to occupy those trenches recovered them. The *Advertiser* for August 1915 told the story of two postcards that had been found in a trench by a soldier in France and he had sent them to the newspaper for identification. The two cards showed pictures of Rotherham, one of the Chapel on the Bridge and the second of College Street and they were addressed to 'daddy' from Gertie and Joseph. Incredibly, within a very short time, the children's father was identified as Sergeant J. Medlock of the 1/5th Battalion of York and Lancaster Regiment, whose wife and children lived at 154 Greasbrough Street, Thornhill. The father was reported to be recovering from his wounds at No. 5 Convalescent Depot, where he wrote:

> I cherished those cards and they kept me going in the trenches and at the time I lost them a German bomb came over and knocked our parapet down, burying all my belongings. There is great credit to lads from Rotherham and Barnsley for the way they stick to their trenches under the worst bombardment, since we have been out here. I would like to thank you for the return of the postcards through your newspaper. When I look at them they remind me of my wife and children and the view of the dear

old town of Rotherham cheers me up and I hope to carry the postcards throughout this war.

A few weeks later, other belongings, which again had been found in the trenches, were sent to the newspaper offices. Lance Corporal J.T. Hague of the York and Lancaster Regiment sent in some articles in September 1916 – photographs of a young woman attached to a number of remembrance cards – which he found in one of the dugouts following the 'big push' of 1 July. He had reason to think that they belonged to a Rotherham lad, although we are not told the reason why. The name Ethel is written on some of the cards and the reporter described the young lady as dressed in white jersey. The verse on one of the cards reads:

> I daily pray that God will keep
> My hero in his care
> And bring him safely back again
> The joys of home to share.

The same week, a set of miniature photographs were sent to the paper from Mrs G. Beighton of 132 South Street, Rawmarsh, which had been found by her brother, once again in the trenches. He was Lance Corporal F. Walker. The miniatures were described as being of three little girls and on the back their names were inscribed; Millicent, Alice and Gladys. These were obviously belongings of great value to the owner. Unfortunately, there is no further information as to whether these were identified or not.

An inscription on a church wall from one Rotherham man prompted another, Sergeant E. Scanlon, to write to the editor of the *Advertiser* in March 1917, stating that when he was billeted with his company in 'a shell battered church, in a much shell battered town, somewhere near Belgium a few weeks ago,' he came across an inscription. It was written on the wall of a corridor in the church from another local man, who had printed his name and address. The inscription was from a John Goodwin, whose address was Marr Street, Denaby Main near Rotherham. Scanlon said:

> I hope that you will insert these few lines in the *Advertiser* as it may meet the eye of the Denaby Main readers amongst whom may be the said John Goodwin's friends. In conclusion I hope the man John Goodwin is alive and well. The *Advertiser* is greatly appreciated over here. It comes to me like a ray of sunshine among scenes of utter desolation. I remain sir, Sergeant E Scanlon.

It was clear that the men of the town shared a common identity with other soldiers and did their best to return lost items. It is hoped that the local newspaper helped in getting these items back to their owners or, in cases where they were no longer alive, served as some form of comfort for the relatives left behind.

Within months of the outbreak of the war, propaganda infiltrated the newspaper's articles and advertisements. One such example, which was printed in November 1915, was an illustration of a young woman pegging onto a washing line a Union Jack. The byline was, 'I peg a Union Jack on my clothes line every wash-day! In other words, I use the purest and

The patriotic Sunlight soap advert.

I Peg a Union Jack on my clothes line *every wash-day!* In other words, I use the purest and best BRITISH SOAP.

**SUNLIGHT SOAP**

best BRITISH SOAP.' From this it was to be deduced that using the soap would uphold the nation's tradition for quality. This advert for Sunlight soap was just one of many such advertisements which appeared in the *Advertiser* throughout the years of the war.

Darker propaganda was seen in the reports of German atrocities, which were in the news on a regular basis. When this coincided with an atrocity like the sinking of the battleship *Formidable* at the hands of the Germans, the press really went to town. On the same page as the news of the sinking battleship was the headline, 'German outrages proved'. The enemies (the 'Kaiser's Huns') were accused of 'inhuman conduct', 'killing men and violating women'. Both the national and local press repeatedly portrayed the German people as violent bullies due to the cowardly invasion of Belgium and because of the invention of gas warfare in 1915. Many felt that these traits would never be seen in an Englishman. All these stories fuelled the idea that the British 'Tommy' was fighting to save the virtue and idealism of the rest of the world.

Some of the eminent citizens of the town with German-sounding names, even those who had lived in this country for some time, were also subject to rumour and speculation. One such publican was forced, on 8 August 1914, to put a notice in the *Advertiser* stating:

> Slanderous statements entirely without foundation have been circulated to the effect that FREDERICK CHARLES SCHONHUT of the Red Lion Hotel has expressed hostility to England and sympathises with the German nation. That Frederick Charles Schonhut is a British subject and his sympathies are entirely with England. Untrue statements have been made that he had taken down a picture of the King from behind the bar of the Red Lion and replaced it with the Kaiser have caused and are likely to cause him serious loss.

Such speculation could have caused him to lose his standing in the community as well as affecting his livelihood. But the most anti-German feelings in Rotherham, and indeed the rest of Britain, were stirred after the sinking of the *Lusitania* by a German submarine, resulting in the death of innocent men, women and children. The Germans had notified the world that it considered the water around Britain to be a war zone from the 18 February 1915 and that all vessels found in those waters were liable to attack. The liner was torpedoed just off the coast of Ireland on 7 May. It took just eighteen minutes to sink, with the loss of almost 1,200 lives. It was this single act that turned many of the population irrevocably against the German people.

After the war, in July 1919, the *Advertiser* printed an account of a medal, brought home by an artilleryman, which had been cast in Germany following the sinking of the ship. One side of the medal showed the ship sinking and, underneath the date of the disaster, a eulogy to German U boats. The reverse of the medal showed a human skeleton issuing tickets to crowds of passengers anxious to board the ship, which is illustrated by an explanation that those who lost their lives had only themselves to blame by ignoring the German warning not to travel.

The news of the tragedy reached Rotherham in May of 1915, when it seems that this, combined with a lack of meat, provoked violent anti-German riots in the town. The events started peaceably enough on the 8 May 1915 when, because of the scarcity of meat, the butchers of the town held a meeting at the Cross Keys public house on the Crofts. They proposed that the butchers' shops be closed from Saturday to Wednesday of every week, but it seems that there was some dispute about this. Being unable to come to a decision, it was agreed that the opinion of the town's butchers would be canvassed and a decision made the following week. On the 14 May, the paper reported that crowds had gathered in the vicinity of St Ann's Road, where an argument broke out in front of a pork butcher's shop owned by Mr L. Fisher.

This uprising was reflected in further riots in other towns of the nation. It had been rumoured that German butchers were poisoning the meat supplied to their British customers and this may have added fuel to the fire of anti-German feeling. It was reported that the crowd was composed mostly 'of women and children', with 'a sprinkling of youths'. In the course of the argument that broke out, someone threw a brick at the butcher's shop window and smashed it. Angry remarks against Germany and the Kaiser were heard and possibly a connection to another butcher's shop in the town was made. The party then moved onto 101 Frederick Street and grew in strength in front of another pork butcher's shop – one owned by Mr C. Hanneman, who was described as 'a man of German extraction'. His window was smashed and the contents of the shop looted. It was reported that the crowd was between 3,000 and 5,000 in number at this point, assembling next on the corner of Doncastergate, High Street, Wellgate and College Street, and once more in front of another pork butcher's shop, that of Mr T.W. Downs. A group known as the Rotherham and District Volunteer Defence Corps were brought into the town and sworn in as special constables to quell the disturbances in these extraordinary street scenes. During the riots, when people were attacking German shops and businesses, it seems that crowds of hostile people tried to get into the Red Lion pub, run by Mr Shonhut. Thankfully they were forced back by police, who had ordered that the yard gates be bolted and shuttered.

The Cross Keys as it is today. Butchers met here to discuss meat rationing, which sparked the anti-German riots in Rotherham during May 1914.

# Anti-German Riots

## Rotherham Joins in the General Rising.

### WIDESPREAD DAMAGE.

### SHOPS LOOTED AND FURNITURE SMASHED.

### BOY KILLED IN THE CROWD.

### MEETING OF MAGISTRATES IN COLLEGE SQUARE.

An account of the anti-German riots in Rotherham.

However, it does seem that in Rotherham the attacks were mainly concentrated around pork butchers' shops. It was reported after the riots that 'four women were seen with the carcass of a pig' on the streets of the town. As a result of the anti-German feeling, which was still in evidence a week later, one of the butchers, Mr T.W. Downes, took out half the front page of the *Advertiser* to announce:

> I am sick of hearing that only a German can effectively cater for the English taste in the pork trade and to prove that an Englishman can cater for English people I have taken a shop just below Mr. Earles in Doncastergate where I purpose [*sic*] making a choice and tempting display of pork delicacies.
> THIS WILL CONVINCE ROTHERHAM PEOPLE THAT WHAT OTHER COUNTRYMEN HAVE DONE ENGLISHMEN CAN DO.
>
> But I need your support. You have given it to me in the past and I shall continue to try to merit it in the future.
>
> NOTE THE ADDRESS: T.W. DOWNES DONCASTERGATE ROTHERHAM.
>
> I shall open Wednesday next.

At the same time, another British pork butcher was doing a roaring trade, serving customers as quickly as he could. Written on his window were the lines 'Be British' and 'We are English' – words that ensured his success.

In the beginning of 1915, the accusation made by Peter Sheridan regarding the amount of young men seen on the streets of the town who were not in uniform, was taken up by the townspeople. In August 1915, Rotherham had three munitions factories, of which, initially, the majority of workers were women; but it appears that more and more men were now being employed in them. Demands for more shells were being received from the soldiers at the front and the town was anxious to supply them. The government agreed that the workers in these factories would have an 'On War Service Badge' to identify them as working in reserved occupations, as well as an exemption certificate or card. In this way, genuine men who had been rejected as unfit for war service would be able to get work in these factories in order to contribute to the war effort and to prevent them from suffering harassment. At first the matter was noted with pride. The newspaper for 7 August 1915 read:

> There was only standing room on the tram cars as many of the seats were occupied by men wearing blue overalls and wearing war medals. Here is continuing argument that Rotherham was doing its bit for the town in industry of supplying shells to the Army and the Navy. To quote Lloyd George 'if every ammunition factory is a trench there are now many trenches in our own district which we see in the new Government Factories now being built in the town'.

Two months later, two men, both described as 'wounded soldiers' on sick leave, visited the office of the *Advertiser* and they too criticised the numbers of young men still on the streets of the town. They called them 'vermin dressed up as men who refused to enlist'. One spoke of a young man lounging around in College Street, who when asked why he hadn't enlisted replied that he 'had more sense than to enlist'. Another had stated that he 'wouldn't fight for no one'. The soldiers on leave said, 'Something needs to be done about these shirkers and cowards and the sooner the better.' The words 'shirkers' and 'slackers' now came into vogue in Rotherham and were used in many of the reports in the *Advertiser*. In December 1915, within the pages devoted to the photos of men who had been reported as being killed, wounded or missing, it announced:

BUT THE DRUMS ANSWERED COME: PICTURES THAT CONVEY LESSONS TO THE SLACKERS

It was not just Peter Sheridan who was incensed about these 'slackers', but also other Rotherham men who had enlisted and faced danger and death on a daily basis at the front. They were critical that young men could work in munitions factories in the town and could earn good money whilst thousands of men were risking their lives for the customary King's shilling. One anonymous letter from the front in September 1915 discussed the turmoil of 'being surrounded by young men with children shot down all around [him], whilst unmarried men are enjoying themselves at home.' As if on cue, in the same paper there was a report that Private George Harvey Smith of 47 St Johns Road, Eastwood, had been killed, leaving a widow and ten children behind. It was a question that would continue to be asked in the town throughout the rest of the war.

By September 1916, a campaign was launched to make sure that all able-bodied young men enlisted rather than work in munitions. The police and the military authorities were regularly raiding places of entertainment, such as football matches, boxing booths and other meeting places favoured by the youths of the town, and demanded to see their exemption papers. If they were unable to produce them they were handed over to the military authorities. The *Advertiser* stated that, 'In Rotherham people wishing to keep out of the war have found it easy by getting "badged" as indispensable to one or another of the large munitions works.' The situation was also aggravated by a report that men from other towns and districts were crowding into the Rotherham, attracted by the high wages of the munitions work. In November 1916, the paper reported different 'patois' that could be heard in the streets of Rotherham. Dialects from Lincolnshire, Norfolk and even from 'Zummerset' had been heard.

It was not just that 'shirkers' and 'slackers' were pouring into Rotherham though; some young men would leave the district in an attempt to evade military service and gain jobs elsewhere. By July 1916 it was reported that over 100 Rotherham men were 'absent without leave' and were wanted by the military authorities. They had either failed to turn up at the appointed army base or had not returned to their unit following a spell of leave. A constable reported to the magistrate that he had called at a house in the Holmes district and found a son who was a deserter there. It seems that he had been absent from his unit for about twelve weeks. The father told the constable that he had tried to encourage his son to go back to his unit, but had been unsuccessful. When the magistrate asked him why he had not reported his son to the military authorities he replied that 'it was very difficult'. The Chief Constable noted that there were many cases like this and he asked the Mayor to deal harshly with this young man, but the Mayor said that as it had been the first case to be brought in front of him he would deal with it more leniently. The defendant was bound over for twelve months. These kinds of cases resulted in the councillors demanding that more enquiries were made into the cases of the 'badged' men in the town who appeared to be fit enough to fight. It was agreed that there would be a move to 'comb out' all those men from the munitions factories. It seems that they were unsuccessful as the following week the newspaper printed:

> The promise of the authorities to comb out of the munitions and armaments works the thousands of men whose proper place is in the army, remain unfulfilled and the sight of many badged young men gallivanting during the week end remain to sicken and annoy the general public. These young men should be compulsory [*sic*] put in their proper place in the army. It is said that some employers are reluctant to lose a single unmarried man who only became an experienced worker since war broke out.

By September 1916, another reason for the numbers of young men on the streets of the town was brought to light, when the *Advertiser* reported, 'A strict enquiry into the credentials of many of the badged men would reveal facts that would startle the Minister for Munitions, Lloyd George and he would immediately demand their removal into the army.' This tribunal, which was appointed in February 1916, would examine all the 'badged' men to ascertain their reasons for not enlisting. Their brief was very specific. The four reasons why a man could claim exemption from enlisting for military service were stated:

> That in the National Interest he should be engaged in other work.
> Serious hardship would be suffered if he enlisted.
> He is in ill health or infirm.
> He is a Conscientious Objector.

Before very long it appears that the tribunal was weighed down by the numbers of Conscientious Objectors (COs) that appeared before them. It seems that a lot of men were coming forward and stating that their religious beliefs would not allow them to fire at another human being. For this reason they were going into munitions work instead. These included some COs who, it has to be said, were not treated with much respect. Some of them were forced to go into uniform, and if they refused an order from an officer they were liable to be shot as a traitor. In the *Advertiser* the names of such men were not published; they were just described by their age or occupation. The tone of the reporting was very harmful. For example, a thirty-one-year-old CO from Thorpe Hesley stated to the tribunal, in March 1916, that he would not shoot a German. He was a joiner, undertaker and contractor and belonged to the sect known as the Plymouth Brethren. A lady member of the tribunal asked him, 'Suppose that the Germans were over here and were violating the honour of your mother or sister what would you do? Strike them or shoot them?' The CO replied, 'I would not shoot them,' to which the woman exclaimed, 'Then you are hopeless!'

His claim for exemption was dismissed, but as he was prepared to undertake some alternative employment they ordered that he be placed in a position where he would not have to take up arms to fight. The tribunal informed him, 'You will be placed in a position where you can perform your duty of love and service without the violation of your conscience.'

Mirroring the patriotic fervour of the town, the *Advertiser* continued to condemn the COs:

> There was an astonishing large number of young men holding principles that will not permit them to protect their country or their children when attacked. One has heard of timid ladies and other representatives of the fair sex who would not kill a crawling black beetle, but one never expected so many men. That so much religious asceticism should be paraded by unmarried men makes one wonder whether it is not used for a coward's cloak.

The following week it was reported there were sixty-three cases at the tribunal sitting on Wednesday, 8 March 1916. It took six and a half hours to hear all the cases. One CO, when asked if he would consider munitions work, refused to do war work at all, stating that he might as well shoot the shells if he was making them. He was asked, 'Are you prepared to clear out of the country?' and when he answered in the affirmative the unsympathetic response was, 'Well I think its time you did.' His application was denied, but once again he was recommended to go to a non-combative section of the services. Such was the feeling against these men that the *Advertiser* printed a letter written to them in April 1916 from Sergeant A. Clarke of the Sherwood Foresters, 'stationed somewhere in France'. Addressing the COs he said:

> I don't suppose these few words will make any difference to you. Shall I call you men? You are a long way from manhood. You don't seem to realise the country is at war and that good men are staking their lives for such as you to benefit after it is all over. What should we do if we were all like you? Let the Germans serve England as they have served this country? The likes of you who are afraid to fight for your country and those who are dear to you are not worthy of the name of men. You should be bagged. I myself have left my wife and three children and have been constantly under fire since November 1914. Act like an Englishman and not like idiots.

The position of these COs would not improve very much, even with the onslaught of the Second World War. They were given little sympathy and were, in the main, very misunderstood. For the duration of the war, and for five years following the Armistice, these Objectors were punished by being disenfranchised. Many of them who went into non-combative work were heroes in their own right, undertaking dangerous positions such as ambulance drivers and medical orderlies and subsequently losing their lives in battles. Considered cowards, many others were imprisoned for their beliefs until the end of the war, serving sentences that often included hard labour. Evidently there was strong criticism against the male munitions workers, but this was not the case for the women workers of the town, who were praised for their dedication and patriotism.

# 4

# THE ROLE OF WOMEN

In the early months of the First World War many people thought that the only way in which women might be able to contribute to the effort was by developing a knitting or sewing circle. In September 1914 there was an announcement that a group of Dinnington women were trying to encourage females to join them in knitting socks and sleeping helmets for the boys on the front line. The *Advertiser* announced, 'Mrs. Althorpe and Mrs. Holliday would be pleased to hear from anyone who can help them in this task.' However, some women wanted to take a more active role in the war effort. By June 1915 it was announced that a national munitions factory would be opened in Rotherham and that a large workforce of women would be needed to make the shells. It was reported, 'In order to accomplish this, seven days of recruitment will take place at the Municipal Offices in Howard Street.'

The following month it was decided that instead of one factory, two munitions factories would be opened. It was announced that the two Rotherham premises which would be switched to munitions were those owned by Messrs John Baker & Co. Ltd and Messrs Owen & Dyson Ltd. These businesses already had installed lathes and equipment that was necessary for shell production and it was further agreed that they would work very much like a co-operative. Part of the shells would be made at one factory and the remaining part at the other. The intention was that they would produce 100 shells a week.

Women took to the work very readily. Now, for the first time, they would have the opportunity to be more financially and socially independent. The munitions workers were earning quite a lot of money and, although female workers did not earn as much as men, it was more money than a woman had been able to earn previously. The Minister for Munitions, Lloyd George, instituted a rate for women workers, which was printed in the *Advertiser* in July 1916:

| Premium Hours Workers | Rates for Workers when customarily on time are |
|---|---|
| 18 years and over: 4*d* hour | 18 years and over: 4½*d* hour |
| 17–18 years: 3½*d* hour | 17–18 years: 4*d* hour |
| 16–17 years: 3*d* hour | 16–17 years: 3½*d* hour |
| under 16 years: 2½*d* hour | under 16 years: 3*d* hour |

Presumably the extra rate was a reward for the more reliable workers. In the event the *Advertiser* reporter felt that this was still a 'sweated wage'. In Rotherham it seems that male workers could earn 24s a week, but female workers were earning a mere 16s a week. These wages, however low they seem to us, ignited a storm of protest from the widows and wives of men who had, or who were, serving at the front. There was some feeling that by employing women in factories the Rotherham Council was not taking seriously the financial plight of widows and mothers with children to feed. One widow protested to the *Advertiser* in April 1916 that her husband had been killed, leaving her with four children and that she was struggling to survive to bring them up on the pension issued to her by the government.

In order to 'do their bit', many Rotherham women joined the YMCA. This national organisation had been involved in providing support for soldiers since the Boer War. In Rotherham, a great new opportunity presented itself in October 1915, when the paper announced that a new YMCA munitions canteen on Sheffield Road would be

The typical dress of female munitions workers, 1915.

opened the following week to cater for the large numbers of workers already employed in munitions. The large wooden structure would be opened by Countess Fitzwilliam and would 'provide meals all day until the early hours of the morning.' The YMCA had a lot of experience at providing hot meals and drinks for soldiers coming from or going out to the war. It had been agreed that women, who were volunteers, would staff the wooden structure and that they would provide nourishing meals, costing as little as 6d to 1s each, for the workers. The Countess, whose husband, the Earl Fitzwilliam, was serving in France under General French, opened it with great ceremony. The scheme proved such a success that the Countess visited and inspected the canteen once again in April 1916, when she praised the women who had worked tirelessly to keep the canteen running smoothly. She was 'delighted' to tell them that there was going to be 'a royal visitor in about three month's time'. The royal visitor turned out to be Princess Victoria Helena of Schlesinger Holstein, who was the patron of the YMCA. It was, therefore, a great coup for the Rotherham volunteers when she attended in July 1916. After inspecting the canteen, the Princess declared it to be 'one of the most complete in the country'.

Rotherham women now found themselves experiencing more financial rewards; not only by working at the munitions factories, but also because they were fed more nutritious and healthy meals at the YMCA. In October 1916 there was a report undertaken by the Health of Munitions Workers Committee, investigating the kind of food served in the YMCA canteen. Mr Leonard E. Hill MB, FRCS, who carried it out, praised the good meals that were supplied to the workers at reasonable prices. He reported that for the heavy munitions work, it was important to make sure that the calorific value of workers' meals was sustained at very low costs. In Rotherham it was revealed that for 6d, workers would be served with roast mutton, boiled potatoes and cabbage and a pudding of syrup roll. A breakfast consisting of three rashers of bacon and tomatoes would cost 7*d*; three slices of bread and jam would cost 1*p*, or a meal of sausage roll and a sandwich made of ham or cheese would cost 6*d*. Main meals were estimated to have 1,448 calories, which seems stodgy to our modern palate, but generally it was found that the food supplied was of very good quality and extremely good value. But there was a caution: 'The drinking of strong tea several times throughout the day will affect women workers and they should take note that it is physiologically unsound.'

By the end of 1914 the YMCA were given permission to extend their service of provision of rest, meals, entertainment and religious services to the troops in France. In order to do this, huts were built or buildings were commandeered to provide services for the soldiers fighting at the front. These buildings, sporting the now famous red triangle, were behind the front line, but still within the range of shelling. The soldiers would use them as a place of rest and recuperation, away from the trenches, until it was time for them to return to the fighting. There they would be supplied with free paper, stamps and envelopes and encouraged to write home. Concerts would be put on for them and for a few hours they were allowed to forget about the war. The YMCA and the military authorities had realised how important these base camps were for the soldier's morale. For this reason, many respectable local women elected to go out to France to entertain the troops. Rotherham women who wished to serve with the YMCA had to report to a female officer and would then be dispatched to where she was needed most. Naturally, these women were treated with the utmost respect. No doubt the sight of a woman in France was a boost to the fighting soldiers and would remind them of their relatives back home.

The *Advertiser* sent one of their reporters out to describe these camps in October 1917. The first hostel that the reporter saw was described as 'a hotel with three adjoining villas'. It seems that the first thing the women did was to decorate the recreation room which the reporter said had 'gay posters on the walls'. The rooms were large and airy and the soldiers looked relaxed and happy. He noted that there were rules pinned up on the wall about what was and wasn't allowed. The women volunteers were not allowed to wear ribbons or trinkets and all colours were forbidden with the exception of the French national colours. The volunteers were allowed to decorate their bedrooms, 'so long as they remain[ed] neat and tidy.' The women shared the bedrooms and there were usually three or four beds to a room. It seems that the beds were comfortable but hardly luxurious; they were described by the reporter as having 'up to four blankets each during the winter months, but no sheets were supplied'. The regime was fairly strict and a typical timetable showed what the women were expected to do:

| | |
|---|---|
| 7 a.m. | roll call |
| 8 a.m. | breakfast (bedrooms were to be swept out each morning) |
| 1 p.m. | dinner |
| 6.15 p.m. | supper |
| 8.45 p.m. | roll call |
| 9 p.m. | bed |
| 10 p.m. | lights out |

A typical menu for the day indicated that the meals were basic but filling. Breakfast was tea, bread, butter, boiled ham and jam. Dinner would be thick brown stew, potatoes and cabbage, with bread and butter pudding afterwards. Tea was bread and butter, jam and cheese. Supper would be toad in the hole, bread and jam. These meals would be the kinds of diets that men and women were used to in their daily lives back home. When interviewed, one unnamed Rotherham girl said, 'I love the life since I came here in May.' The reporter responded that it would be difficult not to enjoy the life, as when the women were not working there were concerts, dances and whist drives to organise and attend. They would also cheer up the soldiers in the local hospitals with concerts. Curiously for the time, women were allowed to entertain men in their own quarters provided they got a pass from the authorities. This seems incredibly broad-minded, especially considering the concerns regarding women's moral behaviour back home. The volunteers were also encouraged to attend French classes and YMCA lectures. Life in the camps was very much on the same lines as the hostels except that the girls were billeted in Nissen huts, which were described as 'being made of wood with roofs of corrugating iron which reach down to the floor on both sides.' These huts were used as dormitories for up to ten women, and one supervising forewoman was installed in each room. The reporter stated that the sections for the soldiers were very comfortable, as 'each camp had dining halls, a cookhouse and ablutions hut. Hot water was readily available and each hut had its own electricity and own stove.'

This must have been a real luxury to men who had been living for months in the mud of the trenches. The camp accommodated 500 women and the reporter joyfully noted, 'Those English women are missing their chance if they don't come out here to France and work.' It certainly seems that it was like some kind of holiday camp for young women of Rotherham and as an added bonus there would be more possibility of meeting men, even if they were wounded soldiers.

The opportunities for volunteering during the years of the First World War opened up new avenues for Rotherham woman. Those who wanted to help the war effort were encouraged to enlist as nurses. The Queen Alexander Royal Army Nursing Corps was founded in 1897 and had seen a lot of service at the battlefields. Nevertheless, some of the new nurses in France would find that this was not an easy job by any means. These women would often have to live in tents near the battlefields, drive ambulances and tend to the wounded soldiers amongst the shelling and the bullets. This was definitely not a job for the fainthearted. There were very brave women who undertook this work and one in particular was a very courageous nurse from Rotherham. Known as Nurse Kitchen, she served in Belgium. A letter sent to the editor of the *Advertiser* in June 1915, from Private Tom Senior, shows that she was a celebrated figure. Writing from St Hilda's Hospital at Greenwich, following his return back to England, he explained:

I am venturing to write to you on a subject which will be of interest to the girls of Rotherham. Even in the heat of battle Nurse Kitchen crept on her hands and knees to give water to the wounded soldiers. I witnessed young Davenport of the Holmes in Rotherham who died with his head on Nurse Kitchens breast and many more have had the last kiss on this earth given by her. She is ever ready to pray or to sing to them in their last hour. She always asked the injured men 'are you from Rotherham?' The lads have agreed that if they come back to the town they will buy her the best gold watch in the town.

It was to be hoped that this brave girl managed to make it back home. The reporter noted, 'There are many worthy followers of Florence Nightingale in this town and Nurse Kitchen is certainly one of them.' Many stories like this, telling of these courageous women, were printed in the local newspapers, and so it was with absolute horror in October 1915 when there was news of the shooting of Nurse Edith Cavell. The whole country felt such disgust at the cowardly act and, once again, it added to the anti-German feeling in Britain.

The nurses of the British Red Cross were also singled out for praise in February 1917. Describing himself as a 'Rotherham gentleman just returned from a visit to Northern France,' a soldier wrote to the editor:

> It is marvellous and splendid that thousands of ladies have given up their lives of ease and luxury...caring for the wounded soldiers. They receive no pay for their services and are called to duty all hours of the day and night. They do all sorts of work from treating the wounded and driving 50 horsepower ambulances. In future my mite will be gladly given to the British Red Cross because I will be supporting a cause deserving of every support.

Some patriotic local women chose to work as Voluntary Aid Detached (VAD) nurses. VAD nurses were required to treat wounded soldiers who had been returned to this country to convalesce. Due to the severity of the fighting, many hospitals were required to undertake this work. In December 1915, Mr Colin M. Smith offered to lease to the town council's Oakwood Hall, a magnificent mansion off Whiston Road, for this purpose. This was an opportunity to serve as voluntary nurses and orderlies who were to be trained by the Red Cross Society. Many local women took this chance. Mr Smith's very generous offer was taken up and the building was placed on a military basis. Lieutenant Colonel Connell was enlisted to command the hospital and to take over the finances. A group of local women was organised as the committee, headed by a president, Mrs Coward, who was the ex-Mayor's wife. For many years, grateful soldiers would recuperate from their wounds in this beautiful house, surrounded by these kind and helpful nurses. The picturesque grounds would have aided the soldier's recovery, so it was with great sadness that it was announced that the house was destroyed

by fire in June 1918. The *Advertiser* explained that the people of Rotherham had looked with pride on this beautiful mansion and the great achievements made by the hospital and staff in such a short period. The reporter noted, 'The medical and nursing staff have earned themselves an enviable reputation and the loss of the

Nurses uniforms during the First World War.

hospital is a great tragedy.' The following month it was agreed that the hospital would be re-opened, and Oakwood Hall remains part of the Rotherham Hospital complex today.

For the majority of women, however, the biggest revolution brought about by the First World War was their emergence into the workplace, where they took on roles formerly undertaken by men. It was during a Rotherham Council meeting on 20 March 1915 that it was decided women could replace some of the male employees. It was reported that the councillors agreed that the work women undertook would have to be limited, as 'they did not want to lose their femininity,' but decided that it would be suitable for them to work in such places as dairies and farms, in brush-making and cloth-making industries and even in armament positions using some of the lighter machines. It seems that these councillors had no idea that, within a few short months, hundreds of women would be working very successfully in the munitions factories soon to be opened in the town. No doubt some of the town councillors were congratulating themselves for solving the employment difficulties when they suggested that in these kinds of occupations women 'could do quite well if not better than men.'

The newspaper requested that any women who were willing to undertake this kind of work should register their details at the local Labour Exchange. Here their names would be recorded on the War Office Register. This scheme appears to have been very successful, probably, in part, because it offered women of the town a shared cause with the fighting men. But for the most part it was an opportunity to go out to work, mix with other women and be financially independent, possibly for the first time in their lives. For single women who were prepared to work away from home, it was agreed that the government would provide housing for them to lodge in as well as satisfactory pay. This clarion call for women offered a sense of freedom not experienced before. I am certain that many single Rotherham women took advantage of this chance and would have signed up in their hundreds. Women at this time took on more and more of the roles in the town. One of the greatest successes came when women were employed as tram conductresses. This was announced in October 1915 and the *Advertiser* reported:

> When women mounted the platform of the trolley buses there had been lots of misgivings as to whether the scheme would be successful or not. No doubt the local Tramway Authorities were congratulating themselves on their success. The travelling public was quite in love with lady conductors who was more neatly attired, more courteous and more businesslike that lady conductors in other towns.

Despite this progression, it seems that the trams were only to be driven by men. It was estimated in April 1916 that over £¼ million had been spent in Rotherham in the industrial expansion of war production and that, 'The people of the town were enjoying a period of great prosperity not seen for a long time.' It seems that women wearing trousers had been a rare sight before the war, but now their trousers were said to be 'no longer a novelty in the town'. Nevertheless, it was recorded in the newspaper that the town owed some gratitude to these female workers and printed, 'History will record that she has helped to save England.'

Lots of women workers had come into the town to work and, as a consequence, several hundred were in lodging houses. Always concerned about the morality of these young women,

## THE ROTHERHAM V.A.D. HOSPITAL.

### VIEWS OF OAKWOOD HALL.

The front of Oakwood Hall.

Oakwood Hall VAD Hospital.

the editor of the *Advertiser* suggested that 'steps be taken to provide a place where these women can find a helpful friend and a refining influence.' Mrs Robinson of Barber Wood took up the challenge and she suggested that a club be opened along the same lines as the YMCA. Premises were found at Chrimes Chapel on Moorgate, which was opened in September 1917. The newspaper judiciously stated that 'it was hoped that the club would provide a counter attraction to the allurement of the street.' A week later, it was announced that Miss Elsie Phillips was to be employed at the club to give instruction on a variety of subjects. It was proposed that a Bible class be formed. Restrictive though this seems to our modern eyes, it would have been a freeing experience for girls to live away from the parental home, probably for the first time. The club would allow her to form friendships and to have a life of her own. Possibly in some cases the freedom went to some young people's heads, which instigated a fear that their morals would suffer. This made the traditionalists in the local authorities anxious that the modesty of these women workers be preserved. It was brought to their attention that Clifton Park had been left open at night to allow the munitions workers a shortcut to get to work and that, as a consequence, young women and youths had taken advantage of this and were making assignations in the dark. The *Advertiser* reported:

> Girls and youth in their teens who would be better in khaki or navy blue are seen standing, sitting or lying down in the most suggestive attitudes. There are no police to patrol the park to rid these youthful invaders with the result that lasciviousness is not only common but carried out unblushingly in most bare faced fashion.

Naturally, this situation could not be allowed to continue and only a fortnight later, after the appointment of a constable to patrol the park, two anonymous young people were hauled before the magistrates for 'unseemly conduct'. They were charged with indecent behaviour on the previous Saturday night by one of the special constables who had been patrolling the park with a view to 'preventing this sort of conduct'. The man was fined 20s and costs and the woman was fined 16s and costs. Matters did not improve and the park continued to be used by young people. In September 1917 a further condemnation of these young people were noted. Men were accused of 'wearing straw hats and gaudily looking shirts which ill become youths with foul mouths and low tastes who pollute the atmosphere with ribald and indecent

A Rotherham tram conductresses
in October 1915.

remarks.' The reporter of the *Advertiser* asked, 'Is it
for such purposes that ratepayers provide a park at
the cost of great beauty, or can we no longer control
the youths and popinjays who have escaped military
uniform?'

One of the few drawbacks to women working in
the munitions factories was the increase of what
we now term 'latch-key children'. As a result of
some of these women working very long hours,
their children were missing school. At a meeting
of the Rotherham Education Committee in October
1916 they complained that the children of these
working mothers were neglecting their education.
Canon Goodall suggested that when recruiting for
the munitions, preference should be given to those
married women without children. The munitions were important but also, he pointed out,
was a child's education. Some women had no option but to work to earn enough money to
support herself and the children.

At the same meeting, Alderman Gummer said he had a case brought before him the
previous week from a woman with four children having to manage on only 23s a week,
which she got from her husband who was fighting in the war, and that she had taken a job
in the munitions factory in the hope of eking out her allowance. He did suggest that perhaps
it might be an opportunity for the ladies of the district to set up some kind of organisation
to take on the responsibilities for caring for these children whilst their mothers were at work.
Interestingly, the concerns were primarily about the lack of education for these children and
not for the dangers of them being home alone, as is more pertinent to our modern perspective.

Most of this chapter has concentrated on the positive aspects of these changes for unmarried
women of the town; very little of it has been devoted to the married women or widows, and
this is simply because there is very little recorded about those groups of women. Certainly
the difficulties faced by women left at home, trying to cope with large families and manage
on a very small budget, contrasted with the freedom that other women experienced during
the war. The severe rationing and the long queues would have been difficult to deal with on a
daily basis. Rotherham, during the years of 1917, was becoming 'a town of queues', a sight
regularly seen in front of several shops in the town. The *Advertiser* noted:

Scarce though food is, there is nothing to justify the spectacle of the needs for hundreds
of people waiting for up to four hours as a time for the staple foods of tea, sugar or
butter. Children and mothers with babies in arms were in these queues. Many women
having got supplies would then join the back of the queue to be served again. Others
who were late arrivals would find the food had been sold out when it was their turn.

A demand for compulsory rationing was called for but the queues continued. By December 1917, it was reported that the queues in the town were becoming 'a disgrace to the Food Controllers both individually and collectively.' Just before the seasonal holiday, it was noted that Christmas of 1917 would be remembered as a 'Christmas of the Queues'. There were queues for tea and butter, which were aggravated by other queues for whisky, turkey and goose. The light-hearted note of the reporter hid the fact that Rotherham, at this time, was subject to limited pub opening times of just two hours a day, from 1.30 p.m. to 2.30 p.m. and from 8 p.m. to 9 p.m. in the evening. The pub owners of Rotherham took exception to this stipulation and ignored the new opening hours. By staggering the times, it was reported that the most hardened drinker with money could usually buy a drink at any time. The police were unable to regulate this and it was said at the time, 'The friend that most townspeople would like to have is the one with a good well stocked cellar who is generous to his friends.'

By January 1918, the queues had not diminished but had in fact grown longer. (Unknown to the people of Rotherham at this time, 1918 would be the last year of the war.) It was reported that thousands of people were now queuing for food before daylight. Shops had lists of provisions they were unable to stock inserted in their windows and many stated, 'No tea, no butter, no margarine, no bacon, no jam and no marmalade.' Shops with small supplies found that their stocks were soon depleted. Some women were heard boasting that by joining several of these queues they had got plenty of supplies, and having taken them home had come back for more. No doubt many of these were sold privately and at some cost to those women unable to queue. Grocers complained that it was the government's fault, as shops were unable to buy supplies of imported food and would be accused of profiteering with the produce they could obtain. Finally the *Advertiser* was successful in its campaign and, by the last week of January 1918, food rationing was introduced for butter, margarine and meat. This came about after it reported that 60,000 people out of a total population of 70,000 were counted in the queues in the town.

The position of women, for many of them, would never go back to what it was before the war. Women demanded the vote and for some it was granted. They also had more power in divorces, more power over their possessions and more rights relating to their children, but these were not achieved overnight. There is no doubt that, due to the effort made by women during the war, their position did change for the better. In Rotherham, it was made clear that once the war was over and the men returned, that women were expected to stay at home once again. But the war had created an economy which could never be the same again. Fewer women would go back to being servants and the years following 1918 saw many complaints from the middle classes about the shortage of domestic help, which before the war had been readily available. Rotherham women had experienced a freedom which they would be reluctant to forgo. Generally speaking, the war years were a time when many people of the town were patriotic and hardworking, doing their best to survive the many hardships. However, there were some who exhibited such bravery that medals were awarded, and others who were purely subversive.

# 5

# HEROES AND VILLAINS

There is no doubt that the men and women of Rotherham were both patriotic and courageous. This was amply illustrated in the huge numbers of men who readily enlisted during the first days and weeks of the war. They went in their thousands to fight for King and Country and their sacrifice will never be forgotten. The King sent a message on the anniversary of the outbreak of the First World War, on 3 August 1916 at midnight. Two days later the *Advertiser* reported the King's words:

On this day the second anniversary of the commencement of the Great War my country and her gallant allies are engaged. I desire to convey to you my steadfast resolution to prosecute the war until our united efforts have attained the objects for which we have in common and have taken up arms. I feel assured that you are in accord with me in the determination that the sacrifices which our valiant troops have so nobly made shall not have been offered in vain and that the liberties which they are fighting for shall be fully guaranteed and secured.

The names of many of these valiant troops who made that noble sacrifice are inscribed on the war memorial in Clifton Park. Every family who lost someone will have their own memories of the relatives that did not come back to the town, but in this chapter I will tell some of the stories of these brave men and the glory that they brought to the town through their courage under fire.

Within days of the war, the *Advertiser* held pictures of the Rotherham heroes fighting at the front line. One of the first men to die didn't even reach the front line. Corporal Edwin Smith of the York and Lancaster Regiment was only twenty-five when he contracted typhoid in the training camp and died at Leys School Hospital in Cambridge. His body was returned to his parents, Mr William Smith and his wife, of 57 Arthur Street, Thornhill. He was buried at Masbrough Cemetery with full military honours. He was an exception, as by the end of the hostilities many of the millions of young men who died, or were missing and presumed dead, were buried in unmarked graves. War grave archaeology is, in this present time, still unearthing soldiers who are unknown, and the occasional few are identified from the belongings that they carried with them. Such a body was identified after the war, in

December 1919, when a photograph was taken of a grave on the road to Elouges. The inscription read, 'Unknown British Soldier. Died 24th August 1914.' A photograph had been found in his hand, clutched against his heart, and at the bottom of the photograph was a message from the sender. After the war this person was traced and the soldier was finally buried under his own name. In this instance, one of the soldiers who had buried the dead man had kept his helmet and, when the military authorities interviewed him, he produced the dead man's helmet, proving that he had died from a shot through the head. All soldiers, what ever nationality, were buried as near to the place where they died as possible. If they carried information that could identify them, it was recorded; otherwise they would be buried under the description 'Known Only To God'.

As early into the war as April 1915, the military authorities recognised that relatives would need to have their loved ones' death recorded in a place where they might be able to visit after the war, and much thought was given as to how this could best be achieved. It seems that there were some early war graves that had been allocated in France. The *Advertiser* described these as the 'War graves where our heroes lie.' A reporter stated:

> When relatives are officially notified of a soldier's death, a sketched plan of these graves showing the formation and the locality of the British cemetery in France is sent to them with particulars of the grave containing the body clearly marked. The greatest care is given to the dead bodies which had fallen in battle.

He went on to describe a military graveyard situated to the west of Vimy, where, at that time, the bodies of 1,330 French troops and more than 600 English men lay. The reporter

A typical training camp during the First World War.

described, '...the earth is bare on most of the newly dug English graves. The French graves are older but the English men now in charge of the place care for all the graves.' Perhaps some parents were unhappy that their sons' bodies would not be returned, or perhaps it was the large numbers of men that were already missing after the 'big push' that prompted calls for a war memorial. Whatever the cause, the following year, in October 1916, the *Advertiser* was requesting that a memorial be erected in Rotherham, containing a tablet inscribed with the names of the fallen soldiers. The reporter stated that it had not yet been thought of in Rotherham, and wrote, 'It is unlikely that the County Borough will neglect to perpetuate the memory of the gallant men who have fallen and distinguished themselves by voluntarily serving in the Great War.' The question of what form the memorial would take was discussed at great length in the council chamber, but it was not until after the war that a memorial was erected to the brave men of Rotherham who had died in the service of the King and Country.

The First World War spawned many heroes from Rotherham. It was, therefore, not surprising that in August 1915 the name of the first Territorial to be awarded the Distinguished Conduct Medal was announced in the *Advertiser*. Private Gwynette of A Company 1/5th Battalion of the York and Lancaster Regiment's deed of valour was described thus:

> During the heaviest period of the bombardment on July 10<sup>th</sup> when stretcher-bearers were isolated from the company. Private Gwynette attended to 20 wounded men. By his general bearing and conduct he did much to keep up the spirits of the rest of the men. He also got a party together under heavy fire and buried several dead left by the battalion who had previously occupied the trenches.

The following year, in April 1916, Leading Seaman James Malin of Rotherham won a Conspicuous Gallantry Medal, described as 'almost a Victoria Cross'. It was claimed that Malin would have the Victoria Cross (VC) if he had been less reluctant to talk about his deeds. The newspaper stated that 'the officer who could have corroborated his story was at the bottom of the sea.' His failure to fully describe his part in the gallantry delayed the announcement of the award, and the first Malin knew about it was when he arrived home in the early hours of Saturday morning on 8 April, to find his home on Nottingham Street decorated for a hero's return. The town's dignitaries agreed that there must be some kind of commemoration for the award and a subscription was started. Shortly afterwards, the town celebrated again when news that another of its sons, Sergeant F. Jessop, had been awarded a double Distinguished Conduct Medal (DCM) and clasp for his bravery under fire. These celebrations resulted in a very warm welcome in June 1916. The town was in a fever of preparation, waiting to greet not one, but both local heroes. Malin of the Anston Battalion Royal Naval Division and Jessop of the 1/5th York and Lancaster Regiment arrived in the town to full military honours. Malin had received his medal in connection to the landing of the troops at Suvla Bay, Gallipoli, for the Battle of the Dardanelles. Jessop had been awarded his for 'special gallantry on two occasions': he had attended to the wounded under fire in a gas attack at Ypres on December 1914 and had shown further bravery during a counter attack in the same place in July 1915.

It was reported that there was a large turn out to greet the two heroes, who were led by the Mayor to the Town Hall. Here he pinned the medals onto the two heroes' chests. Many former workmates of Malin, from the Rotherham Main colliery, were in the crowd. The Mayor spoke for the multitude when he said that Rotherham was very proud of the men who had shown such gallantry whilst under fire from enemy bullets. He said that not many men had managed to win the DCM twice.

In August 1916, Private George William Chafer of the East Yorkshire Regiment was awarded a Victoria Cross, the first for Rotherham. The *Advertiser* recorded that the medal had been awarded for:

> ...the most conspicuous bravery during heavy hostile bombardment and attacks on our trenches. A man carrying a most important message to his Company Commander was half buried and rendered unconscious by a shell. Private Chafer at once grasped the

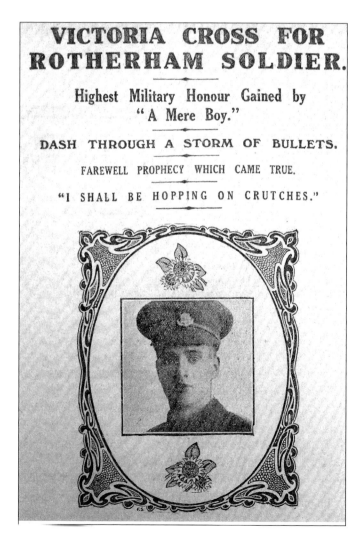

How the *Advertiser* announced its first Victoria Cross.

situation on his own initiative took the message from the mans pocket and although severely wounded in three places ran along the ruined parapet under heavy shell and machine gun fire and just succeeded in delivering the message before collapsing from the effects of his wounds. He displayed great initiative and a splendid devotion to duty at a critical moment.

The *Advertiser* pointed out that Private Chafer was very slight in build, standing not much more than 5ft high and weighing in at only 9 stone, and was also one of the youngest to have received such an award. The reporter reflected that Rudyard Kipling's description of Lord Robert applied here, quoting, 'He's little but he's wise / He's a terror for his size.' When Private Chafer had enlisted, his friends had thought that he would be rejected as unfit due to his sleight build, but to their amazement he was accepted. They also shared with the reporter a story about Private Chafer; that when he went into a Rotherham men's wear shop, the kindly assistant showed him to the children's department.

Private Chafer was likened to another soldier who had recently won the DCM, a Private Clements, who was also very slight. Despite their size they both proved themselves to be heroes. The people of the town had to wait until 13 December before they could show their appreciation for Private Chafer, who had also been awarded the Russian Order of St George as well as the VC. The celebrations began at the station at Masbrough when the Mayor welcomed him home. The news about his arrival had only reached the Town Clerk's office the day before, so arrangements were made very quickly and a program of celebrations was put together. It was reported that he arrived at the railway station at exactly 11.30 a.m. and was greeted by a band of the York and Lancaster regiment. He was then escorted into a car that was decorated with flags and driven to College Square accompanied by uniformed escorts, including a contingent of Royal Defence Corps and a parade of police and special constables. Surrounded by cheering people of the town all waving flags, he was then taken to the council chamber, where he was given a great reception. Following this he was driven to Ravenfield, where another reception was held for him, this time with his former workmates and his family.

The burgeoning flying service had its first air hero from Rotherham when Captain Leslie P. Aizlewood was awarded the Military Cross in September 1916. He was announced as, 'The first airman to win this prize for Rotherham and probably for the whole of South Yorkshire.' The reporter stated proudly, 'It is a case of Rotherham being in the front again.' He related that an illness had caused Captain Aizlewood to leave the trenches on the Western Front, but that he did not intend remaining inactive for long and soon after joined the Royal Flying Corp. The Military Cross was given to him for his 'conspicuous gallantry and skill':

> ...seeing five hostile machines he manoeuvred to get between them and their lines and then diving on one of them he reserved his fire until he was only twenty yards off. The hostile machine fell out of control, but he was so close to it that he collided with it breaking his propeller and damaging his machine. Though it was barely controllable he managed to get back to our lines.

That Rotherham was proud of its heroes could never be disputed. More and more soldiers went on to gain medals; indeed, there are too many to list here. But their bravery was not forgotten and their names are inscribed on the war memorial, which the town erected to show their pride in the townspeople who showed exceptional bravery under fire.

But not all people of the town were patriotic. In April 1916 it was uncovered that a spy had been found. Towns such as Rotherham and Sheffield would attract such people as there were munitions works and other businesses making armour plating for ships and tanks. Albert Robert Bright was arrested under the Official Secrets Act for attempting to get industrial information from several Sheffield firms. Albert Bright, aged forty-nine, offered a local man, Harry Brooks, £100 to obtain secret formulas used in the munitions factory of Messrs Vickers of Sheffield. The charge against him was read out in court when he was accused of obtaining, and attempting to obtain, certain charge sheets containing formulas of armour plates, lyddite guns (an explosive that gets its name from the town of Lydd in Kent) and steel shells.

Bright lived at Moorgate Hall in Rotherham and had become acquainted with Harry Brooks through his friendship with Harry's father, Ben Brooks. He was an engineer by trade, but described himself as a merchant. As early as 1905, he had Brooks get him copies of these charge sheets, although what he was preparing to do with these was not clear. During February 1916, Bright called to see Brooks and asked him if he would get him the latest charge sheets. Brooks told him, disingenuously, that he was making lyddite guns now and shells, and that he was not on the armour-plated section. However, he agreed to get him the sheets and arranged to meet at his sister's house on the following Sunday to hand them over. On Thursday 2 March, Bright asked Brooks if he had got any charge sheets, but Brooks told him that he hadn't been able to get any, so Bright asked him if he could remember any of the formulas that were written on the charge sheets. Brooks dictated as much of the information as he could remember and Bright wrote it down, but it seems that his memory was at fault and, fortunately, he did not give Bright the correct information. Seemingly Brooks could neither read nor write and so, unbelievably, he asked the man working on the shells to write down the information, which he gave to Bright. On the 11 March Brooks obtained four of the charge sheets and left them at his sister's house for Bright to collect.

Bright now asked Brooks for some more sheets, who replied that he was unable to for the next week as he was on nights. Bright then offered him £100 for the information, a massive amount of money in those days. Brooks promised Bright that he would have them in just over a week and they agreed to meet in the Royal Britain public house on John Street, at 6.30 p.m. on the 27 March 1916. Fortunately, Brooks, blessedly unaware of the seriousness of his position, had mentioned to one or two people what he was doing and the information was relayed to his brother-in-law. When he heard about it he went to see Brooks and told him that he had placed himself in a very difficult situation and he could end up being shot for treason. Brooks belatedly realised the position he was in and, on advice from his brother-in-law, went to see his foreman, who related it to his manager Mr Johns. The newspaper reported that 'since that time he had been acting under the instructions of Mr Johns and the police.' Brooks was given thirteen sheets, or partial sheets, and was instructed to pass them onto Bright. On the appointed day, Bright went to Brooks' house, which had not been the plan, but Brooks kept his nerve and they both went to the Royal Britain, as arranged, where plain-clothed detectives were waiting. In sight of the detectives Brooks passed the sheets to Bright who put them in his coat pocket.

Moorgate Hall, where Albert Robert Bright lived in April 1916.

Detective Inspector Fretwell, upon seeing the transaction taking place, attempted to arrest Bright, but he denied all the charges. Fretwell and Bright struggled, but eventually the papers were taken from him and he was arrested. Fretwell searched Bright and found that he had several charge sheets in his bag dating back to 1905. The next day, when he appeared before the magistrate at the Court House, the charge sheets were examined in private and the case was adjourned until the following Tuesday. Meanwhile, the police searched Moorgate Hall and discovered that, seemingly, Bright had no money. The only paper money he had in the house and on his person was forged. The following Tuesday he was tried and found guilty, then sent for trial at the next assizes. The next month, Bright was put on trial and he pleaded guilty. There was much debate about why Bright had been collecting the sheets, as it was obvious that he had not benefited from them since he was 'in impecunious circumstances'. As the prosecution pointed out, the prisoner would not have collected them without intending to profit by it. The judge told him, 'You stand a confessed traitor to this country,' before sentencing him to penal servitude for life. It seems that it was only the fact that he had not passed the information onto the enemy that saved him from being shot.

Some of the unsung heroes of the war were the thousands of ordinary townspeople from Rotherham who aided the war effort by subscribing to buy war bonds. In August 1915, the government realised the incredible amount of money being spent daily on the war, and it introduced war bonds as a method of raising funds. People were encouraged to invest their money at 4 per cent as a loan to the government. The advertisements stated that these bonds could be bought at any post office and at prices that most people could afford. They were offered at 5s, 10s or £1 and people were encouraged to buy as many as they could afford. This scheme was very successful, not only in Rotherham but in other towns of South Yorkshire. In order to encourage the public to buy, many towns would have weapons such as tanks and guns exhibited to advertise the need to buy war bonds and to intrigue the passing townspeople. A tank toured the country and lists of how many war bonds had been sold in other towns were posted near to the tank to encourage inter-town rivalry with subscriptions. At the height of the war the people of Rotherham were also asked to buy war bonds to enable the government to buy ambulances, a battleship, a destroyer and an aeroplane. These were usually given the name of the town, and the amounts collected exceeded all expectations in nearly every case. It started in March 1915, when a motor ambulance was requested to go to the front line and it was stated that it would cost £600. The money was quickly collected and the ambulance bought. Somewhat ironically, what was not revealed until after the war was that this ambulance had been sunk on a boat taking it to France. Under the circumstances, it had not been felt appropriate to announce it at the time. In February 1918, it was ambitiously agreed that Rotherham would be encouraged to buy enough war bonds to supply a destroyer. A week, starting on 4 March, was designated for the sale of the bonds, which would need to be the equivalent of £150,000. Thirty-two other towns including Sheffield, Manchester and Birmingham were enrolled to pay for their own destroyer and a competition was in place. In fact, the scheme was so successful that Rotherham collected a total of £461,117 in a week, enough to buy three destroyers. This was an enormous sum of money from a town that, despite the boom in munitions, was still quite a poor town. It indicates how the townspeople felt part of a common cause with the lads actually doing the fighting in France. By donating money for war bonds they were able to do their bit for the war effort.

One very important band of men who volunteered in the town was the special constables. They volunteered during the war to aid the police in keeping the peace. There was no age limit for this group of men and people who were too old or too young for service were welcomed to their ranks. Initially they had no uniform, just an armband signifying their rank. Part of their work was to guard sensitive areas that might be open to attack and to patrol the streets with the regular police force. Like the Home Guard of the next war, they would also be on the look out for lights left on, as these could be seen by the zeppelins and aircraft in the skies over the town. As we have seen, they were also used to patrol Clifton Park. Two months before the announcement of the Armistice, in September 1918, it seems that all police constables had been given a day's holiday for the first time since the police force was established in the town. It was deemed a great success as no one had been arrested during that day, and it was reported that for the first time in many years the charge sheet was blank for the Rotherham magistrates on the following Monday morning.

These are some of the heroes and villains of the First World War in Rotherham. They were certainly no worse or better in other towns. War brought out the best and worst in people as ordinary men and women pulled together in an attempt to aid the war effort. But I would hazard a guess that many more unsung heroes of the town continued performing heroic and brave acts that went unlisted and unrecorded.

# 6

# ZEPPELIN RAIDS AND THE NEW TECHNOLOGY

The First World War became known as a war in which the development of new technology was accelerated. Cavalry officers, who had seen the horse as a vital weapon, now saw weaponry taking its place. At a time when there was no Royal Air Force, the embryonic Royal Flying Corps (RFC) came into being. The RFC was seen originally as being a branch of the army, and aeroplanes were originally attached to an army battalion, their main use as reconnaissance. The pilots would sketch the ground beneath them as they flew over the battlefields, so they could give the position of the enemy lines on their return. Only when aircraft started shooting down zeppelins was the machine recognised as a weapon of destruction; and so the struggle for air supremacy began. It was not until April 1918 that the Royal Air Force became a service on its own.

The aircraft most remembered from the First World War are the zeppelins, which were ideal for night-time warfare. Like the aircraft, they had first been used as reconnaissance, but by the outbreak of the war the Germans also swiftly realised their potential as bombers. Described as cigar shaped with an aluminium structure covered with cotton, they would silently steal over a sleeping town. These were the machines that engendered the most panic for much of the population, as people feared they would be murdered in their beds. All too soon their fears would be realised, although initially it was warships that launched the first attack. In December 1914, news reached the town that German warships had attacked the East Coast, carrying out 'murderous raids'. In Hartlepool it was stated that the numbers of dead and injured amounted to hundreds. In Scarborough and Whitby it was noted that the 'German murderers' had attacked defenceless men, women and children, resulting in the deaths of 119 people. Zeppelins were soon being used regularly, and in February 1915 it was decided in Rotherham that this threat had to be addressed. It was agreed that precautionary measures should be in place for the townspeople and these were the orders, as reported in the *Advertiser*:

> If German aircraft visit Rotherham you must take shelter in the nearest house, preferably in the basement. You are not to stand around in large groups or to touch any unexploded bombs which might be dropped. The Rotherham Watch Committee

has decided to re-introduce the old buzzer, which will be set off for at least five minutes if the airship is spotted. People are to shelter and for their own protection to shut off any gas supply and pull down blinds in order to make a less conspicuous target.

The report went on to state that the people of the town did not need to be alarmed – the chance of air attack was very remote – and announced the buzzer would be tested the following day at twelve o'clock. A funny sequel to this was reported in the paper of the 27 March 1915. It stated that the previous Sunday (21 March), the buzzer had been activated about midnight. It was described as loud and continuous. Many of the town remembered the warning and recalled drawing their curtains and going into the cellar, where they stayed shivering all night. Others dressed and went into the streets to see what they could see, but it was reported that the majority stayed where they were in bed. The column went on to report that although the buzzer was loud, the fire brigades in Rotherham and Rawmarsh did not hear it and, as a consequence of this, failed to arrive until one and a half hours after the buzzer had been sounded. By February 1916, it was discovered it wasn't just the people of the town that could hear the buzzer (or not as the case may be); the enemy would hear it too and could use it to identify the position of the town. Therefore the Chief Constable announced that the gas and electricity suppliers would now notify the presence of zeppelins. On spotting the raiders, the gas and electricity companies would turn down the supply and then increase it three times in succession; then the supply would be reduced and finally extinguished until the following day. What this plan failed to take into account was that if the raid happened while people were in bed, with the supplies turned off, then they would remain in ignorance of the impending attack. Despite all the warnings, it seems that most people believed that if zeppelins were spotted they stood a better chance of escaping attack by going outside, preferably to an open space, where they believed it would be less likely for aircrews to see them.

Later that month, orders were received to reduce lights in the town in order not to give away the position to hostile airships or aircraft. Posters indicating the difference between British and German aircraft were posted around the town. The Rotherham Fire and Watch Committee issued a warning in January 1915, stating that if an air raid took place over Rotherham that the population must seek immediate shelter. It warned that an anti-aircraft gun 'will fire from Wincobank Hill and fragments of shells may hit persons remaining out of the shelter.' It was advised that lights in tramcars be reduced by the use of blinds and car headlights subdued whilst travelling along the streets of the borough. Arc lights were also forbidden. For the duration of the war even the lights of the clock towers were discontinued. In February 1916, Fred Kelley of St George's Hall spotted zeppelins over the town. It was thought that they had been searching for the towns of Sheffield and Rotherham, but because of the lack of lighting they were unable to target the towns. Mr Kelley stated that he had been on watch duty when he heard that the zeppelins about. He saw the places of amusement being closed down and the people sent to their own homes. He said, 'I would have liked the Germans to have seen the look of contempt of the airships by the people involved.' However, the men lighting up pipes or cigarettes as they left entertainment venues ruined the effect. He warned that a single match could be seen in the dark and said, 'That's all it would take to undo the sterling work done by the Chief Constable and his warnings about lights.'

The fear of air raids continued and in August 1915, the news that zeppelin raiders had been seen over Goole and the East Riding was heard with some trepidation. The fear of these machines was not misplaced. In the war years they were spotted many times over Britain. Their down side was that navigation of these huge lumbering giants was not very accurate and, if hit by anti-aircraft guns, they were liable to blow up. The risk of fire as these great machines exploded in the air was very high. The later crash of the R101 emphasised the fragility of these giants. What is less well known is that the framework for the R101 was made in the premises of Messrs J.J. Habershon & Sons at Holmes Mill in Rotherham. It was printed in a works magazine that, 'All the main ribs and longitudinal end members of the frame, in fact every part called upon to bear the great strain was made from strips rolled at the Holmes mill.'

Using these big machines at night meant that it was difficult to find targets and captains were often unable to identify towns in unfamiliar terrains. But it seems that one of the greatest defects of the zeppelins was their reliance on the weather. They could not be flown on nights when winds were high or conditions stormy. The environment had to be perfect, and so there was usually only a few days of flying a month. Nevertheless, they inflicted massive loss of life and damage costing millions of pounds.

In a report of a zeppelin raid on Rotherham, which for security reasons was described as 'a North Midland town', we can get an idea about what these zeppelin raids felt like. The reporter revealed that shortly after the air raid warning had sounded, the whole town had been plunged into darkness as the noises of the zeppelins' engines were heard. They were approaching from the north-east direction, but due to the dark the raiders missed the town completely. A short time later, the townspeople heard audible sounds of the zeppelins returning. Thousands of people left their homes for the fields, parks and darkened streets, where it was felt they had a better chance of survival. They heard the whirring of machinery in the air and then saw flashes of fire, resembling lightening, illuminating the sky. Apparently these were followed by the sound of bombs exploding in quick succession. Thankfully no damage was reported in this raid but, more to the point, the reporter noted that there was no panic among the people. Finally, to the relief of the townspeople, the 'murder dealing monsters of the air' moved off.

Local people were very excited in February 1916, when it was announced, 'The town will shortly be taking charge of a 77mm German field gun captured at the

Mr Kelley and the zeppelin raid over Rotherham.

## THE ZEPPELIN RAID.

### IMPORTANCE OF SUBDUING LIGHTS.

### ROTHERHAM COMPLIMENTED.

To the Editor.—There is no doubt that the Zeppelins which were out on Monday night were looking for Rotherham and Sheffield, but owing to the splendid way in which the Chief Constable dealt with the lights at Rotherham, Rotherham, I am sure, owes its safety. I was on duty when it was decided to ask the places of amusement to close, as we knew Zeppelins were very close, and it was thought advisable that people should get to their homes as quickly and thus minimize the risk of large numbers being together. I want to congratulate the people on the splendid way in which they left the houses of amusement and went straight home under most difficult circumstances. I hope, should future occasion arise, the people in these places will always show the same splendid, cool spirit.

I would only have liked the Germans to have seen the rotten contempt the crowd showed for their airships, but I hope no one will consider I am exceeding my duty if I address a word of serious warning to those people who frequent these places of amusement. The moment everyone came out, the men-kind, with one accord, struck matches, and the ladies seemed to all have flash lights. Now it is well known that a match can be seen perfectly well from an airship, so one can imagine what hundreds would look like. It would be a fearful disaster if those very matches had allowed a Zeppelin to have found Rotherham, and yet they might have done.

Is it too much to ask men to wait until they get home before striking matches, as it would be most cruelly unfortunate if, after the splendid way the Chief Constable and authorities had dealt with the lighting and the patriotic attitude of the works in at once damping down, had the simple match betrayed us?

My pen must be careful what it writes, but, if I am correctly informed, had other places been as dark as Rotherham, the Germans would have had reason to ask themselves if they had found England at all.—Yours faithfully,

FRED KELLEY, Capt.

battle of Loos.' It was planned that the gun would go on display in College Square. The gun had been captured by the 15th Division on 25 September 1915, and had been on display at a few towns on its journey from York. When the gun arrived on Tuesday, 22 February 1916 there was a great crowd assembled in College Square. Men from the Heavy Artillery had brought it from the station into the town, where there was a ceremonial handover to the Mayor. He said that the gun would be the memento of all the brave young men still away fighting at the front, and it would also be a reminder of what 'our boys [had] to put up with on a daily basis.' For many people it would have been the first gun they had ever seen and, no doubt, it was an object of curiosity for a long time.

For the first time, in 1916, there were reports of tanks being used in the war. Tanks had been developed as a machine that could cross thick mud by having caterpillar wheels. Heavily armoured, it proved to be a great success at the front line. Unfortunately, because of the weight of the vehicle, it was often bogged down in the mud of the battlefields. A war correspondent, Mr Malcolm Ross, reported to the *Advertiser* that the New Zealand Regiment at the Somme had used the tanks. He described:

On Thursday our new engine of warfare began to crawl slowly to the front line. Several out of these were allotted to the New Zealanders. In the evening our 'heavies' far behind the line suddenly opened a furious bombardment. A large column of British troops went forward in the dusk singing as they went. In places our batteries were so thick that in wandering around in the open you had to keep a careful watch or you were in danger of getting your head blown off. The men spent a cold night in the trenches – even with a blanket it was cold and one would frequently wake. Out of the sky at dawn came our aeroplanes like bats looking for the enemy.

Tanks had first been used in the Battle of the Somme, in September 1916, to somewhat limited effect. These early tanks were very clumsy and the interior, which usually held a crew of ten, was reported to be hot and dangerous. Nevertheless, they caused a great disturbance to the Germans. In December 1916 the *Advertiser* gave an account from a soldier on the front line:

Tanks rolled in front of laughing cheerful cheering men. These land 'ironclads' walked cheerfully through the wire and the positions guarded by wire. Now and then they overlooked something and turned back casually to obliterate a stronghold. One sat down on a German battalion dugout and a German commander coming out to see what was happening to his ceiling had a scare, surrendered and was hauled into the tank to continue his battle in 'the belly of the whale'. Soon the troops and the tank had won the fight and news came that a tank was ambling down the main street of Martinpuitch with a yelling army behind it. From every dugout the Germans in scores emerged and threw up their hands. The tank went in jauntily blazing right and left.

Despite the frightening new technological advances, the people of the town, who had suffered such great privations during the war, had reason to believe by August 1918 that at last the war would soon be over.

# 7

# PEACE AT LAST

At long last, the Armistice was announced on the 11 November 1918. The *Advertiser* led the celebrations on the 16 November; the news of the war ending had reached the offices of the newspaper that morning and the headline read, 'The Greatest Day in the World's History'.

More news filtered in from other sources, making it certain that the hostilities had finally ceased. People began to celebrate in the streets. Reports stated that munitions workers, 'not even waiting for a lunch break', downed tools and began congregating around the town. Girls and women, still dressed in their work clothes, walked around the streets arm-in-arm, singing patriotic songs and encouraging others to join in. The reporter of the *Advertiser* stated that by noon 'all industry had ceased in the town'. It was not long before flags began to decorate shops, and houses and factories vied with neighbours to outdo each other in

The end of the First World War.

Decorations for the Peace Celebrations at the works of Parkgate Iron & Steel Co.

their show of patriotism. It was reported that shopkeepers soon sold out of red, white and blue flags and so at this point people made their own decorations. At first cars were held up by the human traffic in the town centre, but when the news was more widely circulated the cars were parked up as drivers joined in with the joyous occasion. Finally, the tram drivers and conductors left their trams in the streets and were caught up in the festivities.

It is difficult for us to imagine the massive strain that the town had been under for four years. The news must have been welcome to almost everyone. The celebrations were muted for those who had lost relatives, but peace was looked forward to by all. The realisation that war had ended was confirmed when the bells of Rotherham parish church, which had been stilled for four years, now began to peal once more. It had been agreed that all the church bells would be stilled for the duration of the war and would only be heard again at the end of the war or in the event of invasion. They would have been joined by the bells from the churches in other parishes, and no doubt people from other areas would have come into the town to join in with the revelry. The *Advertiser* reported, 'A trio of Tommies wearing their gold braid were marching down Effingham Street and singing whilst the police constables and the specials looked on smiling. No one would forbid them their moment of joy today.' Thousands of people were expecting some kind of civic announcement and congregated in College Square, but it seems that the Lord Mayor Alderman Gummer was at home ill and alternative arrangements had to be quickly made. It was not until evening that the Salvation Army band appeared and Alderman Grundy spoke to the cheering crowds. He spoke of his 'relief that the Armistice had been declared and the slaughter which had been going on for so long had now ended.'

No one was going to deny the town citizens their part in these celebrations, and for the first time in four years fireworks were let off, bonfires built and effigies of the Kaiser burnt.

The following day a service of Thanksgiving was held in the parish church, which concluded with a rousing rendition of the 'Halleluiah Chorus'. By Monday, there was no rush to go back to work as it was clear that munitions would no longer be needed, and so the party atmosphere went on. By Tuesday, the festivities continued in a more organised fashion. The lighting ban had now been lifted and so fairy lights surrounded posters with the slogans 'Peace with Victory' and 'Make a Happier World for the Boys who will Soon Return'. The Mayor finally sent a message from his sickbed:

A New World has been created. The Hun as he existed will have no place therein. Let us not engage in vainglory. We have suffered too much and there are too many sad hearts in our midst. We have drunk deep of sorrow and can take Victory with thanksgiving. Let us concentrate our thoughts on the future and make the new world that is opening out a happy and brighter one for the boys who will soon return.

The *Advertiser* praised the actions of the Territorial Battalions, stating that when the Rotherham Territorials heard the call to war, 'they were one of the first battalions to respond'. The newspaper requested that when they return back home that a parade be organised where they march in full uniform 'straight from the battlefields of France to a rousing welcome from the people of Rotherham.' It was also arranged that in the first week of January 1919, a service would take place in the parish church. This would include a ceremony in which

People congregated in College Square waiting for the official announcement of the civic celebrations at the end of the First World War.

the colours, which had been kept safe for the last four years, would be handed back to the Territorials. But the return of the battalion was delayed by the celebrations in France, and it was not until June 1919 that the town was able to show their gratitude for these brave men. The soldiers arrived at Masbrough Station at 12.25 p.m. and there were masses of people to greet them. Discharged soldiers and sailors who had already returned home, now made their own parade along with the band of the 5th Battalion of York and Lancaster Regiment. Both squads arrived at the station at the same point as the Lord Mayor, just in time to greet the men as they alighted the train. The glorious Territorial Army, which had marched out from the town in its hundreds four years ago, described as 'a sea of faces', now consisted of only five officers and twenty men. Nevertheless, the parade proudly marched along Main Street, High Street and College Street to reach College Square, where, after singing the National Anthem, speeches were heard. The Mayor announced, 'It is my proud privilege on behalf of the town to tender you our warmest congratulations on your safe return and to offer you as a representative of all those returned previously, a very hearty welcome home.'

It is without doubt that there would have been great sadness for people in the town who had lost relatives. But it was also felt that the celebrating soldiers and their families were mindful of their lost comrades throughout this time.

The main event of the Peace Celebrations, following the signing of the Armistice, was held on 1 December 1918 on Grand Mayoral Sunday. The parade consisted of mounted police, the bands of the York and Lancaster Regiment, the West Riding Royal Army Medical Corps, soldiers on leave, returned prisoners of war, wounded soldiers, the St John's Ambulance Brigade, special constables, fireman and members of the council. The parade once again ended at College Square. No doubt the celebration went on long into the following week and deservedly so. Rotherham had put up with privations and sadness for four long years and had suffered the loss of many people of the town. Tables were also erected in church halls to celebrate the end of hostilities.

Very few families were left untouched by the war, but if they thought that the troubles of the town were over, they would be mistaken. Rationing continued for some time and there was still the dilemma of what to do with the wounded and able-bodied soldiers returning back to the town in large numbers, all expecting to get their old jobs back. Everyone involved in the war was aware of the high price that would be paid, none more so than the soldiers who were wounded and sent back to England. Men who were blinded or who had lost limbs could no longer take part in the fighting. Many of them would have qualified for a pension, but these heroes made it very clear that they wanted jobs, not handouts. As early as February 1918, a meeting was held between the Ministry of Labour and the Welfare Joint Committee at the Employment Exchange in Rotherham, to organise a way to find work for the disabled sailors and soldiers. It was agreed that all disabled men wishing to return to work would be interviewed by the Exchange clerks and that local businessmen would be approached to provide work. It was requested, as a matter of priority, that all these men register with the Labour Exchange, in order that they could understand the numbers of people involved. The success of the scheme was clear when, a fortnight later, they were able to inform the Minister of Labour that twelve disabled soldiers had been found work so far. But as the war came to an end, the numbers of these soldiers and sailors increased and more pressure was put on local businessmen to take on the discharged men.

Tables laid out to for the Peace Celebrations.

It was not only the discharged soldiers and sailors that were now returning back to their hometown; these ranks were slowly being swelled by the numbers of prisoners of war who, having managed to survive the conflict, spoke out about the Germans and the atrocities they had suffered at their hands. In the first year of the war, in October 1914, Private Arthur Hattersley of 22 Bradgate Lane, Rotherham, was reported as being missing. His wife was later informed that he had been taken as a prisoner by the Germans after the battle near Aisne. It was reported in the *Advertiser* that, 'His wife was naturally anxious about the fate of her husband, but was glad to know that he was captured as a prisoner rather than dead,' In August 1917, Private Hattersley was returned home in exchange for another prisoner. It was reported, 'During his imprisonment he lost his reason and returned to England mentally deranged.' As early as January 1915, stories revealing the ill treatment of prisoners were being reported. One article, published in the Paris newspaper *Bulletin des Armes*, came from a Swiss man who had visited a camp full of French prisoners in Germany. He wrote:

They are badly fed only being allowed 250 grammes of bread a day, vegetables were not cooked and the supply of soup was reported to be inadequate. Nevertheless they are put to very hard work and they stagger under their burdens. They receive blows from the guards' sticks or have their dogs set on them. The quarters where they live are unheated and there was only a thin layer of straw for a bed. There were many cases of sickness reported and the death rate was high.

He then stated something that would be echoed by many of the returning prisoners: 'It is better for a soldier to die with their arms in their hands than to be made a prisoner.' Throughout the war pictures of captured soldiers had been received at the *Advertiser* office and were regularly printed. Pictures of five Rotherham men who had been interned in Holland were displayed in December 1914. These five men had undergone the Siege of Antwerp and had been forced to cross the Dutch border. Another picture was taken of prisoners in Doeberitz in Germany, where it was stated that most of the prisoners were from the Rotherham area. The photograph had been taken by the Red Cross and sent to the police force with queries about the identity of the men pictured. Detective Sergeant Harrison asked the readers of the *Advertiser* that if they recognised any relatives to 'please let [him] know their names and [he] would relay the information to the Red Cross.'

By July of the following year, more details were emerging in the *Advertiser* about what life as a prisoner of war was like for the men of the town. Sometimes the experience was not as bad as was at first thought. An unnamed prisoner described the conditions as being 'very difficult when we were first captured, but as soon as it was seen that our capture would be a prolonged one, huts were built outside the town of Gronigen by the Dutch authorities in a large field.' He described that men of all classes, some with ability, turned it into an ideal garden village and he added, 'We have excellent string and brass bands.' He told the newspaper that the barbed wire and armed guards were 'not conducive to a happy state of existence', but 'the food was the worst part'. He commented:

> Every morning there is an ample supply of black coffee and the men are given a small quantity of coarse brown bread. Those who desire breakfast can have a small bowl of what I can only describe as 'meal', for dinner, potatoes, a few peas and horse meat and for tea the rest of the bread and 2oz of cheese. For supper you can eat anything that you have managed to save from the day's meals.

These fairly positive reports, however, were in the minority and more disturbing reports about the way the prisoners were held captive, from a French prisoner who had managed to smuggle his letter out, were published in September 1915. He revealed that the men were 'practically starved, beaten and knocked about', to such an extent that many died or were 'driven mad'. He wrote:

> Men are little more than wild beasts where food is concerned. For any misdemeanour we are strung up between posts for between two to four hours and flogged. Heaps of fellows have no clothes as what they had was taken or have been exchanged for bread. The enemy guards are harder on the English prisoners than other nationalities.

He also described the meagre allowance as being worst for the British prisoners, and the only thing they had to look forward to were the parcels and gifts from home. The *Advertiser* had been quick off the mark to start a subscription to provide these food parcels for the prisoners in July 1916. It announced that relatives should give the names of Rotherham men who had been captured by the Germans either to the *Advertiser* office or to the offices of George Gummer at his Effingham Brass Works, Rotherham. The reporter pointed out

## INTERNED IN HOLLAND.

Reading from left to right: W. Porritt, 129, Psalters lane, Holmes; T. Round, 128, Psalters lane; G. Bamforth, 134, Hesley lane, Thorpe; E. Band, 68, Lindley street, Rotherham; and (seated) J. Fenton, 8, Harrison street, Holmes.

Five prisoners of war who had been interned in Holland.

that food parcels were already sent by friends or relatives but many men did not have any friends or relatives to send them anything and suggested that a subscription would ensure that these poor men at least had 'the bread of life'. By October 1916, a more concerted effort was put into organising the delivery of parcels to the British prisoners of war in Germany and Holland. A letter was sent to the editor of the newspaper from Arthur Stanley, the chairman for the Joint Prisoners of War Committee, which had recently been established by the Red Cross Society and the Order of St John. He stated that this committee should make the necessary arrangements for coordinating and controlling the work of the various associations and individuals, to present a system of sending parcels to British prisoners of war in Germany and other enemy and neutral countries. His letter outlined the objectives:

That every prisoner shall receive an adequate supply of all the comforts in the form of food etc.

That the excellent work being done at present by associations and individuals be disturbed as little as possible.

That overlapping and consequent waste shall be reduced to a minimum.

In order to attain them, the following arrangements were also summarised:

All parcels shall be sent through the Central Committee or an association authorised by it. A list of such associations will be put up in every post office.

Individuals are requested not to send food parcels but to arrange that to be done by recognised association shown in the list.

By January 1917, the Prisoner of War Committee had a system which ensured that each man imprisoned would receive six parcels of food and provisions to the value of £1 16d each month and also a supply of bread equal to 1lb a day, to the value of 7/6d a month. These arrangements were gratefully acknowledged by a returned prisoner of war from the Duke of Wellington Regiment in September 1916. He wrote to the *Advertiser* to thank the people of Rotherham for the parcels of food that had been sent out to them:

> Sir, I again want to thank you for your kindness to us when I was a prisoner of war in Germany. I can assure you your parcels were a great help...were it not for such people as you I can assure you that all the English prisoners of war would die of starvation.
> It is simply impossible to live on the food the Germans give the prisoners. I remain yours C. W. Cox

Two pictures published in the *Advertiser* in 1918 speak volumes about the returning Rotherham soldiers who had suffered at the hands of the Germans. The images, printed side by side, showed Sergeant James McCormack of 41 Holmes Lane, Rotherham and were of very poor quality. The photo on the left-hand side was of a smart, well setup lad who was very athletic and had gone to France as part of Kitchener's army. The right-hand photograph, however, showed evidence of the malnutrition and ill treatment which he suffered whilst in the hands of the Germans. On his way home to Rotherham, he told his parents that he was 'looking forward to some local bread having not tasted any since before December 1917.'

At the same time, two other unnamed prisoners had written to the editor telling him that they were also on their way home and were at that point in Holland. Whilst they had been imprisoned in Germany they had been subjected to German women spitting in their faces when they were first held captive. They were forced to work in iron mines and subject to insults, jabs and knocks from the captors' rifles. It was reported that, ironically, the food shortages in Germany now resulted in these same women begging for food from the parcels sent out to the prisoners from England. These women were so desperate for food for themselves and their children that they asked the soldiers for their discarded food tins. The prisoners asked the editor 'to imagine the women of Rotherham licking out empty, thrown away food tins'.

The stories being told by these prisoners made harrowing reading and resulted in much bitterness. One such prisoner, Seaman George Beal, was interviewed by the *Advertiser* in November 1918. He told the reporter, 'There were times when I wished I had stopped a bullet instead of allowing myself to be taken prisoner.' Beal, of the Royal Naval Division, lived at 13 Norfolk Street, Rotherham and had been imprisoned for four years in Germany. Not unnaturally, he was very hostile towards the Germans and stated that they were 'not fit to live and should be exterminated'. He spoke of being forcibly marched for miles and he told the reporter that the German soldiers had a habit of taking pot shots at the British lads, killing several just for fun. The remaining prisoners were then made to bury their comrades. When the prisoners arrived at Hamburg they were set on by a stick wielding, mud slinging, spitting mob that made efforts to lynch them. But what angered Beal and his comrades most was that the Germans were saying that they 'had single-handedly captured the British Navy'. Beal and his fellow prisoners had then been sent to the smelting furnaces near Berlin in cattle trucks, where they were locked up for the three day journey. On reaching his destination he fell sick, and when he protested after being knocked about by the guards he was put in a prison cell for four days. His last seven weeks of captivity had been spent working in a coal mine. He described them as being the worst weeks of his life. All the time the guards were taunting, insulting and assaulting them whilst the men were working eighteen-hour shifts, seven days a week. The men had been deprived of soap and water and, as a consequence, were 'verminous with wasted frames and death like faces, resembling living ghosts.' He told the reporter that many men had ended their suffering by committing suicide. He also praised the Rotherham Prisoner of War Committee for sending out the parcels of food, stating that many more men would have died without them.

After the hostilities ceased, the priority for the Red Cross was to ensure that the prisoners of war were returned home as quickly as possible. Hundreds of prisoners brought home pieces of the black bread they had been forced to eat as souvenirs. Thankfully, the prisoners returning back to Rotherham spoke about the warm welcome they had received when they landed in Hull, where they were given a joyous reception. They enjoyed further celebration at Ripon, where they were sent to a camp before moving back to Rotherham. They said that every station they had passed on the journey was alive with cheering civilians, but when they got to Rotherham there was nothing. Perhaps the reason for this was that no one had informed the Town Clerk that they were coming. Alderman Gummer, the Mayor, apologised to them and announced that they would receive a warm civic welcome as soon as it could be organised; a 'welcome home that would do them credit'. A couple of weeks later the Mayor kept his word and the men were paraded around the town on Grand Mayoral Sunday.

What infuriated many of the men was the good treatment that had been given to German prisoners of war in England. In August 1918, one English prisoner wrote of his disgust at the German prisoners of war having 'cricket and tennis tournaments in this country with tables groaning with food when our boys were starved and beaten to death in their country.' It would be a long time before such atrocities would be forgotten by the townspeople and, unfortunately, the next war would show that little was learned about more effective ways of treating prisoners of war.

The returning soldiers and sailors had been promised a 'Land fit for Heroes', but on their return to the town things looked very different; the condition of the town during this period was dire. Massive overcrowding had taken place, which had been accelerated by the opening of the munitions works. In May 1917, Dr Robinson, the town's Medical Officer of Health, stated:

It is impossible to estimate the present population due to the numbers being swelled by the munitions workers in the poorer parts of the town in particular Thornhill, Masbrough and St Ann's. 85% of the houses in those areas contain at least two and many contain three families all living in the same house. The poor housing, the scarcity of empty houses and the difficulties of displaced tenants being unable to find alternative accommodation exacerbated the problems of overcrowding.

This information was not lost on the local authorities. They had plans for new housing schemes, but these were impossible to put into practice until the end of the war. The state of the overcrowding was emphasised in a letter sent to the editor of the *Advertiser* in October 1917, which said:

> Dear Sir,
> I see according to the papers that two discharged soldiers, their wives and two children are living in a pig sty in Sheffield. I left Rotherham in August 1914 to go to France. My wife was unable to keep the house open and feed the bairns on the separation allowance and was forced to go to live with her parents in Durham. I have now returned to Rotherham and am unable to get a decent pigsty, so I am forced to live apart from my wife and bairns after serving the King and country for four years. Yet there are large homes in Alma Road which are empty, but the rent is more than I can afford.
> Signed NAPPOO

The debate about the overcrowding did not disappear and another letter to the editor, signed 'Cramped Up', described living in such overcrowded housing in Rotherham in December 1918:

> The house where I live (not from choice) consists of four small rooms 12 feet square. There are two small children in the kitchen along with table, dresser, fireguard, armchair and sofa (which is necessary for a man who works 12 hours a day) so you will see there is not much elbowroom. The baby's pram has to remain outside for most of the day in all weathers until bedtime when it is brought in. The parlour has a fire, which is only used for guests or on Sunday but is very drafty due to ill-fitting skirting boards. It will be very difficult when the baby starts to toddle around. We have a carpet but it is difficult to keep clean due to the beetles and the clay soil on the floor. It would have been better to have cupboards instead of pots and pans on shelves and to have an indoor bathroom for every house. Lets hope that our MP's are able to get better homes for the working classes.

Slowly life returned to normal in Rotherham and the town was proud of the men who went away to fight a war in which many thousands died. The war had forced the town's population to forge a real community; but after the trials and adversity faced by the town, the promised 'Land fit for Heroes' was non-existent. For the next twenty years many would have to fight for the rights of the working man against bureaucracy. Nevertheless, this was a story of great heroism both in France and in the town itself. People put up with food shortages and the fear of being bombed, but kept their patriotism and gave generously to the War Bonds Committee during times of great austerity. The *Advertiser's* role was crucial in keeping the town of Rotherham at the forefront of the soldiers' minds, while also telling the people of the town what warfare meant to the lads at the front. No one could envisage that Rotherham would be at war once again within a few years. But meanwhile, the interwar years would prove to be a hotbed of industrial strikes, riots, the rise of Bolshevism and the very real fear of revolution.

# PART 2

# THE INTERWAR YEARS

## 8

## THE AFTERMATH OF THE WAR

After four years of hostilities, Rotherham finally began to return to normal. As the town settled down and the men began to return home, people gradually realised that the war was finally over. The official Peace Celebrations were to be spread over three days in July 1918. On Friday 18 July, the celebrations started with a service at South Grove School on Moorgate to give thanks for the end of the war. There was another religious service at Kimberworth Higher Standard School at 11.15 a.m. These services were followed by sports heats in Clifton Park, and at 4 p.m. teas for the children were held in many schools across the town. On Saturday 19 July, the Mayor and other local dignitaries stopped at the Town Hall and paraded to Clifton Park, where at another Thanksgiving service was held 10.30 a.m. The park sported a large display of flags, including the French, English and Belgian flag, with the word 'PEACE' inscribed below. National songs sung by 2,000–3,000 schoolchildren were heard and, later, more children and adult sports competitions were held. There was a boxing exhibition and displays of morris dancing. This was followed by a selection of music from the bands of the discharged and disabled soldiers and sailors. The festivities ended with dancing in the park, by which point it was very late. People who had lost relatives in the war were not forgotten. On Thursday 24 July at 5 p.m., tea was served to the widows and their dependents at South Grove School.

The first Remembrance Day was held in November 1919 at eleven o'clock. People remembered the brave men who had lost their lives and the *Advertiser* described the scene in the streets of Rotherham as 'soul warming'. The reporter observed, 'In College Square the traffic stopped and men took off their hats and every person stood perfectly rigid and even the children and horses remained unmoving. Simultaneously the bugler played the "Last Post".'

Men, women and children wept openly in the streets of the town and in the trams when the two-minute silence was held. It was noted that even at the Magistrates' Court three prisoners, the police clerk, complainants, defendants and witnesses all observed the silent remembrance of the men who had died. The mood lightened a little bit later that evening when fireworks were held in Clifton Park at 8.30 p.m., which the was very well attended according to the newspaper. The following year the Remembrance Day observations were signalled by a buzzer at the Electric Power Station. The local authorities were criticised for this as the buzzer had been used in the town during the war to announce the arrival of the zeppelins. It was strongly felt that it should not be used to call the town's population to remember the brave men of the town who had sacrificed their lives.

In these early days of the interwar years, politicians were counting the cost of the war; it amounted to approximately £7,000 million. The Mayor of Rotherham had pledged that the people of the town would raise £1 million towards the debt. These were to be in the form of victory bonds, which like the war bonds would be bought as an investment in the government. These victory bonds could even be bought in instalments. Remembering how bringing tanks to the town had helped to boost sales of war bonds, the town council arranged for a tank to be brought to Rotherham again. It was hoped, initially, that the tank would be delivered by Christmas 1918, but by the time it arrived it was June 1919. The machine, capable of carrying five machine guns, was transported to its place at Clifton Park by three soldiers and a non-commissioned officer, Lieutenant A.H. Hepworth. The tank must have made an impressive sight as it lumbered along Westgate, High Street and up Doncastergate, entering the park by Birdcage Lodge. No doubt people would have turned

Victory bonds, which could be bought in instalments.

out in their hundreds to see this revolutionary machine. The bandstand in Clifton Park had been dismantled so the tank could stand in its place. A platform had been erected to hold the Mayor and other dignitaries. The Mayor, in presenting the tank to the town, christened it the *Princess Mary*. Although there was brisk sale of victory bonds on the day, the good people of Rotherham were less generous than they had been during the war years.

Despite the celebration of the tank, it was not long before it became a bone of contention for the populace of the town. Many people felt that the bandstand should be returned from its new home in Ferham Park. Others felt that the tank would remind returning soldiers of the weapons of war which they had endured for years. Many just considered it to be an eyesore. Such was the controversy that in December 1926, the *Advertiser* enclosed within its pages a ballot paper to be completed and posted through the door of the office. It read:

I think the tank should remain where it is
I think the tank should be moved to a less conspicuous place in the park
I think the tank should be broken up and sold for scrap

There is no published result to this ballot, but by February 1927 the tank had become very dilapidated and rusty and a decision was made to break it up and dispose of it. Two years later, in June 1928, a new bandstand was opened up in Clifton Park by the Mayor Councillor W. Brookes JP. It was erected on the same base as the previous bandstand and the Mayor told the assembled crown that he took pride 'in giving music back to the people'.

The tank in Clifton Park, which had become very dilapidated by February 1927.

On 18 July 1919, the *Advertiser* published the names of all the men who had died for their country, including those who had died in battle or in captivity. The list is impressive and runs over many pages. A demand for a more permanent reminder, in the form of a war memorial, had been called for as early as October 1916. Local people hoped to be given a memorial hall, but the idea was found to be too costly. The matter came into prominence once more in February 1921, when it was agreed that a cenotaph would be erected listing all the names of the dead heroes from Rotherham. The word 'cenotaph' is Greek for 'empty grave' and would be symbolic of the fact that the only graves for the soldiers killed in the First World War were in distant lands. It was agreed that the cenotaph would be built of Portland stone at 26ft high, and it would cost £50,000. It was to be placed at the entrance to Clifton Park.

By March 1921 three designs were being considered by the local authority and a few weeks later, a design by architect Major J.G. Knight was agreed on. It was hoped that the cenotaph would be unveiled by the Prince of Wales, who was visiting the Electric Power Station in July; however, due to ill health the Prince was unable to keep his promise and the authorities agreed to have the unveiling ceremony on 26 November 1922. The impressive ceremony was attended by groups of ex-servicemen, disabled soldiers and sailors, and ex-prisoners of war – all watched as wreaths were laid on the new cenotaph. The names of the dead totalled 1,304 men, their names inscribed on a brass tablet to the rear of the cenotaph.

Unveiling the war memorial on 26 November 1922.

The *Advertiser* proudly stated that over 10,000 Rotherham men had been involved in the hostilities. A further memorial tablet was erected on the north wall of Rotherham parish church in October 1925, which was inscribed, 'To the memory of all the ranks of the York and Lancaster Regiment who died in the Great War'. On the day it was unveiled, a guard of honour assembled in front of the Town Hall which included bands of the regiment as well as the members of the 284th Howitzer Battery. The bands led the Mayor and other members of the town council to the parish church for the unveiling. Regimental colours were carried proudly as they paraded through the town. The tablet was unveiled by Lieutenant General Sir Charles Harrington in front of a 1,000-strong congregation, which consisted mainly of relatives of the fallen men. The tablet was made of bronze on white statuary marble and had been designed by Major J.E. Knight, who not only designed the cenotaph but had served with the regiment during the war. It was a very moving ceremony and it served to remind the people of Rotherham of the great sacrifice of lives that war entailed.

Since 1916, the *Advertiser* had led a campaign for the 'big push' of 1 July to be remembered separately from Remembrance Day. The newspaper asked people to consider the 'unwavering quick march into a hail of bullets and shells of the brave comrades who were mowed down like grass.' It reminded the people of the town in 1921 that at least two regiments of the 7th and 8th York and Lancaster Regiment were decimated on that day. Both regiments were almost wholly composed of men of Rotherham. The following year it was agreed that the day which was of such significant to the town would be remembered in a military parade. On 1 July 1923 the very first 'big push' parade went from Corporation Street by way of Frederick Street, Effingham Street, College Street and Doncaster Road. The interdenominational service was presided over by Revd W.J.T. Pasco, the vicar of St Paul's Masbrough, and Revd C.H. Sheldrake of the Primitive Methodist Church. They told the assembled crowds, 'We must bow our heads today and silently pay our respects to those men who so light heartedly sacrificed everything for our sake.' Yet by this time, less thought was given to the dead of the town. Following this service the newspaper reported that there was 'much irreverence at the sight of the cenotaph and the former seriousness had gone'. It was explained that young men and boys had been seen in the park looking at the labels attached to the floral tributes and, according to the article, 'they didn't even bare their heads'.

Gradually the town was returning to how it had been during peacetime; the munitions factories closed and new businesses sprung up. Many women returned to domesticity and awaited the return of the men they had not set eyes on for years. Children were also to meet the fathers they had rarely seen before. There is little doubt that men returning back to the town looked forward to a time of peace and prosperity. During the interwar years the town received many visitors – some were heroes and some were royalty – all were greeted with much enthusiasm and warmth.

# 9

# PROMINENT VISITORS TO THE TOWN

As was usual for that period, the majority of the population of Rotherham revered the Royal Family. So there was great excitement in the town when rumours that the King himself was arriving for a wartime visit on Wednesday, 30 September 1915. The visit had been kept very secret but, as these things usually do, the truth came out on the morning that he was due to arrive. Since the beginning of the war, King George V had shown particular interest in visiting munitions factories and meeting the ordinary men and women workers. He had already toured several industrial areas around Britain, but it was still exhilarating that the King himself would be coming to Rotherham. It had been arranged with the palace that His Majesty would offer royal words of encouragement to the munitions workers, 'in their ceaseless endeavours to make the required numbers of shells.' The visit was inevitably compared with a similar visitation three years previously, when the King and Queen had come to the town as part of their visit to South Yorkshire. Bunting had decorated the streets and the children had lined up to greet their Royal Highnesses with great cheers. No bunting was seen on the streets in October 1915, but a few hastily found flags had been placed in the windows of some houses along the route. About an hour before the King's arrival at the unnamed works at Parkgate, women collected at the gates. Arriving precisely on time, a pilot car approached followed by four large cars. The King emerged from one of the cars dressed in the khaki uniform of a British Field Marshall. Several important Rotherham men were introduced to his Majesty, and as he passed through the lines of working men and women they cheered him loudly. Shortly after 10.30 a.m. the King came out of the factory and proceeded to walk through the gates and out among the crowds. No attempt was made to stop people coming over to talk to him. Although the whole visit lasted no longer than forty minutes, it was thought to be very successful and, no doubt, was a talking point in the town for a long time to come.

In January 1919 a rumour circulated the town that the hero of the last war, Field Marshall Douglas Haig, who had been created Earl Haig, was to visit Wentworth Woodhouse, the seat of Earl Fitzwilliam and his family. The programme was published of his journey as many people wished to see him. But Rotherham townsfolk were taken aback to discover that although he was to be received by representatives of Sheffield City Corporation, he

The visit of the King and Queen in 1912.

would then be driven straight to Wentworth. The *Advertiser* questioned why the people of Rotherham were to be left out of the receiving party, stating that Rotherham would also like to pay their respects from the thousands of men of the town who had fought under Earl Haig. No doubt arrangements were made very quickly for Earl Haig to visit the town. At Rotherham's Central Station, the Mayor, Mayoress and some borough officials were involved in a very quick ceremony. They shook hands with the Earl and handed Countess Haig a bouquet of flower. The people of the town probably felt slighted by this and the *Advertiser* printed, '...this was the extent of Rotherham's welcome to the world's greatest soldier. Moreover the Field Marshall saw about as much or as little of Rotherham as the inhabitants saw of him.'

The Prince of Wales, later known as the Duke of Windsor, was expected to visit Rotherham in 1922, but due to ill health the visit was postponed until 28 May 1923. It is difficult now to imagine the charisma surrounding the Prince, who was boyishly handsome and whose visits were widely reported. He had much the same effect on people as the late Princess Diana. The visit, which had been arranged hurriedly, caused the *Advertiser* to state two days prior to his visit that 'last minute preparations are needed for the town to be ready to welcome the Prince.' But there was no need to worry; the town was decorated magnificently. Flags festooned every edifice and rows of paper flags were stretched across Howard Street, Henry Street and Rawmarsh Road. Signs with the words 'A Royal Greeting' and, more familiarly, 'Aye Lad, Tha's reight Welcome' and 'When ta Coming Ageean?' could be seen everywhere. This popular Prince opened the Electric Power Station that was to be called after him and then had lunch with the Mayor and other dignitaries. Once again, the Earl and Countess Fitzwilliam were to play host at Wentworth Woodhouse, where they had organised a distinguished house party in his honour. It was noted that the Fitzwilliam flag was replaced by the Royal Standard whilst he was in residence. The edition of the *Advertiser* published pictures of the Prince of Wales for the next two weeks; so popular had been his visit. In the same edition the newspaper also listed the dates of when other Royal personages had come to the town:

**June 12th 1886** Queen Victoria accompanied by the Duchess of Teck arrived at Rotherham on a visit to Earl Fitzwilliam in order to open the Elsecar Exhibition.

**25th June 1891** The Prince and Princess of Wales, later King Edward VII and Queen Alexander opened Clifton Park.

**September 12th 1908** King Edward VII visited Wentworth Woodhouse as a guest of Earl Fitzwilliam during the Doncaster races.

In May 1933 the Prince had made a stirring speech in the Guildhall at London, urging all local authorities to ensure that slum housing would be eradicated and requesting that they prioritise schemes to get rid of 'the blight on our towns and cities'. The following month, the Mayor of Rotherham sent him a telegram informing that the Rotherham Corporation had taken a decision to proceed forthwith with a scheme for the complete clearance of slums in the borough. The Mayor received a reply:

St James Palace SW
June 8th 1933

Dear Mr Mayor

I am desired by the Prince of Wales to thank you for your telegram of yesterday's date from which his Royal Highness was very glad indeed to hear that your council have passed a resolution initiating schemes for the clearance within eighteen months of all remaining slums in Rotherham.

Yours truly
GODFREY THOMAS
Private Secretary

A SECTION OF THE GUARD OF HONOUR.          Photo: "Leeds Mercury."

The Prince of Wales visit on 28 May 1923. Courtesy of *Leeds Mercury*.

The Prince of Wales paid yet another flying visit to the town in December 1933, in order to see what Rotherham was doing for the large number of unemployed men and young boys of the town. He inspected the bowling green for unemployed men at Masbrough and the Rotherham and District Boys Welfare Club in Nottingham Street. Large crowds flocked to see him even though his visit was only a short one lasting just forty minutes. He said that he was pleased that men were being employed again and he commented positively about the new look of the town with its broader highways, more prestigious shops and the new Chantry Bridge.

In September 1925, yet another royal visitor came to Rotherham. This was Princess Mary, the third child and only daughter of King George V and Queen Mary. She arrived with her husband, Viscount Lascelles, and they were accompanied by the Earl and Countess Fitzwilliam to open a new wing at the Rotherham Hospital on Doncastergate. The road outside the hospital was closed to traffic for the day in order that the assembled crowds would have a good vantage point to see all the royal visitors. The royal procession entered the town at Rawmarsh Bridge, where they were greeted by the Chief Constable, and the party proceeded along Effingham Street to College Square, College Street and up Doncastergate. The visit was a great success with hundreds of people crowding the road to see the royal visitors. In memory of the visit, a new ward was given the name 'the Princess Mary'.

The interwar years in Rotherham saw the development of better housing schemes, the eradication of slums and improvements in health, particularly those of mothers and babies. Government money was dedicated to providing better homes and some of these homes were inspected in October 1927 when the Minister of Health, the Right Honourable Neville Chamberlain, arrived in Rotherham. The man who had served under the Prime Minister, Stanley Baldwin, was accompanied by his permanent Under Secretary, Mr Arthur Robinson. Mr Chamberlain was driven from Sheffield to inspect the housing on the newly built housing estates. He then visited the smaller houses, which were described as 'non-parlour houses'. They were built to provide housing for lower paid working-class families and consisted of two bedrooms and a bathroom; the larger ones were three-bedroom houses. His tour then

Princess Mary in Rotherham in September 1925.

## MINISTER OF HEALTH IN ROTHERHAM.

### VISIT OF MR. NEVILLE CHAMBERLAIN THIS WEEK.

Neville Chamberlain, who arrived on Wednesday, 26 October 1927 to inspect the new housing estates.

took him to the Ferham House Maternity Home, which was reported to be 'in full swing'. He inspected the school medical services and the school clinic, which were all based in the same building. He was then taken to Badsley Moor Isolation Hospital, where on the opposite side of the road he was shown the land where the Herringthorpe playing fields were and where the future housing estate was to be built. His last port of call was a tour of Oakwood Sanatorium. This included a visit to the kindergarten there, where he talked to the children for a short while.

The Mayor, Councillor W. Brooke, welcomed Mr Chamberlain to Rotherham and advised his officials that they should follow Mr Chamberlain's example and look into what achievements had been made in the town. Mr Chamberlain warmly responded to the welcome:

I am glad of the opportunity of meeting the members of Rotherham Corporation and my task today is to unite the relations between the local authorities and the Ministry of Health. I am not here to condemn what the Corporation should or should not do. Indeed the Ministry of Health are guilty of getting it wrong themselves. Rather myself and my Under Secretary Mr Robinson are looking into the sense of community in Rotherham and we see that the local authority are interested in improving the material and normal health, happiness and prosperity of its people. I see that the town has not got the acuteness of housing problems in other parts of the country such as Birmingham or London and that Rotherham has an excellent health record and it is a matter for congratulations for the authorities of the town. I also urge inter-town co-operation such as that with Sheffield which is a larger authority and to work in harmony without caution or jealousy.

Mr Chamberlain then told the assembled audience something of his early working life. He had been employed by the local authority itself and said that he saw no finer form of higher service than that of local government. He implored people to keep the sense of greater trust that had been given to them. He was given a grand applause before leaving for his next destination, which was the East Dene housing estate. As Mr Chamberlain left, crowds assembled to wave him off at the Central Station in Rotherham, where he caught the 6.28 p.m. train to Hull.

Another politician who came to the town was the Minister of Transport, Herbert Morrison, who arrived on Monday, 28 April 1930 to re-open Chantry Bridge. The bridge had been closed for two years and the River Don diverted in order to widen the road for traffic. It was reported that thousands of people watched the memorial event, which had cost the ratepayers £100,000. Councillor Dickenson, addressing the crowd, told them that some very famous people had crossed over Chantry Bridge. He stated that Cardinal Wolsey had passed over the bridge on his fateful journey from Sheffield to Leicester in 1530. He died at Leicester on 29 November, en route to London to be tried as a traitor. A link between Rotherham and King Henry VIII was also spoken of. (Rotherham became the King's headquarters during the Pilgrimage of Grace. This was an uprising which took place in 1536 in response to the Dissolution of the Monasteries and England's break with Rome.) Councillor Dickenson then handed Mr Morrison a gold knife with which to cut the cord and he declared the bridge open. The Bishop of Sheffield led the crowd in a prayer and then Herbert Morrison gave a speech expressing his delight at opening Chantry Bridge. He stated that there was a great lack of such bridges and yet the two remaining ones were at Rotherham and Wakefield, only 20 miles apart. Today, Chantry Bridge retains part of the original road and the modern road runs alongside it.

Herbert Morrison re-opening Chantry Bridge on Monday, 28 April 1930.

Part of the old road over Chantry Bridge as it is today.

In 1933 a less formal visitor to Rotherham, but no doubt just as welcome, was one of its own sons, the comedian Sandy Powell. Sandy had been born in Rotherham in 1900 and by the 1930s was starting his career as a music hall entertainer. By the time he came to Rotherham, he was touring with his own revue called the *Sandy Powell Road Show* and had made several comedy records which had sold in their thousands. He left his revue in Sheffield to visit a local (unnamed) razor-blade factory on Saturday, 6 May 1933. He was listed as 'a world famous comedian and now a famous gramophone and music hall star'. Pictures in the *Rotherham Advertiser* showed him watching a girl worker making razor blades at the factory. He thrilled the workers as he told them, 'I am pleased and proud to see that Rotherham has had the initiative to enter this very important phase of industry and [alluding to the gift of razor blades] I shall always use them.' When he came back to Rotherham again in April 1934, he brought his troupe with him and they gave a good programme to a gathering of unemployed men at the Assembly Rooms. The Mayor, Alderman Kirk, welcomed him as 'a friend and a fellow townsman'. It was noted that he was appearing at the Sheffield Empire and, although he had many calls on his time, he very kindly 'entertained those who could not afford to go out for entertainment out of the meagre income they received as unemployed.'

Sandy Powell later succeeded in breaking into the world of television in the 1940s and '50s, with his famous catchphrase, 'Can you hear me mother?' which had started when he

Sandy Powell, a star of radio and later television, watching a worker at a Rotherham razor-blade factory on 6 May 1933.

The Assembly Rooms, where Sandy Powell entertained unemployed men and women.

# MR. T. W. BURGESS IN ROTHERHAM.

## CIVIC RECEPTION FOR BOROUGH'S CHANNEL SWIMMER.

Photo: "Rotherham Advertiser."

Mr. T. W. Burgess paid another visit to his native town on Thursday, when the Channel swimmer and his wife were given a civic reception by the Mayor and Mayoress (Councillor W. Brooke, J.P., and Miss M. M. Brooke).

The above picture, taken outside the Town Hall, shows (reading from left to right) Mr. John Fellows (a Channel swimming aspirant), Mr. T. W. Burgess, Mr. E. C. Bell, J.P., of Sheffield, the Mayoress, Councillor George Mitchell, the Mayor, Mr. Geo. Hy. Parkinson, Madame Burgess, Mr. R. Reid, and Ald. R. Dewar. On the steps of the Town Hall are Ald. Gummer, J.P., and Mr. W. J. Bradford, J.P. (Borough Coroner).

Thomas Burgess, the second man to swim the Channel.

dropped his script and was killing time in the microphone (he was alluding to his mother's deafness).

A fact not known by many people today is that it was a Rotherham man, Thomas William Burgess, who was the second person to ever swim the Channel, after Captain Webb. He achieved this feat on 7 September 1911 and shortly afterwards he visited the town of his birth, where he was given a civic welcome.

In January 1932, the people of Rotherham had the opportunity to witness a swimming marathon performed by Miss Mercedes Gleitze. She had been another successful Channel swimmer on 7 October 1927 and she then became famous for her endurance or marathon swimming events. On 16 January 1930, she had completed a forty-three-hour swim at Auckland New Zealand. Later, in February 1931, she completed a forty-four-and-a-half hour marathon in Sydney, Australia. On 2 January 1932 she was invited to complete another marathon swim in Rotherham. Thousands of people crowded onto Main Street and Market Street to see her break her own record. Starting at precisely midnight, she swam up and down the baths to music provided by a radiogram until it was announced, at 8.30 p.m.

Miss Gleitze receiving her bronze awards from the Mayor, Alderman Caine.

the following day, that she had achieved forty-four and a half hours. To almost continuous cheering she carried on until 9 p.m., at which point she signalled to three members of the St John's Ambulance Brigade who jumped into the water to lift her out. She had been swimming for forty-five hours. Waving her hand as she was brought out of the pool, she shouted to the people of Rotherham, 'Are you proud of me?' and it was reported that the cheers were deafening. The following day she was presented with two bronze ornaments by Mayor Alderman Caine.

The interwar years were a time of great change in Rotherham. New innovations such as gas and electricity transformed the town, while improvements in health were high on the local authority's agenda. Nevertheless, local people found it hard to forget the deprivations of the last war. Returning soldiers had been promised a 'Land fit for Heroes' and for some of them the changes were not happening fast enough.

# 10

# DISCONTENT

T here had been many complaints from returning soldiers about the lack of jobs available for them after they had fought for King and Country for four long years. The Rotherham Advisory Committee and the War Pensions Committee were determined that returning soldiers would be prioritised for jobs in the town. Despite this, as early as January 1919 it was reported that there were already 233 discharged soldiers and 485 civilians signing on for 'out of work pay' at the Labour Exchange. By March 1919, Major Kelley, the local MP, had persuaded industries in the town to purchase the munitions factory at Templeborough and he joyfully announced that the factory would be shortly re-opened for 'a kind of manufactory where it is to be hoped that it will find employment for between 4,000 to 5,000 persons'. Other schemes were put forward to encourage firms to employ a number of discharged and disabled soldiers. An agreement was made with these firms to have notepaper with a heading that showed their participation in the scheme and the names of such companies were held in a central register by the Ministry of Labour. It was also agreed that the government would take the lead in this scheme by ensuring that 5 per cent of their labour force was from this group. However, the numbers of men returning to Rotherham were increasing daily and the authorities were having difficulty getting jobs for all the men. In August 1922, a letter was received by the editor of the *Advertiser* stating that not only had these men been unable to find the jobs they were expecting, but neither had they found the houses they had been promised by the government. The letter explained:

Officers are now seen out in the town selling oranges in the street. We are forced to witness the desperate plight of many ex-servicemen who expected to live in well furnished homes and who are now living in direst poverty in garrets and basements.

Part of the discontent stemmed from the fact that during war, which had cost millions of pounds each day, the soldiers, decked in their uniforms, were 'heroes'. On their return back to England, however, and with the donning of civilian clothing, they could not find work or anywhere to live. In the 1920s the fear of revolution and the rise of Bolshevism could be felt on a national scale. Many landowners and politicians truly believed that the pre-war loyalty to King and Country had been lost on the war fields of Flanders.

Returning soldiers were very critical of the people who had not enlisted and who spent the war working in the munitions factories earning a decent wage. The Labour Party took a pacifist stance after the war and the *Advertiser* was very critical towards it. When Major Frederick Kelley was elected as the Conservative MP in January 1919, it was reported to be a 'blow to the pacifists'. The situation was exacerbated by the inflaming speeches which could be heard on the streets of the town by members of the Communist Party.

During the interwar years, the *Advertiser*, like national newspapers of the time, focussed in on the threat of the Bolsheviks. This became even more prominent in the news after the Tsar and his family were murdered in Russia on 17 July 1918. People were unable to believe that such an atrocity had occurred. Fear of revolution in England was widespread amongst the government and they came down heavily on people they suspected of spreading sedition. In March 1919, it was announced that advocates of Lenin and Trotsky had been speaking in College Square about 'class war'. According to the *Advertiser*, leaflets had been distributed to 'willing listeners and converts among the ignorant men and women'. It was written, 'These agitators are generally plump well-fed men and their hands bear no marks of toil.'

People demanded to know what the police were doing about it: 'It is not so much about free speech but protecting the workers,' a report in the *Advertiser* stated. More revolutionary speeches were heard in August 1919, once again in College Square, when the *Advertiser* noted, 'The euphemism of free speech is trotted out to incense feeling and mislead the workers and spread an infection of disorder. These people are allowed free rein to go over the country and spread sedition.' In February 1920, a young man named John Frederick Hedley was arrested for making seditious statements in College Square on the morning of 19 January. He was arrested under DORA (Defence of the Realm Act), although there was some dispute about whether DORA, which gave the government powers under wartime conditions, was still applicable after the war had ended. He had been arrested on two counts, for two claims he had made in his speech:

> During the war I was on a British submarine chaser. We deliberately and by instructions sank some of our own submarines not German. What was this done for? Simply to keep up the hatred between the British and German working men. The poor devils who went to the bottom did not know who had fired the torpedo and the Capitalistic press would add one more vessel lost to enemy action. Secondly, you have heard of raids on different towns on the east coast such as Scarborough, Hartlepool and other places. That was done by British battleships not German. We know of cases where our own people have been mowed down, yet mown down deliberately by our own countrymen.

He was brought into the Rotherham Police Court two weeks later and he had now employed a London solicitor to defend him. The magistrates agreed that the rules under DORA still applied and the court session lasted for five hours. His solicitor stated that he had been a stoker during the war, but since then had resumed his civilian life and become a lecturer. Friends claimed that Hedley had the right to say what he felt under the Freedom of Speech Act. One of his colleagues admitted that he had organised a circuit of places for Hedley to visit so he could talk to the workers. When the unnamed colleague was questioned as to whether he had heard Hedley say that he was a revolutionary, the colleague replied, 'Yes, I had.' When asked, 'Are you in sympathy with that?' he replied, 'Most decisively but not in favour of bloodshed as there has been enough of that in the last five years.' The magistrate found Hedley guilty of sedition and sentenced him to three months' imprisonment with hard labour.

Conditions in the town during the interwar years led to the rise of discontent. There were strikes about pay and unemployment, and reports of children of ex-soldiers being unable to go to school because they had no boots. In May 1921, three men were in court charged with making 'speeches calculated and likely to cause sedition and disaffection among the civil population' on the 24 April. The three men were named as James Bown, whose address was given as Don Cottage, Forge Lane, Rotherham; Robert George Murray of 309 Chesterfield Road, Sheffield; and Peter Hannon of 1 Priestly Street, Sheffield. All pleaded 'Not guilty' to the charges. Murray chose to have his case heard separately from the other two, but it was to no effect; all three were found guilty and fined £20 in lieu of a month's prison sentence. Some papers in Murray's hometown referred to him as a 'communist' and there were supporters in court who applauded comments made by the prisoners. Murray was a speaker for the party and he stated that he supported the need to 'overthrow the bossing classes and the need for the working classes to take industry by force', to which there were loud cheers in the courtroom. Defending himself, Murray claimed the right of free speech, but the magistrate stated, 'Free speech is your right providing it does not lend cause to offence or breach of the peace.' Despite the fine, Bown was charged again in May for making inflammatory speeches at Parkgate to a crowd of between 250 and 300 people. He said that England was 'the rottenest country in the world' and that there was 'more poverty in England than you would imagine'. He urged that the people of Rotherham should 'follow Russia'. The magistrates were not amused and sentenced him to be bound over for twelve months on a surety of £50 for good behaviour.

Bolshevism, or Communism, gained popularity due to the many unemployed men on the streets of the town. On Friday, 12 November 1926 at the Rotherham Police Court, it was decided that a meeting to be held the following day, to commemorate the Russian workers' huge victory, would be banned. Fearing the discontent that was still felt around the town, the meeting was prohibited under the Emergency Powers Act. A notice was erected stating that the meeting had been banned, but urging the striking miners to 'Fight on and Win'.

In 1925 an amusing incident took place involving the political groups in College Square. The *Advertiser* reported that on the evening of Monday 24 August, the Conservative Party, no doubt trying to oust the communists 'who had held meetings almost daily', were trying to deliver a speech to the crowd. The Conservative speaker, Mr S. Hardwick, was just getting into his stride when groups from the opposing party arrived and demanded that they be allowed to continue, as they had advertised the meeting around the town. Mr Hardwick refused and told them that they should go away and 'respect the unwritten law of College Square'. A certain amount of heckling took place, but before it could erupt into a situation beyond control, the Salvation Army band arrived to deliver their service, which had been traditionally held for many years on a Monday evening. Ignoring the two parties, they launched into their first hymn and both sides, realising the futility of continuing, gradually dispersed.

The interwar years saw its fair share of inflammatory speakers. On Thursday, 31 October 1935, Sir Oswald Mosley, the leader of the Fascist Movement in Britain, addressed a crowded meeting at the Town Hall. In the *Advertiser* it was reported that he said to the assembled audience:

The Fascist regime only started three years ago but already there were 472 branches and that Fascism was a dictatorship of the will of the people expressed through a leadership of their own choice. As soon as they had between 400 – 500 candidates and the same number of Parliamentary agents then and only then would he countenance them entering the field at a General Election. Fascists would ask for authority to divide industry into great Corporations governed by representatives of employer and worker. The first task of such Corporations would be to systematically raise wages over the whole field of industry.

He blamed the present crisis on the cheap imports, amounting to almost £360 million pounds, which the government had allowed into this country and which had displaced the millions of people who were at that time unemployed. He emphatically stated that the Fascists would combat the power of international Jewish financial services. There followed a question and answers session in which he stipulated that under the Fascists, national newspapers would be compelled to tell the truth and every man and woman would be entitled to free speech. Nevertheless, it was also reported that 'It was a quiet meeting,' which leads us to suspect that the people of Rotherham were well aware of the strict rules under which the German people endured life under its Fascist regime. This feeling was underlined in November 1943, when it was announced that Sir Oswald Mosley and his wife had been released from the captivity they had been under since 23 May 1940 due to medical grounds. Calls for their immediate imprisonment were the subject of a heated debate at the monthly meeting of the Rotherham Trades Council on Tuesday 23 November at the Cross Keys Hotel. It was resolved that a petition, signed by 2,673 people, be sent to the Executive Committee of the National Labour Party to investigate the circumstances of their release. The Rotherham Trades Council stated, 'We view with alarm the discontent to the industrial workers in this area and also the effect it will have on our Fighting Forces seeing they are fighting for freedom.'

The reason given was that if Mosley remained in prison it would cause his death and the Trades Council felt that if the choice was between the life of Mosley and the Fighting Forces who opposed his totalitarianism, 'then Mosley could die'. Mosley was released but remained under house arrest until after the Second World War.

Discontent continued throughout the interwar years and great resentment was felt in the town. One of the biggest contributory factors to this bad feeling was the running of the coal industry. Rich coal owners were trying to reduce the wages of their workmen and, as a result, strikes ensued.

**MOSLEY SPEAKS.**

**Fascist Leader Expounds Policy At Rotherham.**

**BANNING OF IMPORTS FOR NATIONAL TRADING.**

**Socialist Leaders Attacked.**

Sir Oswald Mosley, Leader of the Fascist movement in Great Britain, addressed a crowded meeting in the Town Hall Assembly Rooms on Thursday night, during the course of which he condemned all political parties other than his own, and then, in reply to questions, bitterly attacked the Socialist Party for its indifference to the question of unemployment. It was a quiet meeting.

Oswald Mosley addressed a 'quiet meeting' in the Assembly Rooms.

# 11

# THE COAL STRIKE

The one industry that had continued during the war, in full employment, was coal mining. Strikes were forbidden during wartime, but in the interwar years work conditions and pay were so poor that strikes were happening on a regular basis. Even before the Peace Celebrations had been held in the town a strike had been called. The local newspaper was initially sympathetic towards the one-day coal strike which had been called for on 30 January 1919. The reporter stated that 'one whole day was a day too long' if one simple complaint can bring the whole Yorkshire region to a standstill. It seems that all the miners were asking for was twenty minutes break to eat their breakfast. The paper reported that a strike lasting any longer than a day would paralyse industry with the coal shortage. By August 1919, a longer strike was held and it was announced that 10,000 unemployed miners were on strike pay:

> Although the strike was supposed to be settled by the Miners Federation of Great Britain, Herbert Smith or someone who professes to guide Yorkshire miners was not permitting them to return to the pits of South Yorkshire and the coal shortages had been exacerbated. The local miners had no grievance and had come out in sympathy when ordered out by the Barnsley miners.

Finally, by 16 August, it was announced that the coal strike was over and the miners of Rotherham had returned to the pits.

Part of the aggravation was due to the terrible conditions in the mines. One miner, Frank Lee of 30 Aldwarke Road, Parkgate, wrote to the newspaper about improving the conditions and increasing the output of miners. He had spent most of his life down the mines and made the following suggestions:

> More inspections are needed
> More consideration given to the health of the miners
> More humane treatment in the case of accidents
> Fully qualified medical practitioners at the larger collieries

Bathing facilities should be provided at all the collieries and made a crime for any man to go home in his dirt

More shafts and better ventilation

A man should not have to work in a nearly naked state, so that during a shift he has to empty his clogs of sweat and wring out his socks

Only two months later, on 16 October 1920, a further strike was called about the miners' wages. The following week the *Advertiser* stated that although the strike was only a week old, there was already 'considerable signs of deprivation in the town'. A total of 2,300 men were signing up for out of work payments. On 23 October the coal strike was affecting other industries. It was announced that '2,000 men from the Parkgate Iron and Steel Company will cease work,' and as a result the *Advertiser* predicted that gas supplies would soon be affected. Sure enough, the gas supplies were reduced and it was noted in the newspaper that evening classes had to be abandoned due to the poor lighting. The strike finally ended in January 1921, after twelve weeks, and the newspaper stated that 'the men of the town should be congratulated for the exemplarity way in which the Rotherham miners have conducted themselves.' Nevertheless, further strikes followed as discontentment spread. A thirty-three-week strike was brought to an end in October 1922 at the Parkgate section of the Rotherham Main colliery.

However, all the grievances of the miners and the owners were put to one side on 28 July 1923, when an explosion took place at Maltby colliery. There had been reports of 'gob fires' in the mine, and until they had been investigated it was agreed that the mine would be closed down. This resulted in 2,000 men being laid off. (Gob fires were pockets of gas which were liable to spontaneous combustion.) An investigation party of 120 men and youths were sent underground and twenty-three of them were killed when an explosion took place. Only one body was recovered; it was a man called Original Renshaw, known as Reg. All the rest were trapped. The names of the men were printed in the *Advertiser*:

Reg Renshaw, married with 1 child aged 48
Raymond Clinton Bourne, single aged 18
William Emberton, married with 1 child 28
Ernest Dunn, married with 2 children 28
Aaron Daniels, married with 6 children 46
William Preece, married with 2 children 24
Alfred Fellows, single aged 15
George Hickling, married with 10 children
John Green leaves 3 children
Benjamin Jones leaves 1 child
Jonathon Spilsbury, married with 4 children 33
Richard John Brooke, married with 1 child 25

John Garritty 38
Harold Bourne, single aged 25
John Stoker, single 30
Sylvanus Turner leaves a widow 25
Leonard Meredith, single aged 22
George Brierly, married 3 children 34
B. Beardshall, married with 4 children 29
Albert Smithson, leaves a widow 29
Joseph Best, single aged 19
Joseph Spivey leaves 1 child
James Smith leaves 1 child 35

From the list it is evident that forty children were left without fathers. If anything needed to underline the daily dangers in which the mining community worked, this was an apt example. The Lord Lieutenant of Yorkshire, the Earl of Harewood visited the colliery and offered

Reg Renshaw's coffin. His was the only body to be recovered following the Maltby colliery explosion.

condolences to the widows and families. He also suggested that a subscription be taken up for the families who were left behind and the *Advertiser* readily complied. Messages of condolences were sent by the King and Queen, and the Earl of Scarborough visited the pit and asked Revd B.P. Sheppard to convey to the stricken relatives and families his heartfelt sympathies. The funeral of the one miner whose body had been recovered was well attended by crowds of people. It was said that the remainder of the bodies might never be recovered. No doubt the crowds at the funeral of Reg Renshaw held many wives and families silently grieving for their lost relatives. By December, it had been impossible to deal with fires from the explosion and it was agreed that the pit would be flooded. Grants of between £10 and £30 each were issued to the miners' wives and families in January 1924 for the loss of their relatives. It was reported that these families were also receiving payment out of the County Fund and that they had 'plenty of money to enable them to live with a reasonable degree of comfort.'

Still the unrest in the Yorkshire collieries continued and a national strike was called to take place on 1 May 1926. On 24 April a notice was pinned to the gates of all South Yorkshire collieries from the owners, stating the terms under which the miners may continue to work:

> Notice to the workpeople of the offer of employment for the month of May 1926. Notice is hereby given to all workpeople employed at this colliery from May 1st to 31st inclusively the colliery will be open for work on day to day contracts and wages will be calculated and paid in the following manner:
>
> The owners give a guarantee that there should be added to 1911 basic rate a minimum of 32%.
>
> The owners also give a guarantee that the Subsistence Wage award of his Honour Judge Stavely Hill (dated March 12th 1925) will continue in operation as a protection for low paid adult day wage workers.
>
> The minimum percentage and Subsistence Allowance will only be paid on condition that any subvention payment granted by the government shall be received in full by Yorkshire collieries on the same basis as other collieries.
>
> All underground piece workers will continue to receive in addition the 12.2% as hereforto in respect of the reduction of hours in July 1919

On 1 May Yorkshire miners ceased work and the coal strike commenced. The *Advertiser* reported that there were 266 Yorkshire pits involved, comprising 153 in South Yorkshire and 113 in West Yorkshire with a combined weekly wages bill of £500,000.

At first the strikers were very optimistic. May Day celebrations were held in Eastwood Miners Welfare Institute by the Rotherham Labour Party. There were speeches made to enthusiastic crowds and two pit ponies on loan from the Silverwood colliery led a parade through the town centre, accompanied by trade-union officials and a handful of communists. Councillor Hutchinson, the president of the Rotherham Labour Party, said in his speech, 'Fraternal greetings to the workers of all lands who are on this day demonstrating their international solidarity in the cause of socialism and pledges themselves to the abolition of capitalism, Imperialism and war.' He called upon workers to 'unite in a demand for a living wage'. A week later the *Advertiser* was apologising because it was only eight pages long instead of sixteen, due to a strike by the Topographical Association, who had joined in the General Strike.

But there were angry scenes of violence reported in Rotherham in July 1926 when a riot broke out, resulting in ugly scenes in the town centre. There had been some debate with the workhouse authorities as to whether single able-bodied men would be able to receive relief during the industrial distress caused by the coal strike. It seems that a group of men from Wath and West Melton had decided that they would take matters into their own hands and they demanded entry to the Rotherham Workhouse. There was apparently between 300 and 400 men there and the workhouse master was unable to allow entry to all the men; only those who were exhibiting signs of malnutrition or destitution were allowed entry. Thirty men were found to be eligible and were admitted by the workhouse medical officer. The rest were sent on their way and they congregated on the piece of spare land near to Alma Road School, where it was decided that they would march to the police station on Frederick Street. There they congregated, demanding that alternative accommodation be found for them. A delegation of four men was received by the Chief Constable Mr E. Weatherhogg, who pointed out that it was beyond the power of the police to help them. They told this to their colleagues waiting outside and the mob became so unruly that mounted police were called in to remove them. The men were scattered up Howard Street, Henry Street and Effingham Street and the mounted police continued to patrol the streets until a late hour; there were no further disturbances reported though.

Increasingly there was much unrest in the area and it continued to ferment throughout the inter-war years. The following month, three women were charged at Maltby under the Emergency Powers Act, for inciting others to turn over a lorry loaded with 4 tons of coal intended for the works of Messrs Steel, Peech and Tozer. The driver told the police that when he got to a point near Roche Abbey, two youths jumped onto the steam lorry. As it approached a railway bridge he said there was a crowd of people waiting. Thankfully the lorry was guarded by a police sergeant, who calmed the situation down and arrested the three women. The lorry arrived safely at its destination. When the case was heard in court, one woman was dismissed by the magistrates and the other two were fined £5 each or a month's imprisonment. One of the women shouted at the magistrate, saying that surely he 'would not take £5 out of the mouths of [her] children'. Ignoring her, the magistrate ordered the women to pay the fine within a month or go to prison.

By August 1926, a ballot was taken as to whether the miners should go back to work and it was found that the men were divided in opinion. Thurcroft, Dinnington and Treeton miners voted in favour of accepting the offer made by the coal owners. Silverwood, Maltby and Rotherham Main voted against. The votes were 700 to 12 in favour of fighting on. But by

December it seems that most of the men had returned to work. It was reported in the *Advertiser* of 4 December 1926 that 13,083 had returned to work the previous week and a total of '441,570 miners are now back at work in the coalfields of Yorkshire with the exception of Thurcroft and Maltby Main colliery.' On 4 December a peace agreement was signed and all the men returned to work; but that peace was not to last. On 4 September 1928, news came to the town that Rotherham Main colliery at Canklow, which had been open since May 1892, was to close. Notices had been handed to employees, stating that the pit would close indefinitely from the following Wednesday. The letters stated:

> John Brown & Co Ltd
> Rotherham Main Colliery
> 5$^{th}$ September 1928

> Dear Sir
> In handing you notice to terminate your employment with the company I do so with very great regret. It is I believe a well known fact that geological conditions at Rotherham Main are such that the colliery can only prosper when the coal trade is in a normal condition. The present serious depression in the industry makes it impossible to carry on resulting in working at a serious financial loss for some considerable time. After giving the matter much careful thought the directors have reluctantly decided that the working of the colliery must cease.

> Yours faithfully
> Mr A Blenkinsop
> General Manager

As a sop he added, 'If there is an upturn in the trade the work will be resumed and the pit will be kept in condition by a skeleton staff.' This was particularly bad news for Rotherham, as Maltby Main colliery had also been closed 'indefinitely'. It was estimated that this closure would affect between 2,000 and 3,000 men. Including Maltby, there was a total of about 6,000 men and boys out of work. The *Advertiser* noted that this would mean 'stagnation for the town'. It stated, 'There is scarcely a household or business in the immediate neighbourhood of the pit which will not be affected.'

Thankfully, in November it was announced that Maltby pit would re-open but that between 200 to 300 men would lose their jobs. This was not going to be a good Christmas for many families of the town. Matters worsened to such an extent that the following month the Mayor gave a statement to be inserted in the *Advertiser* of 15 December 1928:

> In view of the great distress arising out of the present industrial depression it has been deemed advisable to form a local committee to work in conjunction with other efforts that are being made to render help to sufferers.

The coal strikes had been devastating to the town and deprivation continued. The large numbers of men returning to the town resulted in massive unemployment as the relief systems began to break down.

Cage crash at Kilnhurst colliery.

Once again the Rotherham miners were called out in another national strike held in January 1936, when it was announced that the coal owners were trying to make an offer to increase miners' wages in the districts. The *Advertiser* reported, 'It was hoped that there would be a general offer which will be uniform in character,' and that the 'amount of coal used in the gas and electricity industry alone amounted to 12 million tons a year.' Local pit boys' wages had been increased on Saturday, 24 July 1937 and it was hoped that this would lead to better general wages across the whole of the coalfields. However, this did not prove to be the case. Stoppages occurred at Silverwood on Monday and Tuesday 26/27 July. By Thursday, the unions were negotiating with the miners to persuade them to return to work, pending negotiations. Maltby Main laid down their tools on Wednesday, New Stubbin refused to work on the Tuesday and Aldwarke Main laid down their tools on Thursday. Only Treeton, Dinnington and Thurcroft Main collieries continued to work. At the same time as this there was an accident at Kilnhurst colliery on 28 July 1937; a reminder of the dangerous nature of the industry. A cage crashed into the bottom of the number 2 shaft. The accident involving the shaft, which was 2,000ft deep, resulted in one man being killed and seventeen others injured. The injured men were removed to the Rotherham Hospital and others to the Montague Hospital at Mexborough. The pit was closed on Thursday for officials to visit the site and investigate the accident, but re-opened for business on Friday 30 July. The Secretary for Mines reported the accident in the House of Commons and deep sympathy was extended to the miners' families. The MP for Rotherham, Alderman Dobbie, returned to the town to visit the men in hospital and later paid tribute to the 'amazing fortitude of the injured miners'. He reported:

> The first thing they asked me was how their comrades are going on. It shows the splendid comradeship of the miners. They were all very appreciative of what was being done for them and they told me the accident might have been much worse for them.

There is no doubt that the people of Rotherham experienced great poverty throughout this time of industrial unrest. The town's organisations started subscriptions to get boots for children and soup kitchens were established in order to alleviate as much distress as possible. But the situation was also aggravated by the numbers of unemployed men on the streets of the town.

# 12

# THE PLIGHT OF THE UNEMPLOYED

By the early 1920s, the amounts of relief given at the workhouse to support the massive numbers of unemployed Rotherham men reached monumental proportions. The workhouse officials stated that the situation was 'in such crisis that the whole system has become unworkable'. The Poor Law Guardians had taken out loans which they were now unable to pay and they asked that a new system be devised. The unrest over the lack of jobs available resulted in a decision to take the problem directly to the seat of government and a 'hunger march' to London was arranged. Modern historians are familiar with the hunger marches of the 1930s, but as early as 1922 marches were being organised to the capital. This was to force the newly elected Prime Minister, Bonar Law, to be aware of the depth of concern over the unemployment which faced the country. In November 1922 it was agreed that a contingent from Rotherham would go to London, but the march did not go quite as planned. The marchers from Rotherham, which were estimated to be about 200–300 men, women and children, were requested to assemble in College Square on the 3 November. It had been arranged that they would meet at 4 p.m. and form a procession which would be headed by a pony and cart carrying 'an erection setting out the marchers' objectives'. At the last minute it seems that the pony and cart would not be arriving until after 6 p.m., so it was agreed that the marchers would set off the following morning instead. The men agreed to meet at 6.30 a.m. and would begin the march by taking the cart around the local shopkeepers and asking them for donations of food and other provisions for the journey. By 7 a.m. the men were ready and they marched out of the town singing the 'Red Flag'. They sported a banner decorated with a skull and cross bones and the words 'Rotherham Unemployed' and 'Death is better than Semi Starvation'. It was intended that they would march approximately 12 miles a day and would reach Clowne on the first night, Mansfield the next day and Nottingham the following day. There they planned to meet up with the Nottingham contingent to proceed en masse to Melton Mowbray, Kettering, Bedford, Luton and St Albans. Then all the individual groups would converge in London and meet as a party on 16 November. The following day they would march through Marble Arch into Hyde Park at 2 p.m., where they would join the unemployed men from other counties. On 22 November it was hoped that they would have their meeting with the Prime Minister.

By 18 November it was rumoured that some men had dropped out of the march due to a dispute within the ranks. It seems that five people, Messrs A. Wright, William Briggs,

T. Gunn, B. Flint and McMahon, had dropped out at Oakham in Rutlandshire. They had been collecting money as they walked along the route; they had a sum of £13 8s 0d to be used for accommodation, food for themselves and fodder and shelter for the pony. These five people objected to having to put their money into the communal pot and felt that it should have been divided between the five of them. The leader, Mr Pickering, protested to this and so the five men left the group. Accusations were made that they joined another group and criticised Pickering for this action. When the party arrived back at Rotherham, it was generally felt that these men were in the wrong and the money should have been shared out between all the marchers. But their troubles had only just begun: it was announced that Mr Bonar Law had refused to meet the delegation in London. He sent a message to say that the Minister of Health and the Minister of Labour would attend in his place. The hunger marchers refused to meet his deputies and insisted that he attend. They sent a message, which was reported in the *Advertiser* on 25 November, stating, 'A great demonstration will be held next week and we shall not leave London until he sees us.' They requested a manifesto, asking for other unemployed men to respond to a call for action:

> The movement is engaged in a terrific struggle against the forces of reaction and suppression as a result of the high handed attitude the Premier has taken. The marchers have decided to stay in London until he does condescend to receive them, his elected representatives. In order to keep up the pressure it is imperative that reinforcements of men should take the road to London.

Many of the marchers stayed resolutely in the capital, but by February it seems that Mr Pickering was anxious to return home. He applied to the guardians of the Poplar Workhouse, where some of the men were being accommodated, for money to return to Eccleshall. When considering the question, the clerk to the guardians made the comment that anyone who had marched from Rotherham to London 'should be capable of marching back', but whether the guardians took this comment seriously was not recorded.

To add to the problem of unemployment, by 1928 the town was in the grip of an industrial depression. The government came up with many different schemes to try to get men back into work. One of these took the radical idea of emigrating young single men to places like Canada and Australia. On 11 August it was announced that the first batch of six men left Rotherham to go to Liverpool where the *Cedric* would take them to Canada. The Rotherham Labour Exchange later agreed that married men were allowed to go out to Canada under this scheme as well, providing they could make arrangements to support their wives and families, until they too could move to join the men in their new country. The *Advertiser* noted that ten more applicants were to emigrate on the *Laurentic* the following Friday.

The scheme had been so popular that more than 300 men had applied, but many didn't fit the criteria; candidates who were disabled, unfit, or men who were on part time work were denied. Of the 300 applicants, 65 had been selected for interview by the Canadian authorities, and of these 34 were accepted. It was reported that the remainder were 'to be interviewed as soon as arrangements can be made'.

The government also devised a scheme for men and boys, aged eighteen to thirty-five, to go out to Australia, where they could find jobs in the large farms of the country. Two farms in

Suffolk and Norfolk had been chosen by the Ministry of Labour to train these men prior to their departure and they were then guaranteed a job on their arrival in Australia. It was reported the following week that some men and boys who had gone out to Canada were now engaged in working either for themselves or in shared farms. However, that was soon to change.

Scarcely before some of the men could land in these foreign countries, there were conflicting reports about the treatment of Rotherham men who had taken advantage of this scheme the year before. British MPs attending the Empire Parliament Conference protested about the treatment that these English men had suffered at the Winnipeg Immigration Sheds. Tales had emerged about these emigrants being kept in underground cages and guarded by armed soldiers. The men were apparently 'herded together like sheep' and some men who had found work 'had to work for a dollar a day'. News must have got to the Rotherham men travelling on the *Cedric*, as they refuted the stories, saying that the treatment which had been metered out to them by the captain of the vessel and the crew was excellent. Another positive account was reported in the local newspaper from a man who had gone to Nova Scotia. He said that his employers had 'treated him like a son'. The following week another of the emigrants, John Kershaw, wrote to his parents in Rotherham telling them that Canada was a great place. He said that he and his mate Charlie had settled down really well and described the food as 'ripping'. He told them, 'We could not wish for a better farmer who is only in his thirties and he pays us the equivalent of 16/8 a day with board.' He admitted that the work was hard, with a 7 a.m. start and 6.30 p.m. finish, but they had a lunch hour and breaks mid-morning and afternoon. He ended the letter, 'It's a real man's country and a real man's job.'

On 16 March 1929, Mr H. Horsefall, who had left Rotherham many years before to go to Canada, heard of the poor conditions which the people of Rotherham were enduring. He sent a sum of money to the Mayor to pay for the entertainment of the Canklow miners' children, as well as an open letter. He outlined the wonders, wealth and resources of Canada, stating that, as emigrants, they were 'sharing [their] heritage with these souls in need of [their] assistance which will succeed in developing a scheme to make Canada the greatest nation in the British Empire.'

The scheme was so popular that another programme, for women to train as domestics in Australia, was developed by the Rotherham Employment Exchange. On 11 August 1928, it announced that twenty-five berths had been secured on two ships leaving on 13 October and 10 November 1928. The passage would be free of charge and no qualifications would be expected, as the women would be given training up to a week before they sailed. The women were to be trained at a government hostel at Market Harborough. In the week before they left they were able to visit their families, take their leave of relatives and select what clothes they wished to take with them. The Employment Exchange stated that single girls or married women or widows without children, aged between eighteen and thirty-five, were all eligible for the scheme. It seems that they had more than 200 unemployed women on their books at that time. The following March, another fifty berths were booked on the *Oronsay*, sailing for Australia on 22 June. The ministry advised that early application to the Employment Exchange would be necessary and, once again, a position would be secured and a minimum wage assured. There are no reports about whether these schemes were successful or how many men and women returned to this country. But there was no doubt that for some people it was a golden opportunity to get away from the national depression which was settling over the country.

By 15 December 1928, the situation in Rotherham was so dire that Mayor Alderman S. Hall issued a public appeal for subscriptions for the unemployed men. But the men of Rotherham didn't want handouts. One man, in a letter to the *Advertiser* in April 1930, stated boldly, 'Give me work I don't want the dole. Give me a chance in life.' At that time there were 10,000 unemployed men out of a population of 70,000, 'who daily attend[ed] the Employment Exchange in Westgate'; Rotherham was now officially a depressed area. On 14 March 1931 it was announced that 12,436 men were unemployed; the following month the figure had risen to over 14,000. Matters were, however, about to get much worse with the introduction of the Means Test, which was due to start on 1 November 1931.

On 3 October the Means Test was discussed at a meeting of Rotherham Trades and Labour Council and strong objections were registered against it. This was a clause of the Unemployment Insurance Act, which meant that unemployment benefits were now to be assessed on a means basis. The council resolved to send a protest against the act to the Prime Minister and the Minister of Labour, as well as to all parts of the country. Protests against it resulted in ugly scenes in Rotherham on 10 October 1931. This demonstration resulted in a clash with police on Howard Street during a meeting of the Rotherham Borough Council. Four arrests were made and several people were wounded. It had started with an organised procession of unemployed men, who had been instructed to start from the old fairground on Main Street. They marched along Effingham Street to the Town Hall and four men were deputed to go into the offices and meet the Town Clerk, who informed the demonstrators that they were unable to prevent the act being introduced in the town. The leader, a communist named Thomas H. James, aged thirty-four from Warde Street, Rotherham, told the demonstration, which had now collected at the Market Place, what the council had said. There were boos and catcalls. The men sang the 'Red Flag' and returned to the Town Hall where, by now, a ring of police had been placed around the door. An attempt to rush at the door was made and the police drew out their batons. A further squad of police emerged from the Town Hall and eventually, after much shouting, the mob dispersed. Several men were seen to be lying on the ground and it was reported that several women had fainted during the demonstration.

So much was the opposition to the Means Test that, in January 1932, the town council looked into the matter. It came to light that the test took into account the service pensions of ex-servicemen suffering from physical or mental disabilities, which the councillors found completely unacceptable. It seemed unfair that because these unemployed men had fought in the war and served their country that they would loose 33 per cent of their unemployment pay. The councillors felt that this was unjust and agreed to petition the government to remove this unfair ruling. In July 1932 the Minister of Labour, Sir Harry Betterton, publicly condemned the Rotherham Public Assistance Committee, saying that they had not 'efficiently carried out the duties imposed on them'. He proposed to 'appoint a person to exercise and perform in Rotherham the powers and duties which hitherto have evolved on Rotherham council.' He quoted cases where as much as £10 a week out of work relief had been given to persons already in receipt of other payments. On 4 July 1932, in the House of Commons, Mr William Thorne, the MP for West Ham, asked the Minister of Labour to state the date when he intended to delegate the duties of the Public Assistance Committee in Rotherham. He was told that Rotherham Council had decided 'to comply with the law' and therefore said that no action would be taken for the time being. However, by September, the minister was once again criticising the administration of the Means Test in Rotherham. The local committee that had been in charge of this duty, asked the council to be 'relieved of its task' and it was decided that the matter would be discussed the following week. It seems that they were still unhappy with the means testing of ex-servicemen with pensions and, on 1 October, it was announced that the minister would appoint someone to take over the duties of the Rotherham Public Assistance Committee. The previous committee was accused of being 'too liberal' with relief. Absolute conformity in all cases was demanded.

On Wednesday, 12 October 1932 Mr Kenneth George Holland, a barrister of London, commenced his duty in Rotherham to administer the Means Test on behalf of the Minister of Labour. He told a reporter, 'I propose to stick to the scale laid down by the Minister of Labour. If I think a case demands a departure from that scale I shall not hesitate to make such a departure. Every case shall be judged on its merit.'

Although his arrival didn't provoke any demonstrations, as was expected, a contingent of female workers arrived in the town from Burnley and Teeside, calling themselves the Women's Hunger Gang. They were marching to London in order to take part in a national rally protesting against the Means Test. The reporter for the *Advertiser* did not look on this group favourably, as he stated that the groups of women were '30 strong with a vanguard of about twenty men who were a slouching disorderly mob.' The group was met by Mr T.H. James, the local communist leader. They marched along College Street to the Co-operative Hall, where they were given a meal by the National Unemployed Workers Movement, followed by an evening meeting in the car park on Corporation Street. The women criticised the passiveness of the Rotherham people and then they marched, singing, to the workhouse. Five minutes later, they marched out again having refused to give their names and, as a consequence, they were refused admission. They assembled outside the workhouse and held another meeting. They agreed that they would give their names and so were admitted. The following morning (Friday) they went to the College of Art, where they were given breakfast by the Mayor, Alderman Caine, and Councillor W. Brooks, who told the reporter that the reason they had been given breakfast was because they were women. He commented, 'I think they are misguided and mistaken but still have a right to their opinion and it is my 53rd birthday.'

After breakfast the group proceeded to Worksop for the next stage of the march to London. It seems that this group of people were badly misjudged by the local newspaper. Both Teeside and Burnley had been through terrible depressions in trade and yet reporters tended to treat these protesters as some kind of a joke, criticising them for their slovenly ways and painting somewhat comic scenes at the workhouse. There were many passionate and articulate men and women fighting for justice during the years of the 1930s and marching was a way in which they showed solidarity. The Means Test was universally disliked and many people felt very passionately that it should be abolished.

It was announced on the news on Monday 20 November that Durham County Council had also refused to administer payments in accordance with the requirements of the orders of the Minister of Labour. The minister appointed Mr Kenneth Holland to be one of two commissioners sent to Durham and he appointed another officer to administer payments for Rotherham. This new commissioner was a retired civil servant called Mr A.W. Basham. Throughout March 1933 the debate continued. When the Rotherham MP, Alderman W. Dobbie, made his maiden speech in the House of Commons on the administration of the Means Test in the West Riding, he was applauded. Yet when Sir Harry Betterton rose to answer he was interrupted several times. The following month the Means Test was criticised again by Councillor Ball, who was the agent to the Rotherham Labour Party. He warned of revolution in a speech:

> I believe that unless the government does something to relax the regulations controlling the Means Test Commissioners, our people will get out of hand. Therefore I want to say that collective effort is necessary and it is far better to do what is going to be done as a disciplined body rather then an undisciplined mob. It is trying the patience of working class communities too far and something drastic is going to happen.

Copies of his speech were sent in a letter to the Prime Minister, the Minister of Health and the West Riding County Council.

Despite the strong feelings against the Mean Test, the Rotherham authorities were genuine in their concern to find something for the unemployed men to do. By January 1931, it had been decided that in order to given them some form of work that allotments would be allocated to them. Seeds and equipment would be provided so that they would have something to do and could improve their diet by growing their own vegetables. A meeting was held at the Town Hall on 16 January 1931 and a committee was formed to include one member from the Corporation Allotments Committee, Mr W. Milner, and one of his colleagues from the Labour Exchange. It was agreed that the Rotherham Corporation would buy the land and allocate allotments to the men. Land was identified at Canklow and Kimberworth, which would provide 150 allotments at both sites. Another initiative for the unemployed men was unveiled in June of 1933: unemployed men would build a bowling green on land on the top of King Street, Masbrough. The piece of land was 850 square yards and it was to the rear of Masbrough Independent Chapel. The Mayor, Councillor Ketton, laid the first brick of the wall surrounding the land on which the bowling green would be placed. The men did all the work themselves and the finished green measured 84ft by 75ft, with a path all the way around and a small pavilion in one corner.

In December 1932, in another attempt to get men into work, even temporarily, Councillor Brooks appealed for any employer to consider taking on men for the Christmas holidays. This would at least ensure that the men would be able to provide a meal for their families and maybe a few presents for the children. This scheme was a great success and it was reported that by 23 December, 3,347 men were temporarily back at work. By July 1933 matters seem to have improved; it was reported that there had been a decrease of 2,125 to the figure of unemployed men from the previous month. Many found jobs in tourist destinations such as Skegness and Blackpool, as porters, chefs, waitresses, hall and kitchen porters, chambermaids and housemaids.

A lot of these schemes were very successful and beneficial to unemployed people, although there could be no substitution for full employment. Gradually industry improved and the town returned to normal. However, one problem that was slower to find resolution during the interwar years was the housing situation.

# 13

# HEALTH AND HOUSING

Industrial towns like Rotherham had more than their fair share of disease, and regular epidemics had taken their toll on the population. Some diseases were hard to eradicate. In November 1920 it was reported that Rotherham was still struggling with tuberculosis (sometimes referred to as consumption), which was rife in the town. Oakwood Hall on Moorgate, which had been a Voluntary Aid Detachment (VAD) hospital during the First World War, had burnt to the ground in 1918. Once it was restored, it opened as a sanatorium for patients with consumption. In May 1922 it was reported:

> Its situation at the top of Moorgate faces south in a downward slope ensuring that fresh air and sunshine are in abundance, two ingredients necessary to the health of the town and hopefully for the cure of consumption. Seventy cases of tuberculosis are being treated at the hospital at the moment.

The need for an isolation hospital in Rotherham had been noted as early as 1885 and what was christened the 'tin tabernacle' had been erected in Badsley Moor Lane a few years later. In 1905 a more permanent building was opened and by 1925 it was estimated that it had dealt with a total of 5,298 cases. Enteric fever had been the cause of forty to fifty cases a year. The disease had been practically eradicated due, in no small part, to the transfer of the water supply from Ulley Dam to the Derwent Water Scheme. The better health of the town was also down to the replacement of privies with water closets. It is difficult for us to understand how quickly epidemics took hold of the areas around the town and how futile attempts to stop the spread of infection could be. As an example, an outbreak of smallpox hit the town in autumn 1925 and appeals for parents to have their children vaccinated were made in the local newspapers. The epidemic seemed to concentrate on the areas around Rawmarsh and Parkgate. In January of the following year, there was a reported 230 cases and it was spreading with alarming speed. A Ministry of Health Inspector was sent to Rotherham to examine what measures had been taken to cope with the outbreak and to prevent the epidemic spreading any more. But still cases continued to be recorded, including people young and old. It was estimated that each patient cost £100 in hospital treatment and the costs were escalating. The outbreak, which had amounted to 450 cases, thankfully reached a peak by February 1926, when finally the epidemic was reported to be 'on the wane'.

The worst outbreak to hit the town was the flu epidemic of 1936/7, when Rotherham Hospital was closed to visitors as a precautionary measure. Schools were closed, transport services struggled on with some difficulty and the services at Thurcroft church were suspended. On 23 January it was reported that 15 per cent of the police force had been affected. Local industries reported that between 20 and 25 per cent of their workforce had been taken ill and football matches and social events were postponed.

The poor health of the town and the regular epidemics were blamed on the terrible housing conditions, which had gradually deteriorated during the war years. Worsening rat infestations were also a factor. In August 1919 it was reported that there had been such a large infestation of rats in the town that the *Advertiser* requested:

> If there is any person capable of emulation of the pied piper of Hamelin the Corporation would be pleased to have the use of his services, for which no doubt they would pay handsomely. The rat is to be exterminated in the Borough and they are asking the services of persons to catch and kill these vicious rodents. Rotherham is a rat infested place. It is estimated that there are a thousand rats in the sewers, shops and factories of the town and the numbers have increased in the past few years to alarming proportions. Sums from 2d – 3d a tail are offered.

Unfortunately, the matter did not go away. It was reported in June 1922 that another epidemic of rats had taken hold. It seems that the 'penny pinching local authorities' had decided that the eradication of these rodents was the responsibility of the tenants and landlords of the different buildings and, as a result, had recently dismissed the official rat catcher. By 1926, the matter had escalated yet again and another rat catcher was employed. By November 1930, large numbers of rats were infesting the town once again, but this time it was on the site where slum housing was being systematically demolished. Gradually, as new housing was built, the eradication of the rats became less necessary.

The returning soldiers had not expected to return to the town to find the same overcrowding and shortage of housing they had experienced before the war. Unfortunately, that was exactly what they found. Restrictions on building houses during the war had ensured that the overcrowding had not only continued, but actually worsened. In May 1919, it was reported that scores of houses had been demolished since 1913, but not one house had been built. At that time there were 600 houses in the town which were classed as 'unfit for human habitation'. The *Advertiser* stated that, within a stone's throw of the parish church, a family of eight persons had to sleep in one room. Not far away, a house with two 'ramshackle rooms', unsuitable as a store house, had been used by a man, his wife and two children. The problem was that materials for building houses were very scarce and labour was expensive. A solution was found in March 1919, when it was decided that much cheaper concrete houses would be built on Doncaster Road. By October 1919, the work had begun erecting these houses. Their estimated cost was £500 each. But it was the speed with which they could be built that appealed to the Borough Council; each house could be built in fourteen days. The rents of these houses were suitable for working families who could afford to pay 8s a week. They were designed by Mr A.F. Jeffries, and a reporter from the *Advertiser* gave them the following description:

> The six roomed houses have a picturesque frontage with a large open window, a neat door and a neatly panelled porch. The walls are coloured, the doors are painted green and the windows are steel framed. The houses, being made of concrete, are fire resistant if not entirely fire proof. There is a living room, a scullery, two bedrooms, a bathroom and a small box room.

By June, the local authority was being urged to hurry up with this site and the making of roads and sewers was undertaken. It seems that Rotherham was the first local authority to prepare a housing scheme. The speed with which they worked was phenomenal, as they had the plans approved and the first sod cut by June 1919. But then things seemed to slow down. It December the *Advertiser* reported:

> The first four houses should have been up in November and two more each succeeding week. Another four should have been completed by the end of this month. At this moment there are none finished although four are almost complete. There is ample materials and machinery on site, but there is a lack of labourers although there are 700–800 unemployed men on the books of the Labour Exchange.

The cost of the new housing estates was going to be enormous, and so in April 1920 the local authority issued housing bonds. These were offered at 6 per cent and Rotherham needed to sell enough to pay £725,000 for houses in the first twelve months. The housing problem was not just relevant to Rotherham; it was a national issue. It was reported on 20 March 1926 that Mr Neville Chamberlain, speaking in London the previous day, had said that the situation regarding housing 'was still very serious'. Meanwhile, it was announced at a meeting that Rotherham Council was to borrow a further £144,000 for new houses to be built. The Ministry of Health had given permission for the following sums to be given for the building of houses: at Thrybergh, £23,734; Ravenfield, £23,430; Dalton, £18,700; Catcliffe, £4,578; Brampton Bierlow, £24,431; Bramley, £18,856; Wickersley, £9,430; and Thurcroft, £22,333.

But the houses were not being built fast enough to accommodate the ex-servicemen returning to the town. By February 1921 they were angry with the Housing Committee and one ex-serviceman stated:

> The local authority should redeem their promises made when the scheme was outlined, that ex-servicemen were to be the first tenants of these new houses. Instead hundreds of ex-servicemen are without homes and advantages were given to men in the building trade. Under the present system ex-servicemen will never have a house they can call their home.

The complaints continued and, in July 1922, letters to the editor of the *Advertiser* stated that these new houses had been given to men who had 'never worn a soldier's tunic' and

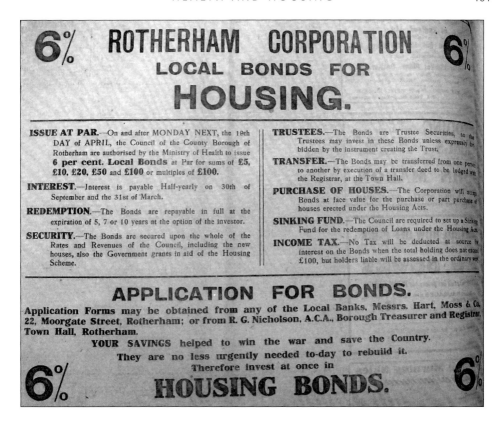

Advertisement for housing bonds.

'families with no children'. The paper called for more houses, stating, 'There is a growing list of applicants waiting to occupy the new houses.' Despite the Corporation's promises, there was an average of less than three houses built a week by February 1925. To make matters worse, later the same month the newspaper described the huts that homeless people were using as dwellings at Canklow. These wretched hovels were placed on the hillside behind the Canklow Hotel and were described as 'a deplorable eyesight'. Families, unable to find accommodation elsewhere, had migrated to this 'bleak spot'. Described as resembling the early settlements of western America, it was reported, 'A small colony of wretched dwellings constructed of wood, turf and rubble has sprung up.' The constructions provided poor protection against the winds and gales of winter and there were no facilities; the only water supply was a natural well on the hillside. Despite these conditions, most of the occupants of these dwellings said they were happy and some were reported as being 'comfortable'. A reporter described one of the dwellings. It had originally been a cart shed but was now 'divided into three compartments, a kitchen, a bedroom and a small apartment used for storing boxes.' He added:

> The inhabitants consist of mother, father and a bedridden son aged 16 who had been
> injured as a result of a bomb dropping from a German airplane in 1917 whilst the boy

had been in school in London. The sleeping arrangements are that the father sleeps in the kitchen and the mother shares the same bed as her son.

By 1925 demand for housing had become so acute that the Rotherham Corporation was investigating using steel houses (known as Braithwaite's, after the engineer from London who designed them). By January 1926 the first Braithwaite houses were open for inspection. The houses had steel walls and could be erected quickly, efficiently and economically. It was estimated that fifty of these houses could be built in twelve weeks, 100 in twenty weeks and 400 in forty-eight weeks. A quote from Mr Coppock, the general secretary to the National Federation of Builders and Operatives, stated, 'Braithwaite housing is a genuine attempt to solve the housing shortage.' These houses were seen as a great success and it was agreed that 1,466 houses would be built at East Dene and further sixty at Meadowbank. A letter sent to the editor of the *Advertiser* in May 1931 stated that the rents for the houses in East Dene were still too high. The writer complained that most of the houses were let to policemen, staff of the Rotherham Corporation and those in regular employment who could afford a 'better rent'.

In December 1929, a decision was taken by the housing committee that eight pairs of what were described as 'non parlour' houses would be built. These were to be flats or maisonettes on the Herringthorpe estate. They would consist of one bedroom, a living room and a combined scullery and bathroom. In a council meeting one person questioned whether these flats would

Houses at Meadowbank as they are today.

be suitable for married couples, as there was a 'distinct lack of provision for this type of tenant'. Alderman Caine stated confidently that they would not. He continued:

> I hope the day will never come when this Corporation will so far degenerate its standards as regards housing to imagine that a living room, bedroom and scullery are sufficient accommodation for young married couples in Rotherham.

Perhaps Alderman Caine was being naïve, as many young couples of the town would gladly exchange living with their in-laws for the first few years of married life for such limited accommodation. The urgent need for housing for young married couples had been taken up by the *Advertiser* as early as May 1919. The reporter suggested that Nissen huts might be used for these starter homes as the military authorities had no more use for them now.

By January 1931 the Rotherham Corporation had announced a five-year slum-clearance plan. One hundred homes were scheduled to be demolished, 'many of which had a demolition order on them for many years' according to the *Advertiser*. However good the intentions of the housing authorities were, houses were just not being built fast enough for some people. On 10 September 1938 the *Advertiser*, which had consistently demanded better housing for people of the town, reported that a man, wife and five members of his family were living in two tents on Wash Lane Aldwarke, Rotherham. The reporter stated that the husband had been employed in a local colliery, but in 1935 had to leave due to an illness contracted when serving as a soldier in the First World War. He had lived in colliery houses for thirty-five years and had always paid his rent on time, but he had been told to leave as his house was now needed for another collier's family. He applied to the council for a house and was told that the only houses available were for people who had been turned out of slums or overcrowded houses and his name would have to go on the list. The family had originally moved in with some friends, but had once again been asked to leave as their friends were not allowed to sublet. Two of the older boys had managed to find lodging, leaving the couple with two girls aged 22 and 8 and three boys aged 17, 15 and 13 living in the tents. A week later the reporter stated, 'There has been no change in the family's position and the man has still not received an alternative offer of shelter.'

Slowly, housing estates developed throughout the town and many of these houses still exist today. Thankfully, the slum dwellings of the town, and particularly the hovels at Canklow Woods, have long since gone. New and better services were introduced as gas and electricity was laid down, but the health of mothers and children remained an important one.

# 14

# MOTHERS AND CHILDREN

As we have seen, after the war, the state of children in the town was the main area of concern for the public health authorities. In May 1919, the unhealthy lifestyle of many families in the town was reported in the *Advertiser*. Children were described as having 'pallid faces and deformed rickety limbs'. It was added, 'In one overcrowded house two young children, no more than fourteen will soon become mothers and the spread of venereal disease and tuberculosis are just some of the many illnesses which affect the town today.'

Some schemes tried to alleviate poverty for even just a short period when long-term solutions were beyond reach. On 2 August 1919, the National Federation of Discharged and Demobbed Soldiers and Sailors (NFDDSS) had organised an excursion to Cleethorpes for 2,000 fatherless youngsters. Leading up to the date of the excursion, mothers had been asked to hand in the names of the children who were eligible to the Federation, which was based at the Old Bank buildings on the High Street. The following week, the mothers had to bring the children to the railway station for 7 a.m. and ensure that they were provided with light refreshments for the journey. They were also asked to provide a small towel so that the children could bathe in the sea. Not surprisingly, it was reported that the outing had been a complete success. The party had met at the Auckland Colonnade, Cleethorpes. Mrs Smalley, the proprietor, allowed the younger children to choose a bucket and a spade each and the older children had ten donkeys placed at their disposal. Sports had been arranged on the sands, with prizes provided by the local trade's people. These included skipping ropes, balls and cricket bats. The return train arrived back at Rotherham between 9.30 and 10 p.m. and each child was presented with a stick of Cleethorpes rock. This outing must have delighted the children of the town, who had probably never seen the sea before.

The determination to prioritise health and welfare of mothers and children led to an announcement, in May 1919, that the former Ferham House was going to be opened as a child welfare and maternity clinic. The Town Clerk was instructed to make an application to local government for a loan of £3,630, for equipment to supply to the new maternity centre. The clinic was formally opened in November 1920 by Major Fred Kelley, MP. Its objective was to bring children into the world under happier and healthier conditions than was possible at that time. However, this service was not free and set fees had been introduced, although it was

Old Bank buildings,
which housed the
NFDDSS in 1919.

announced that 'consideration would be given to personal circumstances'. Nevertheless, the service would ensure that babies were born under professional and hygienic conditions. Once a child had been born, mothers were encouraged to bring their children to the centre regularly for examination and advice. There were separate departments, covering children's throats, eyes, ears and teeth. The hope was that such clinics would reduce diseases and infections so prevalent amongst the children.

The clinic boasted an X-ray department, hot and cold showers, cleansing baths and dentists rooms. In January 1922, there was a reunion of all the mothers who had given birth at the maternity clinic. Major Kelley spoke of his privilege at being present to open the clinic a year ago, and about the great improvements in the health of mothers and children there had been. The Mayoress regretted that she had been unable to attend the original opening due to poor health, but complimented the mothers on the healthy babies that she saw before her. She told the mothers that in the last year there had been 220 babies born, out of which only one child death had been reported. This was considered to be a great tribute to the staff.

Despite this tribute, many children of the town were still living in dire straights. In December 1919 it was observed once more that there were many 'bootless children' in the town, which stirred up a lot of feeling. The remarks had been made by Councillor Caine, who stated that the orphans and children of widows were suffering 'because the pension of £6 a year given towards clothing [was] inadequate for the children of men who had died on active service.' Fred Kelley MP noted this and wrote to the town council from his residence in London:

> ...the statement made that children were unable to go to school because they had no boots to wear, I sincerely hope that the gentleman was misinformed. I shall be pleased if Councillor Caine will give me the names of any children who are so unfortunately

Ferham Clinic, which was opened as a clinic in November 1920.

placed. I am at the moment the custodian of the honour of Rotherham in the House of Commons. I refuse to represent a constituency against which a serious lack of patriotism can be charged, if true. If Councillor Caine sends me the names etc and not one school hour will be lost before I personally shall esteem it a most distinguished honour to send those kiddies to school in the best boots that Rotherham can provide.

Fred Kelley December 4th 1919

The plight of these poor children did not improve, regardless of the promises made by Major Kelley. In October the following year, the editor of the *Advertiser* asked that a subscription be started for boots for the children. He stated that many children were unable to go to school through their feet being inadequately shod and that those who did attend usually had borrowed boots. The Poor Children's Boots Fund was started and, as usual, all the subscribers were listed. Many of the town's children received new boots under this scheme and the newspaper listed some of the families who were the recipients:

Labourer out of work with 10 in the family. Eight children under 14. Income: out of work money with 3 children without any boots

Labourer on short time for 12 months. Five in the family and three children. Income: 24/- (rent 6/6) two children no boots

Labourer with seven in the family, five children. Income: wages 32/-

Blacksmiths striker, nine in the family. Five children under 10. Income: wages £1.14.6d

It was recognised that children suffered the most during times of industrial depression. As a result of the coal crisis in May 1921, the Rotherham and Barnsley Football Club gave a tea for the children of the unemployed men at the site of the football club at Millmoor. Tea was provided for 200 children, consisting of bread and meat, buns and tea. A bar of chocolate was given to each child as they left. Another tea was given in the Kimberworth Wesleyan schoolroom a few days later, where another 230 children attended. It was agreed that during the time of distress that the Masbrough Corps of the Salvation Army would ensure that these teas continued each Thursday. It was reported that on average 200 children would receive meals of soup and bread during these desperate times. Once again there was a period of industrial distress in June of 1926 following the coal strike. The *Advertiser* started another subscription to provide meals for the children. It was noted that, 'Although the distress in the town is not as acute as other districts nevertheless this weaker group needs to be protected.'

At this time the government also recognised that, in order to save lives, smaller families were desirable. Middle or upper-class women had access to birth control information through their doctors, but it was unavailable to working-class wives, who had to bear the brunt of large families. Eight to ten children was the norm for families in those years, resulting in poor health for the mothers and the children, as well as increased mortality rates for both. At some point in 1928, a birth control clinic was introduced to the town. This caused some controversy. At a council meeting held in the council chambers on 7 June 1929, the Mayor spoke about the success of the clinic during the previous year. He stated that he was 'glad that light had been thrown on a subject around which there was much misunderstanding'. He applauded the work that had been done by the clinic and shared his hope that the subject would 'become a recognised part of the Public Health Service' in the not too distant future. Members of the health committee spoke about the eleven centres for birth control in the country and one that had been recently opened in Newcastle. Perhaps the Mayor had spoken too soon. A heated debate took place in the council chamber a few weeks later, when the council received a resolution brought by the Shoreditch Town Council, stating:

> This council recognises that the question of family limitation is one that should be settled by the individuals themselves. It further recognises that a demand exists for working class married woman for reliable, private information on the methods of family limitation. It therefore calls upon the Ministry of Health to allow the municipalities who wish to do so, to provide facilities for such information through public service.

The Mayor conveyed that this subject had been discussed twelve months earlier, but that no decision had been made as to whether this should become a part of the health service. An amendment was put forward by Councillor Mrs Green that pressure should be put on the government to bring the whole matter into the realm of public authority, 'to enable them to provide such facilities and knowledge for all that desire it'.

Councillor Clarke, who was also a doctor, disagreed and stated that it was a very difficult question to discuss. He said that investigations were at that time being made into the whole subject by medical and surgical authorities. He demanded that the matter be shelved until their investigations were completed, as they were unaware of the effect that such limitations would have on mothers. He pointed out that there was also the moral and religious side to such arguments to be considered, as he felt that birth control would inevitably lead to immorality. Councillor Brooks agreed with him, pointing out that marriage was for the procreation of children and that birth control was unnatural. Councillor Mrs Green, who had supported the amendment, stated that what was involved was not the morality of the subject. She believed that those who wanted the information should have it and that Rotherham Council had no right to deny mothers that knowledge. She stated:

> There is an increasing demand from working mothers for such information as there is an appalling lack of knowledge on these matters amongst them. I feel very clearly that the life and health of these women can only be improved by spacing out their children.

Councillor Mrs Moorhouse agreed. However, other councillors did not and they voted against the amendment. It was lost by nineteen votes to ten.

The subject did not go away and exactly a year later, it was agreed that a committee should be set up to look into the matter. It was announced that since the Shoreditch resolution, no fewer than thirty-five local authorities had adopted the resolution for themselves. As a consequence, twelve of these had already put such clinics into operation. There was still no resolution at this time for Rotherham Council though.

Two months later, in August 1930, it was proposed that the clinic at Ferham House should ensure that birth control information was given to married women. But in order to get it, women would have to produce medical evidence to prove that child bearing would be injurious to their health. The birth control clinic, which had been operating in the town for some while, once again came under discussion. The Mayor pointed out that the clinic was run on a voluntary basis and that it should come under the remit of the Public Health authorities. Dr Clarke said that the British Medical Association had recently investigated the matter, on sociological grounds, and had clearly stated that advice about birth control was not to be given. He was overruled, however, and the approval of the Ministry of Health was sought in order to establish Ferham Clinic as a place where advice could be given to married women.

The Ministry of Health disagreed with the council request. Birth control was still seen as a very serious moral issue and according to the ministry, maternity and child-welfare clinics could only deal with expectant or nursing mothers; therefore, it was not the place to give advice on birth control to all women. It was stated that to use the clinic for such a purpose would damage the 'proper work of the clinic' and, therefore, the Ministry would not sanction the giving of advice in all cases. In fact, they made it very clear that advice could only be given to mothers who were already consulting the clinic and who could provide the medical information that was required.

Free birth control book for Rotherham parents.

It seemed then that there would be little birth control information for the mothers of Rotherham. However, within the pages of the *Advertiser*, from February 1933, a little book was publicised called the *Free Book of Birth Control for 1933: The Husband and Wife's Handbook*. It was advertised that this book could be ordered free of charge from the R.A. Hygienic Stores Ltd, 95 Charring Cross Road, London WC2. There is no evidence of what kind of advice was in this book, but it seems that it was all married mothers would get in Rotherham at this time.

In March and June 1939, Rotherham was concerned not only with its own children but with refugee children coming into the town. The *Advertiser* of 25 March 1939 issued an appeal from the Mayor, Alderman A. Buxton, to help the first few children under the Kindertransport scheme. These were Czech, German and Austrian Jewish children, fleeing from their country and the brutality of the Nazi regime. The reporter stated that they were fleeing from Germany following the November pogrom, known throughout the world as *Kristallnacht*. This name, meaning 'the night of broken glass', was given because of the hundreds of windows broken as Nazi troops stormed into Jewish quarters and smashed up homes and buildings. Worried parents were forced to part with their children, not knowing what their fate would be, but trusting that they would be safer in another country. The Mayor discussed the difficulty of transporting children away from their parents and into a foreign country, but spoke of 'one gentleman here tonight who has willingly agreed to take the first refugee boy to come to Rotherham.' He also appealed for hospitality for the children, either permanently or for a holiday period, as well as clothing, blankets and money in order to get them into homes in and around the districts. Over the Easter holiday, four Czech children were entertained in Rotherham and it was hoped that at least one would be settled on a local farm. Four more boy refugees came to Rotherham and were found homes in June 1939. Although little was known about the death camps at this time, there is no doubt that the people of Rotherham rose to the challenge and gave these children a safe home for the next few crucial years.

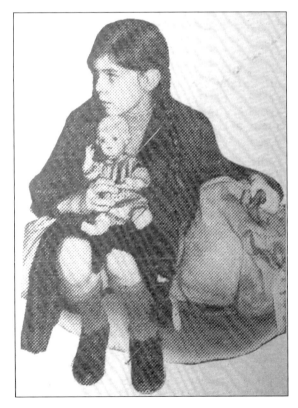

Kindertransport children arriving in Rotherham.

# 15

# ENTERTAINMENT

The interwar years saw great technological leaps in the world of entertainment. In December 1922, the radio, or wireless as it was called then, was very much in its infancy but many people were already expressing an interest in the new apparatus. A wireless demonstration, consisting of a programme of news and music, was broadcast from Manchester to the newly established School for Wireless and Telegraphy at the Borough Collegiate School on Clough Road, which was very well attended. The wireless was described as a 'three-valve set' which was reported to be 'in splendid order until the last few minutes of the demonstration when only a few present could hear what was being said.' Another demonstration of the new wireless was made in February 1922 at Parkgate, to entertain the men of the Rawmarsh Cricket Club. It was recorded that Mr Bool of Rawmarsh Hill, Parkgate had erected a temporary aerial and that the first attempt to pick up signals had been very successful. Children's stories were heard from Manchester and Birmingham, as were sessions of singing and piano playing. These early radio sets had little programming, and the signals that were picked up seemed to be very random. Morse code was heard, which was being transmitted out to sea from Flamborough Head, and later a station at Newcastle broadcast a male voice choir and a cornet solo. This was followed by the news from London and the score of the cricket test match. Such was the popularity of this new technology that by December 1923, regular broadcasts were heard and the *Advertiser* now published details of the weekend programs. On 15 December, a Saturday afternoon concert was listed, which was broadcast from 3.30 to 4.30 p.m. Other programmes included children's hour, farmers' weather forecasts and organ recitals. A Sunday program included a concert, discussions with young people, a religious address and a solo clarinet. Naturally, there was a limitation to this fun as all broadcasts ceased by 10.30 p.m.

The interest generated by these new wirelesses resulted in their prices dropping, and so they became more readily available to every home. In December 1923, sets were on sale in the town at Lilleker Brothers, Wireless Engineers of Howard Street Rotherham, who were selling a Mascot wireless set for 10s. In January 1924, a Brownie Crystal set would have set you back 8s 6d. By February 1925, it had been suggested that a wireless set would be a boon to the workhouse inmates, following an exhibition at Messrs Habershon Welfare Club. Consequently a fund was started to provide a four-valve set to the Rotherham Guardians of the

Poor, for the inmates. At the exhibition it was reported that thirty wireless sets were exhibited. They were described as being 'all different kinds of instruments from simple crystal sets to five valve receiving sets.' Despite the national interest in the new wireless, some people were not impressed. In February 1926, Mr George Auty, the headmaster of Kimberworth Central School, gave his opinion on the new wireless at an 'old boys' dinner. A new set had been presented to the school by the association, but he stated ungraciously:

> At present I am not favourably impressed with the educational position of wireless for children. The human element is lacking and there is too much of effortless entertainment. I am a firm believer in the gospel of work and particularly for boys.

But whatever his feelings, the wireless was a great success as entertainment. The following month, the *Advertiser* asked that the sum of £470 be subscribed in order to provide a complete wireless-receiving outfit for Rotherham Hospital. Such was its popularity that in the first week £300 had been donated by the readers. By June 1933, the programmers were using the wireless to inform as well as entertain. That month a series of lectures was broadcast, given by Judge Rutherford (listed as the world's greatest broadcast lecturer) on his visits to Europe. They were given three times a week on various stations. Lists of the lectures given and the various wavelengths on which they could be heard were published. The titles of the lectures were given as 'The Happy Home', 'The Kingdoms Blessings' and 'Stabilising the World'. The moralising tone of such lectures would be unpopular today, but at this time they were very popular. On 4 November 1933, the local newspaper announced a 'New Page in Wireless History':

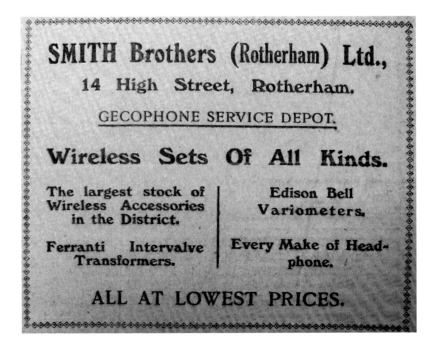

Wireless sets of all kinds.

Over a thousand houses in Rotherham have been wired up to a system operated by Clear Radio Ltd. Some years ago an enterprising gentleman attached a wire to his wireless and carried a loud speaker to the next room. This gave him the idea that he could provide it to a neighbouring house. There are now many of these relaying companies operating in the larger towns who operate a free installation and removal service. Over 100 hours of perfect radio for 1/6d.

Alongside the interest in wireless technology was the development of the gramophone, which at first was used for public entertainment in the town. On 18 October 1928 a gramophone recital was given in the Town Hall Assembly Rooms to a packed audience. The particular machine used in the concert was called the Gilbert Tone Reflector and the recital had been arranged by Messrs J. & W. Hastings Ltd of Rotherham and Masbrough. The gramophones were supplied by Mr Bernard Woods of Sheffield, who brought a selection along to the concert for the Rotherham people to look at. Most of them were priced at between eleven and seventeen guineas and, with the increasingly popular hire purchase terms, they would have been readily available to all. Mr Hastings told the assembled crowd that their Bridgegate shop would soon have its own gramophone department and also a concert room that would accommodate 200 people. The evening was such a success that he promised these gramophone recitals would continue. Two years later, regular concerts were being held at the Hastings shop, where they were still very well attended by people who could not afford to buy their own gramophone. At Easter 1930, one of the records played during one of these concerts were listed as John Stainer 'Crucifixion', written in 1887 and sung by soloist tenor Francis Russell, with Robert Easton singing bass and the choir supplied by the BBC. Admission was free, but no doubt people were encouraged to buy the gramophones that were sold in the shop. The following month, Hastings advertised the Lissenola Radio Gramophone, which was 'standing in the middle of [the] showroom and bringing in music from any European station.' There is no doubt that the Hastings firm readily cashed in on the interest over this new technology, and doubtless people would flock to the store to listen to these new radiograms. To buy one of these machines in an oak cabinet would cost £22, and in a mahogany cabinet £25. This model proved to be very popular. Records to play on them also sold well, including 'Selections from Carmen', 'Gypsy Songs', 'Polly Wolly Doodle', 'Widdacombe Fair', 'Organ Solos', 'Old Music Hall Favourites' and 'Marches by Her Majesty's Grenadier Guard Band'. These were on sale for 3s each. Gramophones were to continue to be one of the prime means of domestic entertainment for many years to come, though the rise of the cinema would present a challenge.

During the interwar years, Hollywood films revealed a lifestyle far removed from the lives of Rotherham people. The extravagances on screen were a world away from the shortages in the town. It had been noted that even in the midst of the miners' strike of October 1920, that attendances at the cinema had not fallen. At that time there were seven cinemas or 'picture palaces' open, so there was plenty of diversity. Popular films of the period were the comedies of Charlie Chaplin and Buster Keaton, as well as the Hollywood musicals of the 1920s. So it was a great disaster when it was announced on Friday, 25 February 1921 that the High Street Picture Palace had burnt down and was totally destroyed. It was estimated that rebuilding would cost between £25,000 and £30,000. It seems that the premises had been locked up

'His Master's Voice' products on sale at Hastings' shop.

on the Thursday evening as usual, but flames had been spotted by PC Taylor on his beat through Clifton Park. The fire brigade was on the scene within a few minutes, but it was noted that the Elephant and Castle Inn, opposite, was covered with embers from the fire. Sparks were reported as far away as College Square, and only with great difficulty was the fire brought under control by 4.30 a.m.

Film censorship was concerning the Rotherham Watch and Fire Brigade Committee in April 1928. They recommended that another special committee be assembled to examine any cinematograph films proposed in the borough that had not been approved by the British Board of Film Censors. But the committee, and the number of people on it, was to cause problems for the watch and fire brigade. There had been some concern expressed about showing that most innocuous of films *King of Kings* in Sheffield. It had been proposed for Rotherham, but the watch committee had asked fifty-one ministers to view the film first, and they had been divided on its suitability. The committee suggested that others be co-opted onto the board if necessary, to make a decision on the matter. One of the councillors pointed out that if the committee had a representative from the Church, the law, press and politics, surely that was representation enough. The Mayor, no doubt annoyed by this lack of decision, ended the argument by stating that he would not go to any outside authority. Enough people had seen the film to make a judgment on it, he said and, as he had been 'elected as a representative of the people', he would bring the matter to a close. Not much more is mentioned about the censorship board or whether the film was shown in Rotherham.

But the fact that large crowds continued to attend the many cinemas in the town proved its popularity as a medium.

The greatest news for Rotherham film-goers came in February 1929, when it was reported that 'talkies' were coming to the town. The newspapers stated that the installation of the necessary equipment at the Whitehall Picture House, which was re-opened on 20 April 1929, would proceed. The success of the 'talkies' resulted in the Empire cinema screening them too. Matinée performances were attended by the Mayor and Mayoress on 30 November of the same year.

Magazines aimed at film fans became more popular. These allowed the film-going public to discover the world of some of their favourite film stars. In July 1933, the *Advertiser* reviewed the *Picturegoer's Summer Annual*:

> Brightly written pen pictures and well produced photographs of the stars who shine in the film firmament are contained in the summer annual of the Picturegoer which is an entertaining 6*d* worth. Joan Barry has some good and sound advice about leaving worries on the doorstep. 'Worry' she points out 'has killed more people than wars, although casualty lists are never published'. An article based on the requirements of a wife by eligible Hollywood bachelors is diverting, whilst the screen star fashions for summer and autumn have an irresistible feel to the feminine mind. An article by a doctor in which he says the cinema is playing an important part in avoiding the condition which leads to neurasthenia is of considerable interest and there are in addition many articles of the inner lives of Hollywood as well as lovely shots from the pick of the pictures. It has an attractive frontispiece with Norma Shearer as the central figure.

Further excitement grew in the town on Saturday, 22 December 1934, when the opening of Rotherham's new 'luxury cinema', the Regal on Corporation Street, was announced. It was to be opened by the Mayor, Alderman R. Kirk, and Rotherham's own star Sandy Powell. The crowds assembled at 7.30 p.m. and it was reported that they were 'awed and amazed by the luxury they found within.' A local reporter stated, 'A sense of ease and well being settles upon the patron when he or she passes through the doors into the cosy and beautiful appointed foyer.' The first feature shown was a Sydney Howard film called *Girls Please*, where he plays the part of a gymnastics teacher left in charge of a girls' school whilst the headmistress is called away. The reporter wrote, 'There are scores of screamingly funny scenes which involve an elopement and a hare and hounds chase.' These kind of mad cap films were shown in their thousands and were possibly the forerunners of the *Carry On* films of later years.

A free form of entertainment, no doubt enjoyed by the people of Rotherham during the interwar years, was the library service. So it was a great shock when people heard that the library, which was then situated in Main Street, had been on fire on 26 July 1925. Ironically, it had been decided previously that the site was not entirely suitable, being attached to the public baths, and a more central site had been called for. Permission had been granted to look for premises in the centre of the town, but before this could be achieved the building was almost destroyed. Damage was estimated to have been between

£15,000 and £20,000 and approximately 15,000 books had been burned. Fortunately for local historians, the area least damaged had been the reading rooms, containing a case of some very old books belonging to a former lending library. The library had been founded in 1723 by Mrs Frances Mansell, who had offered the books 'for the use of the clergy and parishioners of Rotherham for ever.' The case and the contents had been presented by the vicar and the churchwardens of Rotherham in 1893. Thankfully these books had not been damaged.

It was reported that the fire had been spotted by several persons at 6 a.m. in the morning and was brought under control by 10 a.m. A new manager of the baths, Mr T.W. Paine, who had only been there a few days, had woken to find the library ablaze. His wife and two children had only joined him from Frith in Kendal the previous evening. They were unable to save anything apart from a few clothes. Although part of the building was unscathed by fire, water was reported to be running down the stairs of the building and out into Main Street. As a temporary measure, a reading room was provided at Rotherham School of Art and provision was made for the return of books to St George's Hall. The following month, however, it was noted with horror that the library books stored on the top storey of St George's Hall were full of 'verminous insects'. It was agreed that a wooden structure would be erected in Corporation Street to serve as a public library until the new Central Library could be built. It was estimated that the temporary library would 'be open in the next few weeks'.

Two years later, a report was drawn up and presented by the Borough Engineer Mr Boardman, on the accommodation and equipment required to stock the new Central Library. He had brought a rough sketch with him for the approval of the town council. Provision had been made for the stock of 30,000 volumes, of which between 8,000 and 10,000 were to be in the reference section. The new library would accommodate 301 people, with a separate section for thirty female readers. It was also proposed to stock 6,000 to 7,000 books in the children's section. The sketch and the report were accepted in principle. In May, it was announced that the Carnegie Trust had agreed to a grant of £1,000 for the cost of furnishing the new public library, which was to be built on Howard Street at a total cost of £20,000. By May 1930, the new library was still in mid-construction and there were complaints in the local newspapers about how long it was taking. It was reported that the pressure on the library staff at the temporary library had been immense, as there had been a turnover of 47,000 volumes since the library had been opened. This had resulted in long queues and congestion at the shelves during busy periods. Finally, on Monday, 19 October 1931, the new library on Howard Street was opened by the Earl of Elgin and Kincardine. The children's section was in a lower part of the ground floor, and considerable floor space had been allowed for public lectures. It was reported that the building had been wired for radio reception in order to give special broadcasts to schoolchildren in the afternoon. Subscription of almost £10,000 had already been raised at the time of its opening and, with the grant from the Carnegie Trust of £1,000, just £9,000 still needed to be found at that time.

By the 1920s, more and more people were interested in the burgeoning motor industry. Cars were becoming very popular and more families could afford them with hire purchase. The cost of a family car by the end of March 1928 was advertised:

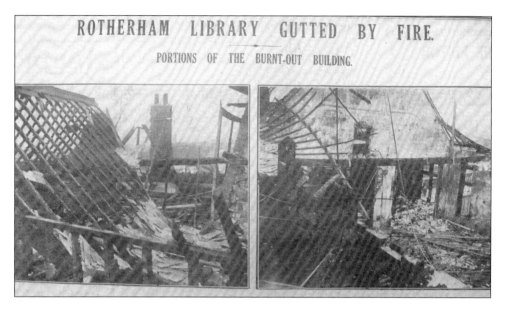

## ROTHERHAM LIBRARY GUTTED BY FIRE.

### PORTIONS OF THE BURNT-OUT BUILDING.

The devastated ruins left by the fire at the library on Main Street in 1925.

| | | | |
|---|---|---|---|
| Austin 7 hp Chimney is for sale for | £135 | Saloon | £150 |
| 12hp Tourer | £255 | Saloon | £325 |
| 16hp G Cylinder Saloon will cost | £434 | | |
| 20hp 4 Cylinder | £515 | | |

The garage stated that there were 'plenty of Easter bargains offering part exchange for older cars or motor bikes.' Driving tests were not compulsory until 1930 so, with limited experience, anyone could drive. Inevitably, several collisions were reported and incidents of 'dangerous vehicles exceeding the speed limit of 20 mph'. One such accident was reported in August 1925 and was one of the first hit and run crimes in the area. It seems that a motor lorry had mowed down two men on the evening of 27 May at Hooton Roberts. Three men – Edwin Thompson, James Bristow and Arthur Griffiths – had been in the Hill Top Inn just outside Hooton Roberts. They left the inn and walked towards the little village. They heard the vehicle behind them, but as there was plenty of room to pass they did not turn round. Suddenly Thompson turned and, seeing the lorry coming at him, leapt into the hedge. The two other men were not so lucky. Bristow was hit and his leg was broken; Griffiths was carried along for 20 yards and then thrown. Thankfully, he only suffered a minor head injury. The lorry did not stop, but carried on hurtling towards Hooton Roberts. A cyclist, Oswald Sale, was coming up the hill and he saw the two men in the middle of the road and stopped to see if he could help. At the same time, a car approached from the Hill Top area and was flagged down by the cyclist. He requested the driver and his passenger, a Rotherham solicitor and his clerk, to attempt to stop the lorry. The solicitor, Mr Leonard Hall Brittain, followed the vehicle, which was reported to be now 'zig zagging down the hill'. He tried to make the driver stop by pulling alongside him, but only by stopping in front of the lorry did he force it to stop. The driver,

The new Central Library on Howard Street.

Leonard Skelton, denied all knowledge of hitting the men, but Brittain could see the man was so drunk that he could hardly stand and refused to let him get back into the vehicle. He also noted that there were two children inside, aged three and four. A policeman was sent for and the man arrested. Due to the injuries of the two men, it was August before the case came to court. Skelton faced three charges: being drunk in charge of a motor car; driving in a manner dangerous to the public; and failing to stop when an accident occurred. For the first crime he was given fourteen days in prison; for the second he was fined £10 with £11 costs or two months' imprisonment; for the final charge he was fined £4 or one month's imprisonment. The magistrates suspended his driving license and he was banned from driving for a further two years.

With the reduction of working hours after the war, people generally had more leisure time during the interwar years. As a result, driving a car or going on a bus trip were popular pastimes for the people of Rotherham. In order to promote bus trips, the *Advertiser* printed details of beauty spots and places of historic interest. These locations could be visited by buses belonging to the Rotherham Corporation Tramways and Motor Department. At Easter 1928, one bus trip included Roche Abbey, Thorpe, Chapeltown, Greasbrough and Conisbrough. Fares were kept to a minimum. The fare to Laughton, for example, would only cost 10*d* and to Conisbrough a mere 9*d*. The same advertisement also offered advice to day trippers:

**DON'T** pluck or uproot the wild flowers. Leave them in their beauty to gladden the hearts of fellow passers by.

**DON'T** leave paper, glass bottles or litter of any kind on your picnic spot. You spoil it for other parties.

**DON'T** throw about carelessly burning cigarette ends, lighted matches etc which may cause a conflagration and serious loss to the farmer or landowner. He will appreciate your consideration.

These trips were undoubtedly a great success. Later that same month, Alderman Caine opened a new motor bus garage to accommodate thirty vehicles. It had been erected on a piece of land near to the Rawmarsh depot. The cost was in the region of £6,000. The *Advertiser* noted:

> ...a quarter of a century has passed since Rotherham placed on the rails its first tramway car and where the Rawmarsh, Thrybergh, Canklow, Kimberworth and Templeborough sections were opened. Nine years later the rail less service to Maltby came into operation and in 1913 the first petrol vehicle was put into commission to operate between Rotherham and Thorpe. In 1919 only five petrol buses were in active service. Now there is no fewer than 42 motor buses in everyday service.

During the day, the depot doors were thrown open to the public so they could examine these new modes of transport. With the increase of vehicles on the roads, better regulation of traffic was required. The Watch Committee adopted traffic signals in July 1929 and by 1933, there were three sets in the town. The traffic lights must have made a positive difference as one local reporter stated, 'I hope that this year the number of signals will be increased considerably.' It was agreed in June that a set of traffic lights would be erected at the junction of High Street and College Street, at an estimated cost of £700, the Ministry of Transport paying 60 per cent of the costs. Around this time, roads were being widened and Rotherham Council started a programme of improvement. Church Street was widened and there were significant improvements made to Ship Hill and Westgate, a notorious bottleneck for traffic.

But for people wishing to travel who were not able to afford petrol and bus fares, there was the two-wheeled variety of transport. Interest in cycling was having an effect on the people of the town, and in March 1931 it was reported, 'Groups of cyclists are regularly meeting in College Square on Sundays. Then, depending on the weather, they decide where to go.' Weekly columns in the *Advertiser*, under the heading 'Local Cycling News', would give information about the clubs in the area, what trips out were expected and news on previous trips. The groups were all individually named and no doubt there was rivalry between them. The Cyclists Touring Club, the Rotherham Plebs Club and the Rotherham Wheelers Club were the groups available. At this time, bikes were becoming fairly cheap and could be bought with easy payments schemes, making them accessible to all. In 1931 a Raleigh 'all steel' bike cost £5 19s 6d and could be paid for with 'no deposit and 1/9d a week'. Strangely, all the adverts show a traditional men's bike; it seems that no women's bikes were available at that time. The first recognisable women's bike was advertised in February 1934 and listed as having a 'chain case and dress guard'. These were available for the princely sum of £4 2 s 9d.

Despite a more relaxed attitude towards Sunday entertainment, some critics demanded that the observance of the Lord's Day should he held solely as a day of rest and prayer meetings. One regular critic was Revd James Fielding, the Rotherham Wesleyan Circuit Superintendent, who sent regular resolutions to the Rotherham Corporation from the vestry meetings. One resolution, sent in March 1931, was that 'Sundays should be given over for the worship of the Lord.' In another resolution he protested against the actions of Rotherham Corporation in 'promoting secularisation by allowing the Town Hall, which belongs to the people of the Borough to be used for political meetings.' The irate cleric then gave a third objection, which was 'for allowing ice cream to be sold in Clifton Park on Sundays'.

In May 1931, an unusual opportunity to take part in aerial flights was offered to the people of the town. The activity was being held 'in a field near to the Kimberworth Toll Bar on Wortley Road' by the Wolverhampton Aviation Company, until 19 June. The cost of an ordinary flight was 5s; a 'stunt flight consisting of a loop, a swing and a roll' was more expensive at 30s. These flights were in an 'Avro 504K fitted with 110hp Le Rone engine', piloted by Captain S. Summerfield and two other experienced pilots. Stunt flying would take place each Sunday afternoon. One of the most breath-taking sights was a person walking on the wings of the plane.

People who were interested in watching or taking part in the stunt flying were told to catch a bus to the Colin Campbell public house (fare 2d) on Wortley Road. The field holding the aeroplanes was 'just a short walk away' and admission to the field was 6d for adults and 3d for children. Another flying scheme was introduced at Whiston in August 1936 by a member of the Air Flying Corps, Mr C.W.A. Scott. The flights were to be held on Sunday 30 August and twenty free flights would be offered as a prize for a competition set by the *Advertiser*. The newspaper stated that it could not 'be held responsible for any entrant who breaks their necks whilst flying.' Mr Scott told the assembled crowd:

> First and foremost I would say that it is a national duty for people to become air minded...Consistent flying is a rich man's sport. It costs a lot of money to buy an aeroplane and even more to maintain it in a satisfactory state of operation. With my display it will be possible for keen amateurs to obtain practical experience.

It was noted that three of Mr Scott's pilots had served in the previous war. They were listed as Captain P. Phillips DFC (Distinguished Flying Cross), Captain J. King and Captain L.J. Rimmer. It was reported that the aeroplanes on show were: two Airspeed Ferries, one Tiger Moth, three Avro Cadets, one Mongoose Avro, one Lynx Avro, one Autogiro, one Drone and one Flying Flea. Although people flocked to see these marvellous new machines, few people suspected that they would be instrumental in the next war.

# 16

# THE GATHERING STORM

During the interwar years, not many people anticipated that the world would soon be at war again. No one wanted to believe that conflict was coming, even though the signs were there from about 1933. One of the first mentions of future conflict was at a dinner given to Rotherham MP Alderman Dobbie, by the National Union of Railway men in March 1933. The secretary, Mr C.T. Cramp, gave a speech on Fascism, stating that while in England the Fascist Party was very small, people 'must not think the same thing is true of the party in Italy.' He pointed out the difference between the British and the Italians, saying, 'We may smile at dictatorship but people are at their wits end in times of difficulty and depression and they often turn to dependable remedies.' Alderman Dobbie must have taken this speech seriously, as in a public meeting at Dalton Welfare Hall on May Day later the same year, he warned of 'the great attempt to introduce Fascism into this country' which could be 'more successful than the average man or woman would understand.' He told them, 'Hitler had been laughed at in Germany but all of a sudden Hitlerism has got a grip on the German people.'

In the *Advertiser* of August 1933, Alderman Hall reported on Hitler's regime in Germany. He had been on a recent trip to meet old friends and stated:

> One cannot wonder at the utter bewilderment of many who are anxious to know the truth. Is it really as bad as the reports seem to indicate? Are the alleged atrocities, the petty meanness and the brutality of the Nazi's grossly overstated? Are the reports of outrages the figment of an overwrought imagination, distilled by a prejudice against the present dictatorship? Some of my German friends had escaped from the Fatherland but if they returned they would be executed. Others were so badly treated that they shot themselves. Another friend escaped from prison and another was shot whilst trying to escape. The need to assist the lovers of freedom and international goodwill against the present tyranny is obvious.

Alderman Hall went on to describe how some of his friends had accompanied him and his wife to the station. This time, he said, 'auf weidersein took on greater significance'; he wondered whether he and his wife would ever see them again. He spoke of his relief at coming back to Britain and said, 'In my heart I thanked God that England was my home.'

Only a year later, the fear that Fascism could come to Rotherham became real. A meeting had been organised in September 1934 between groups of fascists and communists. They were supposed to meet on a piece of land at the bottom of St Ann's Road. On hearing about the meeting, and no doubt realising there would be clashes, the owner of the land, Mr E.H. Lockwood, refused to allow it. Nevertheless, by 7.30 p.m. on Thursday 13 September, a huge crowd had gathered to watch the contest. The communists had borrowed a large kitchen table as a platform and had started the meeting, but they were forced to desist when Mr Lockwood's views became known. About half an hour later, a car drew up containing five fascists wearing black shirts and swastika armbands. Amid considerable booing, they were escorted to Mr Lockwood's house, where he informed them they could not use his land for the meeting. On returning back to their car, the black shirts found the rear tyres were slashed and a crowd had gathered around the car. Thankfully, before the crowd turned ugly and came to blows, and before another twelve fascists turned up, the police arrived. The tyres were changed and the car driven away with the men standing on each side of the vehicle and the communists following behind. This procession went through the town centre, followed by groups of shouting children. The procession made its way back to the fascist headquarters on Wellgate, where a number of them got into a lorry. The lorry sides were protected by wire and the group of fascists screamed slogans at the crowd. The people of Rotherham were not to be intimidated and the crowd retorted with other slogans until eventually the lorry drove off.

One can't help but compare this scene with those we are now familiar with of the German fascists in their lorries, screaming obscenities and attacking helpless Jews in the streets of Germany. There is no doubt that Fascism was disliked by many people of the town, especially as stories of brutality spread. At a meeting of the Trades Council in November 1943, Councillor F. Davies stated that he had once got inside the fascists headquarters and watched in horror at a lecture on the use of knuckledusters and truncheons in demonstrations. He also said that he had vivid memories of a talk given at the Assembly Rooms in the town centre by William Joyce, later known as Lord Haw-Haw. At this time, Joyce was the deputy leader of the Fascist Party in England and was said to be a gifted speaker but a 'savage brawler'. This was evidenced by Councillor Davies who witnessed a forcible ejection of a man who persisted in asking questions. He stated, 'Because Tommy James and I and one or two others tried to help him we finished up at the bottom of the stairs.' These expressions of hatred towards Fascism probably helped to foster the patriotism which emerged during the next war.

Military authorities were already considering the possibility of future warfare. At a meeting in the Drill Hall in April 1936, Major General Kelly, the officer commanding the 49th (West Riding) Division, stated that the York and Lancaster Regiment, which had been so prominent during the First World War, was to cease to exist for infantry purposes. He stated that the battalion was to be converted into an anti-aircraft unit to protect the industrial areas of Rotherham and Sheffield. He warned that future wars would be fought in the air and that Rotherham could not afford to get too complaisant. He warned that townspeople would not have days to man their defences but a matter of hours. In the previous war, all major defences were prioritised for the city of London, but with the improvements made in aircraft, 'no where [was] safe in the British Isles.' The Mayor thanked Major Kelly and stated that it was still hoped that a war would never come, but that if it did, the town of Rotherham would be ready. The changeover to an anti-aircraft unit also necessitated larger barracks. A site on Fitzwilliam Road had been identified by November and these barracks would have the extra space to store guns and other war material. The Drill Hall, which had been in use for over fifty years, had no such accommodation. There was an appeal for recruits to this new brigade, dated 28 November 1936, for gunners and fitters:

> We all hope that war will never come and if we are prepared as a nation and our enemies see that we are prepared it will do more than anything else to avert such a tragedy...We now ask that to help in this vital work of preparing to defend their homes by encouraging men to join this new arm of the service which is essential to the safety of our country and neighbourhood.

Throughout 1938, there was great speculation as to whether or not the country would soon be at war with Germany. Even in May of 1938 there was some ambiguity about the outcome. Neville Chamberlain's famous 'Peace in Our Time' proclamation appeared to some to indicate that the crisis had been averted. Nevertheless, plans were still being made to protect the town and its people. On 1 August 1938, the *Advertiser* was stressing the need for protection from gas attacks and promising that 'everyone in the town will have a respirator as soon as possible.' Alderman Hall, JP stressed the necessity of all these preparations and announced:

> If the relations between England and any other country become so strained as to cause danger of war a state of emergency will be declared and Rotherham along with other local authorities will receive instructions from the Home Office to distribute gas masks to the civil populations. The air raid precautions services will come into operation immediately and in Rotherham the distribution will be carried out within eight hours providing there has been created an efficient service of air raid wardens and other volunteers.

A total of 70,000 gas masks were delivered and distributed by 400 Rotherham teachers as well as other Air Raid Precaution (ARP) volunteers, from 10 a.m. on Tuesday 28 September to 10 a.m. the following day. On Thursday, a demonstration of fitting the gas masks was held at schools and people were urged to ensure they had their gas masks with them every time they left the house. Four new sirens had also been ordered to supplement the one at the Electric Power Station. In the town council meeting, the Mayor stated that Rotherham Corporation had an obligation to provide services. These services would only be effective with a good response from the citizens, he said, and many volunteers would be needed. They discussed the provision of air-raid shelters and Alderman Hall pointed out that to build a large air-raid shelter for the entire population of the town would cost 2½ million pounds and might prove ineffective. The committee felt that the best means of protection for the people of Rotherham could be provided in their own homes. Whilst there would be shelters in the town centre for those unable to return home when caught in an air raid, they would only be splinter and gas-proof and would not withstand a direct hit.

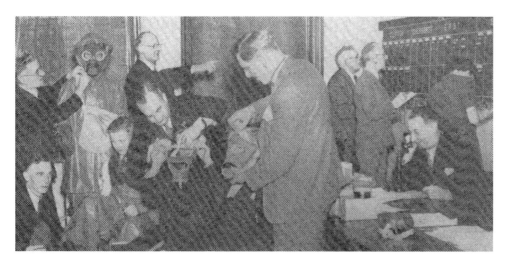

Fitting gas masks at the ARP headquarters.

The following month it was recognised that Rotherham still had a long way to go to have the 2,500 volunteers required to protect the town. A report, prepared and read by the Town Clerk on Wednesday 1 June, stated they had 1,330 volunteers at present and that a much bigger response was needed. On the previous Tuesday, Alderman Hall had attended a meeting of female air-raid wardens and he paid tribute to the 'public spiritedness of the women of all ages who had shown a fine example to the rest of the town.' However, a report about a dug out shelter built in the garden of a house on the East Dene estate by a Corporation tenant was criticised. One of the councillors felt that the tenant had no such right to build his own shelter as he was not the owner of the property. Alderman Caine stated that such 'do it yourself dug outs' were not to be undertaken by amateurs and it was a job for a miner or a navvy, who were used to working in such conditions. Such an attitude was ridiculous under the circumstances and four months later, on 1 October 1938, the *Advertiser* carried details of a personal air-raid shelter, 'constructed of stout timber at the side and covered by sandbags and a corrugated iron roof', which anyone could 'make in their own garden'.

On 13 August 1938, when war was seen as imminent, a mock test for the blackout was tried out in Rotherham. It had been announced in the town council that, for the purpose of the test, all the lights were to be extinguished in the area immediately surrounding the town. Gas lamps were to be put out at midnight and even the smallest amount of electric light was to be extinguished. Lights from railway stations and steelworks were to be screened as much as possible and traffic lights had to be dimmed. As a consequence of the dimmed lighting, motorists were asked to show extreme care when driving. Householders were asked to participate by either putting out their own lights or erecting blackout screens at all windows. It was stated, 'There will be several observers in the town and sightseeing in motor cars is forbidden.' The trial was set to end at 3 a.m. with a siren which would last for two minutes. A report in the *Advertiser* the following week indicated the success of the scheme, revealing that there were no lights at all from Broom Road to the Stag or Whiston crossroads. Looking

The design of a personal air-raid shelter.

from the top of Carr House Hill towards Rotherham, once again there were no lights at all to be seen. Only the dim outlines of the South Yorkshire Chemical works, the Corporation Tramworks Department and the Electricity Works on Rawmarsh Road could be seen. However, the test was not a complete success. The reporter said that three lights were seen on Doncaster Road and Lindum Terrace and two lights on Middle Lane and Middle Lane South. A blazing light was observed from one of the bedrooms of the Hind Hotel on Bawtry Road and another light from the signal box on Rotherham Road could clearly be seen. He then inspected Ferham Road and Meadow Hall Road, but all was in darkness. Returning back to the town, he had been forced to get out of the car at Ferham Park and walked down to Coronation Bridge, where there was a crowd of people watching the ARP services deal with a fire at Woodstock Bower. Within four minutes the fire brigade was on the spot and within a minute or two the fire was under control. Though the authorities were congratulated on their success with this mock test, the reporter came to a different conclusion:

Rotherham will have to be more serious minded on this question.
Railway signal boxes will have to be more effectively dealt with.
A smoke screen was needed for the Steel Peech and Tozer works and should be experimented with.

He cheered on the volunteers, stating that they had 'plenty of enthusiasm', urging them, 'Carry on – you have started well.' He came to the conclusion that Rotherham could be successfully blacked out, and that in the event of raids it would take some finding. Ending his report, he recommended that the experiment needed to be repeated on a moonlit evening, when things would be more visible from the air. A further test blackout was arranged for October 20, when it was reported that guns had been placed at strategic places throughout the district to afford protection to vital spots.

On Monday, 21 August 1939 an RAF spitfire pilot named Sergeant Donald Victor Peacock died aged twenty-five years of age. He had been exercising over Hooton Roberts when he lost control of the plane and crashed into a field. He had been stationed at RAF Church Fenton and he lived at Hinckley in Leicestershire. The plane, which was described as 'one of the fastest planes in the world', was seen to be in difficulty whilst flying over a houses in the village. Witnesses said that it seemed to have overcome the problem and started to rise back up in the air, only to crash to the ground behind Low Farm. People from the farm rushed to the scene but it was obvious that the pilot was dead. Mr Tolson White, who lived at the farm, managed to pull the body free from the wreckage. The pilot's watch had been torn from his wrist and had stopped at nine minutes after midday. His body was later taken back to the RAF camp at Church Fenton. The incredible force with which the machine had hit the ground was evident as the nose of the plane was buried in the ground to a depth of 2ft and only the tips were left showing above the earth. Wreckage was thrown over a large area and the plane was broken in two.

At the inquest, which was held in the West Riding Courthouse in Rotherham the following day, the coroner, Mr J. Kenyon Parker, spoke to his father and three of the dead man's colleagues outside the courtroom. The coroner said that he was not calling a jury, but the inquest would merely identify the pilot so that the body could be released for burial. A more formal inquest would take place later he said. He told the court that it was a matter of record that the young man had not died on active service, but in training for his duties as an officer in His Majesty's Air Forces. The pilot's father, Mr Arthur Thomas Peacock, gave evidence that he had identified the body of his son, whose twenty-fifth birthday had recently been celebrated on 10 August. He affirmed that his son joined the RAF about four years previously. The inquest was then adjourned to Tuesday 29 August and the funeral was held at Church Fenton on the following Thursday.

At the adjourned inquest, the coroner told the jury that a post-mortem had revealed a fracture to the skull and compound fractures in both legs and arms. The RAF also undertook

Coronation Bridge, as seen from the bottom of Ferham Road, and the pharmacy of the Woodstock Bower surgery as it is today.

# SPITFIRE CRASHES IN HOOTON ROBERTS FIELD.

## " Everything Done To Make Flying Safe "---Told Father.

WHEN an R.A.F. Supermarine Spitfire, one of the fastest 'planes in the world, crashed in a field at Hooton Roberts, on Monday, the 25-year-old pilot was killed instantly. The machine was a total wreck.

The crash at Hooton Roberts.

extensive enquiries into the cause of the accident and the coroner informed the jury that they should not concern themselves with technical details. Mr Tolson White described how he went into Wapping Lane, saw the plane flying over Hooton Cliff Woods and heard a 'cracking noise' coming from the engine. Two other witnesses described the engine as misfiring. The machine was a Supermarine Spitfire, which had been put into commission on 24 April of that year; the pilot had been training in flying practice. Flying Officer Thompson, who had been the last person to see Peacock alive, said, 'An inspection of all engines and air frames was made before the pilot was allowed to fly and the machine was examined at 8.30 a.m. on the morning of the flight.' He was asked by the coroner if he could give a reason for the crash, but the officer was unable to offer an opinion. The jury brought in a verdict of Accidental Death and the coroner offered his sympathy to the family of the dead pilot. He also praised the bravery of the rescuers for getting the body out of the plane 'at great risk to themselves'.

On Sunday, 3 September 1939 the Prime Minster, Neville Chamberlain, announced to the nation confirming that Britain was at war with Germany. In Rotherham, Mayor Alderman Buxton paid a tribute to the 'spirit of the townspeople'. He said:

Everything is in readiness to meet any emergency and the people of Rotherham can rest content that as far as is humanly possible their interests are being watched. Our difficulties at the moment can be overcome much more easily if more people will offer their services as air raid wardens or first aid workers. It must be realised that the very heavy burden of responsibility carried by those volunteers would be made much easier if more people would volunteer.

He stated that shelters were being built and the co-operation of local builders was speeding it up, so that the following day, two or three of these shelters would be available for use. The Second World War had begun.

# PART 3

# THE SECOND WORLD WAR

## 17

## PREPARATION FOR WAR

As early as February 1937, Rotherham was preparing for the conflict which would be known as the Second World War. Politicians and military leaders were aware that, this time, more modern technological machines would be at the forefront; gone were the days of the infantry regiments. Now the war would be dominated, and many would say won, by the flying machines which were taking prominence. It was announced in a town council meeting on 17 February that Rotherham would be the training ground for low-flying aircraft. Anti-aircraft divisions were formed by combining the Territorials, the Royal Artillery and the Royal Engineer Battalions for the defence of the Midlands and the North. On Monday 19 September, first-aid posts were established on Doncaster Road and at Park Street Council School. Rotherham was preparing for war.

It had been agreed that warning of any air raids was a first priority and on Sunday 10 September 1939, air-raid sirens were tested in the town at 2 p.m. to make sure they were all in working order. So that people would know it was a test, it was announced that the first blast would be a continuous sound, which would be followed by the 'all clear' sound for two minutes.

There is little doubt that this sound would pierce the hearts of many of the town's inhabitants over the next few years. At first, it had been estimated that the majority of

ARP Volunteers training with the Ack-Ack guns.

people would take shelter in the cellars of their own homes. Those without shelters would use neighbours' houses, and therefore the need for the larger shelters was not necessary. If people were in town when an air raid occurred, they would be able to shelter in the cellars or basements of local shops. A list of air-raid shelters in local businesses was printed in the *Advertiser* in September 1939. Many of these shelters were only available in the daytime; only a few were open for twenty-four hours. The shops in the town centre and the number of people they could hold in the cellars were reported as follows:

BRIDGEGATE
| | |
|---|---|
| E. & F. Fawley Ltd | 100 |
| J. Peck Ltd | 100 |

CORPORATION STREET
| | |
|---|---|
| Rotherham Motor Co. | 150 |
| L.A. Ratcliffe | 35 |
| Quick Press Ltd | 35 |
| Brook Hardcastle Ltd | 30 |

COLLEGE STREET
| | |
|---|---|
| J. Smith & Sons | 100 |
| W. Timpson Ltd | 100 |

EFFINGHAM STREET

| | |
|---|---|
| Prices Tailors Ltd | 90 |
| H. Garnett & Co. Ltd | 60 |
| The Handy Library | 30 |
| Levy Bros | 50 |
| S. & H. Morris Ltd | 20 |

WESTGATE

| | |
|---|---|
| R.J. Stokes and Co. Ltd | 100 |
| Corporation Electricity Department Showrooms | 80 |

HIGH STREET

| | |
|---|---|
| Bradwell Bros | 60 |
| 35/- Tailors | 70 |

ALL SAINTS SQUARE

| | |
|---|---|
| A. Davy & Sons Ltd | 100 |

CHURCH STREET

| | |
|---|---|
| Premises under construction | 750 |

Later, additional shelters available to the public twenty-four hours a day were announced at the following places:

ALL SAINTS SQUARE

| | |
|---|---|
| Tramway shelter and underground conveniences | 200 |

FREDERICK STREET

| | |
|---|---|
| Waterworks Department | 300 |

CHANTRY BRIDGE

| | |
|---|---|
| Under arches of old bridge | 170 |

SHEFFIELD ROAD

| | |
|---|---|
| Bessemer Bridge | 50 |

It became apparent that more surface shelters were needed and it was announced, in September 1939, that these shelters were being erected to hold approximately 100 people. They were to be built in: the Regal car park on Corporation Street; Moorgate car park; Hollowgate; the Crofts; the Gas Works yard; Clifton Park; St Ann's Road; and Francis Street. Shelters to hold fifty persons were built near Greasbrough Town Hall; the Green Dragon Inn at Kimberworth; in Ferham Park; Providence Street; the Browning Road shopping centre; and Badsley Moor Lane.

Chantry Bridge arches, where people could shelter during an air-raid attack.

The council agreed that children in Rotherham were to be evacuated from the more congested areas of the town, due to the fear of attack. In July 1939, the Director of Education, Mr J.A. Mair, announced that mothers and children who wanted to be evacuated could be found billets in more rural areas. It was strongly emphasised that the scheme was voluntary and that no child would be removed without the parents' consent. Parents wishing to avail themselves of the service were required to 'complete a form and return to the Education Department in the Imperial Buildings by Friday July 23rd'. The town council decided that the more industrialised areas, which would suffer the most from air attacks, were around St Ann's Road; Wellgate; Alma Road; Templeborough; Park Street; Ferham and Thornhill Council Schools; and St Bede's Roman Catholic School. The Education Department announced that the evacuation would be spread over two days. On the first day, children would be evacuated with the teachers and helpers and the following day, expectant mothers and mothers with children under five years would be found homes. The *Advertiser* announced that parents wishing to avail themselves of this service should take the children to the school they normally attended, where buses would then take them to their destination. Mr Mair promised that all efforts would be made to keep all the families together where possible. The government agreed to pay all costs of transportation, board and lodgings to the foster carers in the receiving areas. However, parents with young children would only receive the cost of their rent and were expected to support themselves and their children, although those without means would be supported by the government. They also asked for volunteers to help to move an expected figure of almost 4,000 persons. The volunteers would be required to act as escorts, helping children and some adults on and off trains, supervising the children in the reception areas and assisting in games and other recreational sports. On 1 September 1939, 1,600 Rotherham children were evacuated to rural districts. A week later, it was announced that the children were making themselves comfortable in their new and much safer surroundings. The Mayor told the parents:

Children from Well gate Council School are at Wentworth

Children from Ferham and Thornhill Council Schools are in Thurcroft, Slade Hooton,
Laughton and Brookhouses.

Children of Alma Road Council School are at Ravenfield

Children of Templeborough Council School are at Hooton Roberts

Children from St Bede's Roman Catholic School are at Aston cum Aughton

Children from St Ann's Council School are at North and South Anston and Woodsetts

Children from Park Street Council School are at Harthill and Thorpe Salvin

He praised all the people involved in the evacuation. It had been a massive undertaking.

The same month, September 1939, it was announced that evacuated children from some of the regularly bombed cities in the south were coming to Rotherham and districts. The *Advertiser* stated that evacuees who had arrived in the town during the week of 9 September had been billeted to homes in Wentworth, Hooton Roberts, Ravenfield, Thurcroft, Laughton, Aughton, Swallownest, Fence and Aston. Some children had arrived with mothers, others with teachers and helpers. The government had supplied bedding, but camp beds and mattresses were not readily available and many of the evacuated children were forced to sleep on couches and floors. An appeal for bedsteads was made by the Mayor, Mr A. Buxton, as well as clothing for some families of between four and nine children that were now arriving on a regular basis. He requested clothing for children of either sex from tiny babies to fourteen years of age.

The Imperial Buildings, where the Education Department made preparations for the evacuation of the children.

It is not clear whether a steady stream of children continued to be sent to Rotherham throughout the war years, but, strangely, when the war was edging to a close, there were reports that further evacuees were received into the town. On 14 July 1944 it was reported that 800 children from the Greater London area had been sent to the town for safekeeping. Utilising the screens at local cinemas, once again appeals were made for homes and donations for these evacuees. During the evening of their arrival, buses were organised to take them to several rest areas. These were at St Ann's, St Michael's (Northfield), East Dene Welfare Hall, St James (Clifton) and Eastwood Methodist Church. The evacuees and the helpers spent the evening at the rest centres and, on the following day, were examined by doctors and nurses to ascertain their fitness. A few children could not be billeted in private homes due to medical reasons; they were evacuated to Oakwood Hospital. The children were supplied with emergency ration cards for their stay in the district and the steady stream of evacuees continued. On Saturday, 26 August 1944, the *Advertiser* noted that:

On Saturday, 8 July 1944 fifty-nine boys aged about fifteen years arrived in the town from the south of England. They were taken to two rest centres at Thrybergh and on Sunday were given a hot meal before being taken to their billets. Forty of them were found homes at Thrybergh and the rest were billeted at Wickersley and Bramley. For the remainder of their stay it was arranged that they were to attend Maltby Grammar School.

On Tuesday 11 July more mothers and twenty young children arrived and were billeted at Thrybergh and a few on the outskirts of Dalton.

On Thursday night, 13 July a party of thirty mothers and thirty-nine children arrived in the town.

On Saturday 15 July about seventy children were received at Swinton and stayed at the Masonic Hall overnight, before being delivered to their new homes the following day.

Another thirty arrived on Tuesday 18 July.

On Wednesday 19 July, twenty-four young children between the ages of five and seven arrived at Parkgate from the Ashhurst Park Nursery School, Kent. The children were to be looked after by four nurses at the Nursery School, France Street, Parkgate and a warm welcome was extended to them by the Rawmarsh Women's Voluntary Service (WVS) who cooked for the children until a cook could be found. It was reported that the children were settling in well to their new surroundings.

On Sunday 20 August, a further 634 women and children, some just babes in arms, arrived in the town from the south. This large group was taken to rest centres at Kimberworth Central School, South Grove Central School, Spurley Hey Central School, St Ann's Council School and St Mary's School, where they stayed overnight.

Thankfully the response for billets had been very good and it was reported that all the evacuees had been found good temporary homes throughout Rotherham and the districts. The Mayor of Rotherham visited some of the evacuees and talked to mothers at one rest centre on Sunday 20 August. It was reported that the group consisted of several grandmothers, some expectant mothers and thirty-nine unaccompanied children; the youngest evacuee was a child of three weeks old. The response had been good and within a few days most of the group had been found billets.

A reporter visited the same rest centre and found one mother who had been evacuated with her family of eight children. Mrs Lillian Hobdell told him that she had left her husband, who was a builder employed in repairing bombed-out buildings in London, with her eldest son. She asked the Rotherham billeting authorities for a house where she could look after all her children (aged eight months to fourteen years) 'as she had always done'. She told him that the children didn't used to worry about the air raids in their hometown, saying 'it was always me'. The children had enjoyed the journey to Rotherham and were running around the St Ann's rest centre 'without a care in the world'. As to the reception she had received in Rotherham, she said, 'I couldn't have been looked after better. I can't get used to being waited upon.'

At the end of the war evacuees began returning home. On the morning of Wednesday, 6 June 1945, the *Advertiser* announced, 'The last of the evacuated children has left Rotherham on a special train to return them to their homes. The train called at Sheffield before transporting the children to their homes in London and the south.' Several of the mothers, the children and the billeting officers gave thanks to their hosts and extended their gratitude to all the people of Rotherham for the help they had received during their stay in the town. Many offers were made for their hosts to come and visit in London. The Mayor arrived at the railway station to see them off and spoke to several of the mothers. Mr W.I. Dale, the billeting officer, also came to see the party off. It was reported that several WVS helpers were also there to hand out sweets and toys to keep children entertained during their train journey.

It was also recognised, in the early discussions about the defence of the town, that there would be a need for many Air Raid Precautions (ARP) volunteers. A new recruitment office was opened in the Old Technical College building in Effingham Street in September 1937 where men and boys, under eighteen and over fifty years of age, came flocking in to offer their services. Such was the response that as early as 15 January 1938, the *Advertiser* announced that Rotherham's Air Raid Precautions were well advanced. Alderman S. Hall stated that at least 2,500 volunteers had been recruited. These local men with knowledge of the area were essential for certain roles:

Auxiliary firemen who will deal with fires caused by incendiary bombs and high explosives.

Special constables to assist the regular police force and also act as messengers and dispatch riders in case of breakdown in communication lines or to summon aid necessary for any special section.

Air Raid Wardens who will distribute gas masks and give information as to the correct fitting and adjustment of the same and how to prepare a gas proof room.

In order to ensure the swift mobilisation of these large numbers of ARP volunteers, it was decided in July 1939 that a test would be carried out at some time between the hours of noon on Thursday 14 July and 8 p.m. on Friday 15 July. Within half an hour of the air-raid siren sounding at 2.50 p.m. on Thursday, it was reported that between 800 and 900 volunteers

## BRITAIN'S CALL TO BRITONS

### A DUTY TO PERFORM

Have you given all that's due?
Are you like good Sister Sue?
Do you want to get the Nazi Blighter
    down?
Then think of what is needed
Ere Freedom's cry is heeded:
There's something to be done in every town.

Hear you Poland's coronach?
See that Nazi maniac
With scourge and death a nation's wealth
    demanding.
Then think of what is needed
Ere Freedom's cry is heeded.
Bring justice all triumphant and commanding.

*To our Readers we say:*

### BE PATIENT;    BE CALM;    BE BRAVE

and help in the protection of your town, your neighbours and your country.

Your services are needed.                **"We must be free or die."**

*If you have not yet enrolled*

## JOIN THE A.R.P. SERVICES NOW

Appeal for ARP volunteers stating, 'We must be free or die.'

were 'ready for action in case of an attack from the air'. Major Vincent Turner, the Borough Engineer, was very satisfied with the result. He told a reporter:

> Immediately when the siren went off scores of Corporation workmen downed their tools and proceeded to their posts by bike, car and buses to the Highway Dept Depot on Greasbrough Road or the Anti Gas School on Mary Street. At each place they reported for duty and obtained their equipment and waited for messages from the control centre in the basement of the Municipal Offices ordering them to 'stand down'.

By June 1940, it was once again felt that many more ARP recruits were needed. In a discussion which took place in Rotherham Town Council chamber on Wednesday 5 June, Alderman Hall stated that there were some volunteers who believed that the war would soon be over, but their numbers had gradually fallen away, leaving some very dedicated workers who attended meetings and regularly gave up their time to volunteer. He gave his thanks to this dedicated group, but stated that more men and women were needed. At that time they urgently needed drivers, first-aid workers and mobile units. He continued, 'I think it should be the duty of every member of the council to do all he can.' They devised a plan where they would approach people who worked for the council and try to establish what they did for the war effort. If they were found to be not giving any service, they should be asked the reason why and encouraged to volunteer for some branch of the service.

Air-raid wardens were now regularly patrolling the streets, ensuring a complete blackout. Fines of 40s were imposed on those found guilty of showing lights and on 8 June 1940, the *Advertiser* reported nineteen district cases in one day where fines of between 10s and £1 were issued. At the second court held on the same day, seventeen Rotherham people were fined for 'displaying unscreened lights, visible from the outside, in their houses during the blackout periods.' Inevitably there were accidents in the blackout. One such case involved an elderly woman who was knocked down by a trackless tram in January 1942 on Broom Road. The eighty-three-year-old widow, who lived on Browning Road, was taken to the hospital where she later died of her injuries. An inquest was held before the coroner, Mr W.J. Bradford, JP on 5 January 1942, when a verdict of Accidental Death was brought in by the jury. The driver stated that he had left Worrygoose and was approaching Rotherham at 6.12 p.m. doing only 18mph. He described how he slowed down as he approached Fraser Road in case passengers were waiting, when he spotted a pair of light coloured stockings through the window and then felt a bump. He got out of his car to find the deceased woman lying parallel with the footpath about 2ft from the kerb. The hospital doctor gave his opinion that the woman had died from a compound fracture of the skull. The coroner, in his summing up, told the jury that the driver was not to be blamed in any way for the accident. Accidents continued to occur throughout the war years due to the poor lighting and people were asked to 'be more vigilant when going out at night'.

As we have seen, there was a very real threat of attack from bombs. It was quickly established that fire watchers would be required around the clock and that ideally there would be two for every street in Rotherham. The fire watchers' role was to eliminate the incendiary bombs which burnt brightly and provided targets for the heavy bombers which usually followed. All householders were urged to have sand readily available so they could put out any fires started by incendiary bombs.

Training for fire watchers, which taught volunteers how to deal with these kinds of emergencies, was given at the fire station. In June 1940, the Chief Constable spoke about the wonderful response from volunteers, but urged that many more were needed. It seems that due to the lack of numbers, it was the same people who were on duty night after night. The chair of the council meeting, Mr Johnson, stated that in a heavily populated district like Masbrough, which contained about 2,500 people, there were only forty-one fire wardens to protect them. In Thornhill there were forty wardens for 2,470 people; in Kimberworth there were ninety for 5,000 people. He stated, 'As English men and women they should not wait to be made to do work of that nature but they should do it voluntarily.'

Another councillor, Mr Fowler, told them that on the estate where he lived, old age pensioners had formed their own fire-fighting brigade and had told the authorities that they could take care of themselves. In a later recruitment campaign of January 1941, it was put forward that every man and woman had a duty to protect not just buildings but the personal safety of the individual and the community. It was felt to be particularly important that the centre of the town and properties which were mainly unused during night-time hours were protected. In order to ensure that the town centre was guarded, it had been divided up into twenty-seven zones, with a fire-watching leader appointed to each zone. The unit occupying the zone would be provided with bedding at their base, as well as sand and stirrup pumps to extinguish any small fires which might develop. Business premises were encouraged to provide

Men dealing with an unexploded bomb which had fallen on Rotherham.

their own fire watchers and it was agreed that keys for all business premises must be available in case an incendiary bomb was dropped.

Most districts had fire-watcher rotas and fines were issued to people who didn't turn up for duty. In May 1942, two men were accused of missing shifts and they had to pay a fine of £1 per shift at the Borough Police Courts. In the 'Observer's Observations' column of the *Advertiser* grave hints were made about the people who had been found asleep during their shift. The reporter stated, 'Anyone not fulfilling his "alert" period when on fire watching duty is deserving of severe punishment. He is not showing the slightest consideration for his country, his town and his fellow men.' He warned that those people who checked up on the fire watchers should be more vigilant, commenting that if they were 'they might find plenty to interest them'. In June 1942, the fire watchers were criticised again in the *Advertiser*, when the reporter stated that it was well known in the area that fire watchers were 'becoming adept at cards, darts and dominoes', but he questioned, 'How many of them know where the fire fighting equipment is?' Perhaps it was because of these sorts of criticisms that by August 1942, compulsory training for fire guards had been ordered by the Ministry of Home Security. The training was delivered at the public library on Howard Street and it was announced that it would consist of both theory and practice and would include:

> The object and method of incendiary attack
> Types of incendiary bomb
> The method of dealing with bombs
> The reduction of fire risks in buildings
> The use, care and maintenance of equipment
> Elementary rescue and first aid
> General fire fighting hints

The practical part of the training was to take place at the building they were allocated to watch, so that the trainers could see that the men had knowledge of the building and where the equipment was kept. The Ministry of Home Security promised that they would make every effort to ensure that adequate training was provided at a time to suit the individual. But the onus of responsibility was on the owners of the buildings to ensure that the men were properly trained.

In the early years of the war, Emergency Feeding and Rest Centres were established for the numbers of people that could be bombed out of their houses. The centres were usually held in churches and schools and were placed in different areas of the town. The *Advertiser* listed them in December 1941:

The Junior Instruction Centre, Brinsworth Street
St Mark's Sunday Schoolroom, Psalters Lane
St Paul's Sunday Schoolroom, Midland Road
The Methodist Sunday Schoolroom, Lister Street
St Cuthbert's Church, Herringthorpe
Bethesda Church, Tenter Street
Baptist Hall, Wortley Road
Temperance Hall, Wellgate
Unitarian Chapel, Downs Row
The Salvation Army Headquarters, Fitzwilliam Road

It was intended that the rest centres would give people who had been bombed out some breathing space, of between twenty-four and forty-eight hours, before the family decided whether they wanted to go back to their immediate locality. Many of the families of bombed-out houses would load as many of their belongings as they could onto a cart in the hope of being re-housed.

These were the kind of preparations that the town council made during the early years of the Second World War. Although the appeal was made for more and more volunteers, it is a matter of record that the people of the town pulled together to protect themselves and the community. At the peak period there were well over 8,000

A homeless, bombed out family. But at least the goldfish was OK!

Rotherham people involved in the Home Guard and 7,000 in the Civil Defence Service. Most of these volunteers had regular full time work to do during the day also. As well as offering their services as volunteers, not many families of the town were without relatives serving as soldiers on the front line.

# 18

# SOLDIERS

Whilst the town was engaged in preparing for war on the Home Front, many of its sons were already fighting for the freedom of Britain. There are too many brave people to list in this book, so I have just chosen some at random. Many stories of bravery and courage would have been heard before the war was to end. Each one of these soldiers were people of the town who had often gone to local schools and worked for local firms before risking their lives on a daily basis. Many brave lives will be left unheard, as Yorkshire men are not good at baring their souls. Some of these accounts might be shared here for the first time.

One of the first reported casualties was a Maltby sailor, Able Seaman Robert Johnson, the son of Mrs Chappell of 2 Cromwell Lane, Hellaby. He was reported 'missing presumed drowned' on Wednesday, 7 February 1940, after the ship he was on, *Stanburn*, had been sunk by the enemy on 29 January. Seaman Johnson was believed to have died along with Captain Ellis and twenty-five of his comrades, when the ship was attacked by a German Stuka dive bomber. It was reported that the pilot dropped three bombs onto the ship before turning machine guns on the survivors of the wreck. Such was his passion for navy life that Seaman Johnson had lived with his grandparents at North Shields, to be available to report for duty on any ship. He was only twenty-five when he died, but had lived a very full and adventurous short life. He had once walked from Lands End to John O' Groats and subsequently had been interviewed for the programme *In Town Tonight*. He had also appeared on a London stage, singing with another Maltby youth.

Previously he had served on the *Gothia*. This was a ship that patrolled Spanish waters during the Civil War. In a last letter to his mother, which she received at Christmas, he told her of the many comforts and gifts he had received from friends at Maltby over the festive period.

Naval casualties were mounting up in 1942. News of another Rotherham sailor, whose ship had been torpedoed, reached the town in August. A Merchant Navy radio officer, Harvey Edward Cooper, was missing for twelve days before news of his safety was given to his wife and parents in a letter. He described how his ship had been torpedoed twice before the crew was told to 'abandon ship' by the captain, who was the last to leave. The crew of thirteen men had spent the next twelve days in a 27ft lifeboat, covering almost 600 miles before landing in West Africa. Food had to be rationed and the men survived on

6oz of food and a small drink of water per day. He told his wife and parents that they had
survived some terrible weather at sea before landing safely. Radio officer Cooper was a native
of Greasbrough and had attended Rotherham Grammar School. He was the son of Mrs
Cooper of Fitzwilliam Road, Rotherham and his late father, Mr Albert Cooper. He had joined
the Merchant Navy at seventeen years of age and made one cruise to India via America
before returning back to Rotherham, where he took up a post working for the Borough
Engineer Department. Married with one child, there is no doubt that his wife and mother
were relieved to see him return back safely.

The sinking of the German pocket battleship the *Graf Spee* had been a great victory in
the Second World War and it was gratifying to learn that two Rotherham men had been
involved in the battle. On 17 February 1940, it was announced that the two Maltby men
had returned to the town and received a hearty welcome. The heroes had been in the crew
of the *Exeter*, which had famously taken its part in the sinking of the 10,000 ton *Graf Spee*.
The battle had taken place on 13 December 1939 and sixty-four of the crew had been lost.
Extensively damaged, the *Exeter* had returned to Plymouth on Thursday 15th for a complete
refit. The news of the sinking of this German battleship had been heard in the town and
the crew received a heroes' welcome at the Guildhall, Plymouth the following day. Such was
the news that Winston Churchill himself greeted the men. As First Lord of the Admiralty,
accompanied by Sir John Simon, the Chancellor of the Exchequer, Churchill brought a
telegram of congratulations to the crew from the King. The welcome of Churchill and the
telegram from the King would not have been as warm as the welcome from their hometown
a few days later. The two Maltby men were Able Seaman Horace Cooper, the youngest son
of Mr and Mrs Cooper of 12 Rosston Road, Maltby, and Able Seaman William Woods, son
of Mr and Mrs J. Woods of 12 Carlyle Road, Maltby. Cooper had been in the navy for almost
two years and Woods had served for three. Prior to the outbreak of war, both men had been
on a voyage which had lasted eighteen months and were due to take some leave. This had
to be cancelled when war broke out. Both of these brave men had also been involved in
rescue work following the Chilean earthquake of 24 January 1939, which caused the death
of around 30,000 people. Both had also been educated at Maltby School before working at
Maltby Main colliery, then joining the navy.

The people of Maltby were determined that the two heroes would receive a welcome to
remember in their hometown. The men were guests of honour at a concert on Sunday at
the Maltby Picture House, along with another Maltby hero, Able Seaman Albert William
Marshall, son of Mr and Mrs J.T. Marshall of 93 Victoria Street, Maltby. Marshall was home
on leave with the rest of his crew from his ship the *Cossack*, which had liberated 300 British
seamen who were being taken to prison of war camps on the German ship the *Altmark*. The
prisoners had been captured from ships sunk by the *Graf Spee* and were hidden in the hold of
the *Altmark*. Despite the great honour showed to the heroes, unfortunately only two of them
were present. Able Seaman Woods had not been able to get leave, despite several calls from
local dignitaries to the military authorities. Not to be dismayed, the two seamen, Marshall
and Cooper, were received in the Mayor's Parlour in Rotherham and later feted at the Maltby
Progressive Club. But the greatest celebrations were at the Maltby Picture House, which
was so crowded that many patrons had been forced to remain outside. The sound of 'Rule
Britannia' was drowned by cheers when the two men came onto the stage, accompanied by

local MP Mr Dunn. He told the audience, 'Here are two boys of our own village, born here and educated at our schools and who have worked at our own colliery.' He then went on to relate the battle:

> For three months the 'Exeter' along with the 'Ajax' and the 'Achilles' had been engaged in tracking down the 'Graf Spee' which had sailed from Germany at the outbreak of war. The ship had spent its time murdering British seamen and British merchant men in the South Atlantic and had attacked neutrals crossing the sea on ordinary trade. After the sinking of the 'Graf Spee' the 'Altmark' had remained behind to take 299 British sailors to Germany. The ship was tracked down by the 'Cossack' and the rescue was carried out in the way of Nelson, Drake and other famous seamen had made their names.

The speech ended in rousing applause for the two Maltby lads. Mr Dunn had tried to get the Under-Secretary of the Admiralty, Mr Geoffrey Shakespeare, to attend the celebrations, but although he was unable to be present, he sent Maltby his congratulations for 'sending the navy three such gallant boys.' 'It just shows what grand stuff your miners are made of,' he wrote.

Mr Dunn also asked the audience to remember the 458 other Maltby lads and two girls who had gone to do their bit 'in this great struggle'. A collection was taken to provide cigarettes for the two heroes, who it was reported left Maltby later in the week to rejoin their ships.

Photographs in the *Advertiser* of the men on active service.

Throughout the war, regular lists of photographs were inserted in the *Advertiser* showing pictures of men and women engaged on active service. Photos were also shown of missing men. Thankfully, on at least one occasion, a soldier was found safe and sound. Driver Colin Bucknall of the Royal Army Service Corps was in the dining hall somewhere in France when he met a man who knew him from Wickersley. The man informed Bucknall that his photo had been in the *Advertiser* and gave him a copy of the paper, showing him the headline, 'Badsley Moor Soldier Reported Missing'. He immediately wrote to his parents informing them that he was safe, stating that as he wrote he had a copy of the paper in front of him. He had been a fugitive for over five months, but when he got to British territory one of the first things that he did was to go to see Ginger Rogers in the film *Batchelor Mother*. He told his parents that he was hoping to be back home in Rotherham for Christmas and was at that time waiting for a convoy to bring himself and other soldiers back to England.

Other soldiers were not so lucky. Private Victor Douglas Beighton from the King's Own Yorkshire Light Infantry (KOYLI) was reported missing in Norway on 23 April 1940. Recently married, Private Beighton was the son of Mr and Mrs W. Beighton of 22 Burns Road, Rotherham and his wife lived in the town at 15 Bernard Street. He had been educated at South Grove Central School before being employed at Parkgate Iron and Steel Works. Also reported as missing in Norway was Private Lawrence William Beaumont, also with the KOYLI. His wife and child lived at 55 Lindley Street. The families of both men stated that they would welcome any news of the men from any member of his regiment.

The *Advertiser* also provided regular reports of servicemen meeting comrades and relatives on the field of battle. One such story was printed on 8 June 1940. It described how two brothers had met on the fields of Flanders. Private David and Horace Jessop had both been with the Royal Scots Fusiliers for the previous eight years, although they served with different units. Their parents were Mr and Mrs H.C. Jessop of 258 Effingham Street, Rotherham. The two brothers shook hands and wished for good luck. Only later did David hear that his brother, Horace, was reported as 'missing in action'. Private David Jessop had been shot in his right leg and was shipped back to Cheshire in England, where his parents travelled down to the hospital. There his mother and wife told him that his brother had returned to Rotherham safe and sound. After a short leave Horace returned to his regiment. Did the boys return home safely after the war? I have been unable to find any further mention of these two brave men.

The body of a Dinnington wireless operator, who had been killed in action off Dover on Monday, 23 September 1940, was returned to his hometown for burial. Many parents and relatives were not able to have the body of their loved ones returned, so no doubt this ceremony was particularly poignant. He was Sergeant Joseph Henry Dowley, aged twenty-five years and recently engaged to Miss Sylvia Brooks of Crewe. He had been educated at Woodhouse Grammar School where he was the head boy, before he joined the RAF two years previously. The funeral was held at Dinnington Cemetery on Sunday 29 September. His father had been killed in the First World War but his mother, Mrs Dawson, was in attendance and the 'Last Post' was played at the graveside.

Many historians have written about the rescue from Dunkirk of the British Army cut off from their French allies by the Germans. Winston Churchill appealed to boat owners to rescue men trapped on the beaches. A motley group of vessels managed to rescue over 338,000 troops, who were forced to leave most of their heavy guns and vehicles behind.

On 8 June 1940, a reporter interviewed a Rotherham hero who returned from Dunkirk. Stoker James Andrews told the reporter that he had been engaged in evacuating the British Expeditionary Force (BEF) troops and refugees off the beach at Dunkirk in one of the Royal Navy destroyers. He told the reporter, 'Tens of thousands of people were delivered from the jaws of death in countless journeys undertaken day and night.' He saluted his comrades, telling the reporter, 'The greater the peril the harder they work.' Stoker Andrews was a plumber in pre-war life, employed by Messrs Andrews Baldwin & Co. in Rotherham, before enlisting for the navy in March 1940. He had gone to Masbrough National School. His younger brother, Harry, was in the KOYLI.

Four more Rotherham heroes returned from Dunkirk over the next few weeks. They were Major R. Elmhurst, Private R. Liversedge (both belonging to the York and Lancaster Regiment), Sergeant K. Gregory of the Royal Army Ordnance Corps (RAOC) and Corporal George Moore of the Coldstream Guards. All the men were given a few days leave before rejoining their regiments.

The following week, another soldier at home on leave, Corporal J. Jeffs of the East Yorkshire Regiment, reported an account of the escape from Dunkirk. He told a reporter from the *Advertiser* that he had seen houses collapsing around the escaping men, who were showered by bricks and glass. His company had been split up in the melee, but himself and another soldier managed to make it to the beach by 1 a.m. on the Sunday morning, where they found another wounded comrade. About dawn they saw 100 boats lining up to take soldiers on board and they made sure that their wounded colleague was placed on one of them. The Germans attacked the beach again shortly after dawn, but the two men managed to find a ship's raft which, along with another non-swimming comrade, they pushed out to sea. They were finally picked up by small boat, which took them to a minesweeper. They had lost all their possessions and, having removed their shirts and jackets, were left with only their sodden trousers; but they were alive.

It was inevitable in wartime conditions that misinformation was received by the authorities, although sometimes this was done deliberately as propaganda. In March 1940, a sailor, Leading Stoker Bernard Round, who was home on sick leave, told the truth behind the inaccurate message from Lord Haw-Haw regarding the sinking of the *Ark Royal*. It seems that throughout the war, stories about the ship being sunk were regularly heard on German radio. He told a reporter that the ship had been in combat with seven German aircraft after it left Scapa Flow in April 1940. Some of *Ark Royal* aircraft went into battle and managed to keep the rest at bay, but one plane got through and attacked the ship, although the only damage was to plates and crockery. A fortnight later, the ship was in battle again after a torpedo was seen off the stern. There was a massive explosion but the ship was not seriously damaged. Destroyers surrounded the *Ark Royal*. Depth charges were dropped, forcing the German submarine to the surface, and the crewmembers were taken as prisoners and the submarine sank. It was only after this battle, when the ship was heading for home, that the sailors heard the announcement that the *Ark Royal* had once again been sunk. Stoker Round told a reporter that the message announcing that the ship had been sunk was relayed to the men on board through the ship's theatre. The news was greeted with boos and catcalls from the *Ark Royal* sailors. Stoker Round said that his favourite comedian was Lord Haw-Haw and he described that life on the *Ark Royal* was just like living in a town like Rotherham.

Many stories were coming to light in the town about the heroism displayed by Rotherham men and women. Those involving the Air Force were particularly prominent. One of the first glider pilots who took part in the British airborne landings at Arnhem spoke about his forced landing in Holland when he returned to the town in November 1944. Glider Pilot R. Gerald Evans told his family of how his crew had hidden in haystacks when surrounded by Germans, after the towrope of his glider had snapped and he was forced to land. The men only went out at night to try and gather apples and water, which they lived on for six days. They decided to attempt escape, but due to the large numbers of German soldiers in the area were forced to seek refuge in a sewer pipe measuring 20ft long and 4ft in diameter. After three days of hiding, the Germans moved into a farmyard at the side of the sewer pipe. Evans' crew had to endure three days without food and water, hardly daring to breathe. To their dismay, the Germans were then set upon by the British troops and shells were exploding all around them. With just a short break in a barn, the men eventually found out that British troops were on the outskirts of the village and they gave themselves up. It was reported, 'Glider Pilot Evans is having extended leave at his home at 79 St Johns Road, Eastwood where he is hoping to put back on the two stone he lost whilst in hiding in Holland.'

One of the first air crashes of the war took place in March 1940, killing a Kilnhurst RAF pilot in Northants. The pilot, Robert Shiria Spratt Black, was the twenty-four-year-old son of Mr David Black of Beechwood House, Kilnhurst, who was the manager of Kilnhurst colliery. Robert Black's colleague, James Fife Wales, aged twenty, from Cobham in Surrey, was also killed in the crash. The inquest was held on 5 March at Oundle, Northants. A witness, farm labourer Thomas Alfred Pell, told the jury that he had heard the crash and seen the wreckage in a nearby field. He ran towards the plane to see if any of the occupants were alive, but before he got there the plane burst into flames. Flight Lieutenant M.W. Moore gave evidence stating that all planes were regularly checked before take off, and in this case it was a dual-controlled plane piloted by Black with Wales as the passenger. The coroner asked him to give an opinion on what the cause of the crash had been, but because the plane had been so badly damaged he was unable to. Flight Lieutenant G.P. Smith, a medical officer, said that their deaths would have been instantaneous due to the impact. The jury recorded a verdict of Accidental Death.

Pilot Sergeant Black had been a mechanical fitter at Metropolitan-Vickers works in Sheffield before the war, and it was reported that he had been flying since he was seventeen years old. He had been a member of the volunteer reserve of the RAF for some years, serving at Hull, Brough, Doncaster and other centres before being called up for active service. The bodies of these young men were so badly damaged that little could be found in the wreckage. One way of bringing some kind of closure for the parents of such men and women who died on active service was by holding a memorial service. Such a service took place on Saturday, 7 February 1942, when family members gathered to remember another pilot, Sergeant Ronald Walter Duke, who had been killed whilst taking part in flying operations over Germany 'some time ago'. Friends, relatives and ex-work colleagues attended Kimberworth Parish Church to pay tribute to the bravery of this young pilot.

The rise of the RAF during the Second World War was acknowledged by Churchill, who spoke of these air pioneers in his speech on the eve of the Battle of Britain. He stated, 'We shall fight with growing confidence and strength in the air.' On 16 August 1940, Winston Churchill informed the nation that 'so much [was] owed by so many' to these brave men.

As in the First World War, the news that local men had been taken prisoner was a double-edged sword. Many relatives were pleased that their men folk were now out of the fighting, whilst others wondered what kind of treatment they would receive in the hands of their captives. One of the earliest reported prisoners was Captain M.C.M. Athorp, who had formerly lived at Dinnington Hall. In a week of mid-May 1940, which was described by the *Advertiser* as a 'week when the melancholy news of war casualties [had] started to filter into Rotherham and district homes,' the family received the sad news that he had been taken prisoner from the American Embassy. It seems that Captain Athorp had been taken whilst fighting in Norway with his regiment, the Sherwood Foresters. The Embassy informed his family that he was 'in good spirits'.

At first it seemed that the prisoners of war were being treated quite well. A photograph of ten prisoners, taken at Stalag IX C in Germany, had been sent by Lance Corporal Arthur William Sigger to his Rotherham parents. The photo, which was printed in the *Advertiser* on 5 July 1941, shows a group of soldiers looking fit and healthy, all dressed in uniform and smiling at the camera. The other captured soldiers were unknown to the family, but it was hoped that some of them might be recognised by relatives. Lance Corporal Sigger had been serving in France with the Highland Field Section of the Royal Army Medical Corps and had been reported missing on 11 July 1940. He arrived back to a rapturous welcome on Friday, 5 November 1943. He told his parents that the treatment meted out to the British prisoners had gradually improved, explaining that when they first went into captivity they were transported in cattle trucks. When it was decided that they would be repatriated, the men were moved out in private coaches. He arrived home and told the *Advertiser* that for eighteen months he had worked in a German military hospital, where the doctors and other members of staff had treated him very well.

Mr and Mrs Thickett of Broom Lane, Rotherham were also delighted to hear from their son, Sergeant Air Gunner Sewell Thickett, who had written to them after being reported missing following the 1,000-bomber raid on Essen in July 1941. Almost a year to the day since he had joined the forces, they received a letter from him stating that he had been taken prisoner in Germany. Despite the fact that he had only been flying for a year, Sergeant Thickett had been on his seventh operational flight, having also taken part in the mass raid on Cologne. He told his parents he was being treated very well as a prisoner, but as the German authorities censored all mail, there was little else he could say. In August 1942, the *Advertiser* printed advice for relatives writing to men who had been captured and held prisoner. Reporting for the Ministry of Information, it stated that relatives must be careful not to give away information to the enemy. They were advised to avoid mentioning air-raid damage, location of factories, camps or aerodromes, movement of troops or anything that could be of use in warfare.

It was not until later in the war, in December 1942, that the truth about conditions in the camps was heard from soldiers returning back to the town. Mr David Turner, a former Rotherham man who was captured after the *Manchester* sunk, had been released from an Algerian prison camp in Laghouat by allied forces. He was staying with his wife at a relative's house on Chaucer Road when he spoke to a reporter from the *Advertiser*. He told him that he was one of the last to leave the ship and had spent four hours in the water before being picked up by a German lifeboat. Four days later the captured men arrived at the camp. The prison had been very cramped, holding 900 men in a 400-yard square enclosure, bordered with 'barbed wire netting 4 feet thick and ten feet high'. Meals were scant: a cup of coffee for breakfast and bread and soup at midday and 5 p.m. They had been kept in accommodation built to house twenty-five Algerian troops, and even the officers received no special treatment. He praised the Red Cross parcels that had kept them alive with extra rations, although he revealed that sometimes the men did not receive them at the supposed time. The eighty officers on the camp, made up of RAF and army personnel, did have access to six taps that were turned on twice a day. The rest of the men had to make do with horse troughs. The camp was surrounded by desert from which it was impossible to escape but, thankfully, Turner only spent three months there before being released.

In October 1943, news was heard that some Rotherham prisoners were to be repatriated and they received messages of welcome from His Majesty King George VI. The men were among a group that reached England in October. Those who were able made their way back to the town they had not seen for some time. Others were kept in hospital in south-east England whilst they recuperated. Among those who returned immediately was Sergeant Cyril Bennett of Maltkiln Cottages, Westgate, who arrived on Thursday 28 October after nearly three and a half years as a prisoner in Germany. Perhaps fearing for the fate of his comrades still being held captive, he said nothing about the conditions in which he had lived, but he too praised the work of the Red Cross. However, he did tell the reporter there were to be further repatriations in about four months and that he hoped 'many other Rotherham lads [would] return to the town.' He also revealed that whilst in captivity, the men had kept themselves occupied by reading, playing games and learning from qualified schoolmasters. Sergeant Bennett was given a well-earned twenty-eight day rest before returning back to his regiment. It was reported that on Friday, 29 October 1943 he begun a tour of the town – the first since 1940.

Meanwhile, other men were due to return. Sapper Robert Marsh from 16 Rockingham Road, Rawmarsh, who had been in captivity since June 1940, told the *Advertiser* reporter that the food in the prison camp was poor and that they would not have survived without the Red Cross parcels. The first parcel he received was on Boxing Day 1940. 'It had certainly made up for the Christmas dinner provided by the Germans which was sauerkraut,' he said. The meals that had been provided during their captivity were usually 2-inch-thick slices of bread with a very thin potato or barley soup. Occasionally, cheese was served, but as they 'could always smell it coming when it was 100 yards away', they rarely ate it.

Ex-prisoners of war were generally given a great welcome home, not just from their families but from civic dignitaries. On Thursday, 4 November 1943, the Mayoress gave a tea to warmly welcome the men back to the town. She also took the opportunity to thank the committee of the Comfort Fund, who had sent out small gifts to prisoners of war, for their sterling work. The returned prisoners thanked the committee as well, telling them about how the comfort parcels and the Red Cross food parcels had saved their lives. The following evening, the group of repatriated men were invited to the Regent cinema, where the Mayoress distributed gifts that had been donated by local businessmen. Stories were told of how many soldiers had walked for days to arrive at the camps, with very little food. In one case, the only water available to the prisoners was that from the River Rhine. Some of the men were later moved to Poland in cattle trucks, with fifty men squeezed in each vehicle. The German soldiers told them that Rotherham and Sheffield had been 'bombed to the ground' and no longer existed. On their journey back to Britain, the soldiers spoke of the fantastic reception they had received in Sweden. One man told a reporter that military and Salvation Army bands had greeted them when the ship docked and that thousands of civilians cheered them on. The Crown Princess of Sweden had also greeted the men and talked to as many of them as she could. Sapper Marsh said he couldn't believe they were returning home and that, when they did, the reception they got in England was overwhelming. He told a reporter that he didn't believe he was a free man until he got back to Rotherham and saw the town for himself.

Of all the returning soldiers, medal winners were especially celebrated in the town. On 18 January 1941, a twenty-three-year-old Rotherham soldier was awarded the Military Medal. He was Lance Corporal Harry Forster, whose parents Mr and Mrs J.A. Forster of 11 Western Road, East Dene went to Buckingham Palace to receive his medal from the King. He had served in the Royal Engineers for two months, after three and a half years in France and Belgium. It was reported that before being rescued from Dunkirk, he had been a dispatch rider. He was educated at St Ann's School, South Grove and then Spurley Hey School in Rotherham. Lance Corporal Forster was married with one child and had been a bricklayer before joining the army. A DCM was awarded to another Rotherham soldier, Private Harry V. Wordsworth, from the RAOC, aged twenty-three. He was the son of Mr and Mrs M. Wordsworth of 16 Deepdale Road and had joined the army at the age of eighteen, after being educated at Kimberworth Central School. Before joining the army he was a coppersmith at the Rotherham Boiler Company. He was first sent out to Palestine, where he was involved in the Battle of Sidi Barrani, which became known as the Western Desert Campaign. He had a brother, Sergeant A.R. Wordsworth of the military police, who was a prisoner of war in Germany.

A DSO was awarded to a Thorpe Hesley Soldier in September 1943. Flight Lieutenant Phillip Robert Coldwell, the only son of Mr and Mrs J.G. Coldwell of Thorpe Street, Thorpe Hesley, had written his mother a letter stating that he knew he had 'another gong' coming to him but 'didn't dream of a DSO'. He had been awarded a medal the previous July as an 'Honorary Polish Observer', for his work serving as an instructor to the Polish Squadron. Prior to that he had been awarded a Distinguished Flying Medal. He was born in Rotherham and educated at Thorpe Hesley Council School and then Rotherham Grammar School, before going to Durham University. He joined the RAF in 1940, aged twenty, and quickly went through the ranks, becoming a warrant officer, a pilot officer and flight lieutenant. He had been in sixty-nine operational flights. These brave men, who had ordinary occupations in the town before the war, now returned as heroes.

Another Rotherham hero, who was in the Commandoes, was awarded the Military Medal in October 1942, following the raid on Dieppe. The proud parent of Sergeant Irving Portman of 42 Deepdale Road, Holmes heard the news on the 1 p.m. news bulletin on Saturday, 3 October 1942. Sergeant Portman, aged twenty-nine, bravely took over command of his men when all officers and the Sergeant Major had been wounded, until a more senior ranking officer could relieve him. When that officer, Captain Porteous VC, arrived, Sergeant Portman had led an attack on a German gun-pit. He had dispatched the gun crews and demolished the pit. He took home with him a German helmet as a souvenir, which was then taken to the works of Messrs J.J. Habershon & Sons Ltd, where a collection was made for the Mayoress's Comfort Fund. Within several weeks, £3 16s had been raised. He was the fourth son of Mrs M. Portman and the late Mr T.E. Portman. Having been educated at the Kimberworth Central School, he had joined up when he was eighteen and had served for seven years, spending three of those in Hong Kong. He had then become a reservist until the outbreak of war, when he rejoined the army. He became a Commando soon after the unit was formed and saw action in Lofoten and St Nazaire.

News reached the parents of another Commando, Sergeant Frederick Preece, that he had been awarded a Distinguished Flying Cross for bravery in July 1942. Sergeant Preece, who was only twenty-eight years of age, had been attached to the Dragoon Guards for the past eight years and had seen much action abroad. He had been in the reserves and was recalled to his regiment from his home at 2 Crescent End, Thurcroft when war broke out. He had served with the British Expeditionary Force in France, where he received injuries to his right foot. But this hadn't meant his days as a soldier were over. On his return to duties, he joined the Commandoes. His parents Mr and Mrs J. Preece were delighted to hear the news about their eldest son.

One of the warmest welcomes was extended to the servicemen following the D-Day landings on 6 June 1944. This was one of the turning points in the war. Many men had been injured and some of them were installed in Rotherham Hospital. The Mayor of Rotherham, Councillor Mrs F.L. Green, visited them on Wednesday, 21 June 1944. It was reported that thirty-six soldiers and sailors who had been wounded in the landing field and the battlefields of Normandy were 'recovering from their injuries'. A reporter visited and spoke about how the wards 'rang with laughter as the patients called out to each other'. Some of the patients had reached Rotherham on the weekend of the 17 June and others came in steadily during the following week. Many of those who only had slight injuries told the reporter of their determination to 'get back and into Berlin'. The men were from all over the country, many of them southerners and Welshmen, only two coming from Yorkshire. Nevertheless, they were given a good welcome with gifts from the Comfort Fund. They spoke about their experiences whilst under fire, and the bravery of the medical teams who worked for twenty-four hours as stretcher bearers and medical orderlies. One of the soldiers told the people of the town that if one of their relatives was injured in Normandy that they would 'lack nothing in the way of attention'. He said,

Sgt. I. Portman.

Commando Sergeant Irving Portman, who was awarded the Military Medal

'Nobody is left for a single minute and the medical teams are performing miracles. At least 90 per cent of our lads are being got back safely to this country.'

These were some of the brave men who fought to defend the town, and just some of the heroic acts which local men endured whilst fighting. Many, many more remain untold. But the protection of the town itself was given to the brave men who defended these shores; the men of the Home Guard.

# 19

# THE HOME GUARD

The Home Guard was formed in 1940, to act as a second line of defence against invasion by the enemy. They were originally called the Local Defence Volunteers, but due to a nickname the service undeservedly acquired ('look, duck and vanish'), it was changed to the Home Guard. What comes to mind for many people when referring to the Home Guard is the excellent series written by Jimmy Perry and David Croft, *Dad's Army*. This shows a group of bumbling men and boys throwing themselves into different antics whilst trying to preserve the peace. The men of the Rotherham Home Guard were groups of patriotic men who, unable to enlist due to their age or for health reasons, demonstrated their commitment to the defence of the town and districts.

It was thought in the early years of the war that invasion from the skies was probable. At a meeting held in the town in 1940, an assembled crowd were told, 'There is now a great fear that parachute troops might be landed.' It was thought that they might evade detection by landing in the more rural areas of the districts. On the morning of Tuesday 21 May, the Home Guard Group Commander, Captain A.S. Furniss, had been informed that there was 'an imminent danger of troops landing', and so he was assigned 'to assemble volunteers to have patrols on duty to guard vulnerable points of the town.' The men were issued with hand grenades and other such equipment, in case they needed to protect the town from invasion. Thankfully, enemy troops did not land and regular exercises were held to prevent such landings.

A recruitment meeting at the Town Hall, on the evening of Friday, 24 May 1940, was organised to enlist men for the Local Defence Volunteers. Captain Furniss had been warned in advance that an attempt by 'fifth communists in this area' would be made to wreck the meeting. They had spread a rumour around the town that the meeting was to be cancelled. Captain Furniss commandeered a van with a loud speaker attached. He drove around the town, stating categorically that it would be taking place. The meeting was an enormous success, with 600 men volunteering and another 300 men left outside waiting their turn. Captain Furniss and the Mayor of Rotherham, Councillor G.A. Barker, addressed the meeting. The local MP, Alderman Dobbie, gave a very patriotic address to the assembled people, saying they were meeting in perhaps the most desperate moment of their lives and that he was confident there was no feeling of despair among them. He urged people to

Rotherham Home Guard bayonets charging during training.

demonstrate they were 'ready, able and capable of defending the things that had been won for [them]'.

To noisy cheers and hurrahs, he concluded his speech by telling the assembled crowd, 'Whatever danger you may have to face I want to share it with you.' The men were not equipped with uniforms or weapons and for a while had to utilise anything to use as a weapon. Despite this, nearly 850 men signed up at that meeting, of which it was estimated that approximately 70 per cent were ex-servicemen. At a Unity Demonstration held at Clifton Park in July 1940, another sixty-one members elected to join the Home Guard. Gradually, over the next few months, khaki uniforms, armbands and guns were issued. As a result of the threat of 'fifth communists', said to be a 'very grave danger' in the town, all applicants for the Rotherham Home Guard had to present references. Captain Furniss told the volunteers that the forms they would sign for the Home Guard would include the name of two people who were householders and would be prepared to vouch for the volunteer's work and behavioural history. He stated that there would be six companies of Home Guard volunteers in Rotherham, comprising of 140 men each, overseen by seven officers. Up to that point, there had been 1,240 volunteers, and it was agreed that all these men would have training in using hand grenades and rifles with trained instructors. Separate recruitment meetings were held in each district, and it was announced that a meeting would be held at the Estate Hall, Springfield Road, Wickersley the following night at 7 p.m., to recruit for 'A' company. Another meeting the same day was held at the Miners Institute on Broad Street, Parkgate at 3.30 p.m.

The first large parade of the Rotherham Home Guard was on Sunday, 22 September 1940. The men were cheered as they marched past and were accompanied by a mobile and armoured car section. The Bishop of Sheffield, Canon Waring, spoke of his pride at being

In the early days the Local Defence Volunteers were without weapons and had to utilise other implements.

The Rotherham Home Guard in training, with full uniforms and weapons.

appointed as honorary chaplain to the Home Guard. He said that the magnificent impact the men of Rotherham had made by joining had been an inspiration to everyone. He told the congregation:

We are part of a great commonwealth out to overcome the enemies of freedom and raise the banner of truth and liberty throughout the world. We are taking our part in the overthrow of our enemies of all that Christianity and religion stand for. We go forward inspired by that great vision, looking forward to the day that our task will be accomplished and a new day of peace shall dawn for the world.

The march concluded with the singing of hymns, accompanied by the band of Silverwood colliery.

The men were trained for battle but, inevitably, with the use of weapons and armoury, accidents did occur. Such an incident took place at Swallownest in March 1941, when

Private Archibald Wallis was killed during a machine-gun practice. On Tuesday 17 March, a member of the Home Guard, named Sergeant Albert Ernest Copley, got up from the ground where he had ben demonstrating how to set the tripod of a machine gun, when the gun went off, firing a shot of live ammunition. It hit Private Wallis. In a previous exercise live ammunition had been used, but this had been taken out and should have been replaced by 'dummy' bullets. The coroner criticised the fact that both live and dummy cartridges were kept in the same container, but he knew that the person who put the live cartridge in the machine gun was unaware of his mistake. How anyone could mix up a dummy bullet, made of wood, for a real bullet, which was heavier and made of brass, was not explained.

A man named Arthur Lowe (the same name as the actor who played Captain Mainwaring in *Dad's Army*) was a fully qualified machine-gun trainer and had been instructing the platoon for some time. To his knowledge, no bullets had been loaded for the demonstration and he suggested that the bullet must have remained in the gun, since the previous training when live ammunition had been used. Private Albert Edward Burnett told the court that the men watching the demonstration had gathered round the gun in a semi-circle and that he had sat on his heels next to Private Wallis. The coroner told the jury that this was a pure accident and he praised the work of the Home Guard. He stated that no one could feel anything but gratitude towards this body of men serving to protect their country. The jury agreed and brought in a verdict of Accidental Death. The coroner asked military authorities to ensure that such an accident was prevented from happening again. Private Wallis's funeral was held on Sunday, 23 March 1941 at Aston Cemetery, where a large crowd, including his widow and daughter, saw the body interred.

Unfortunately, this was not the only accident caused by misuse of equipment. A year later, in April 1942, a man lost both his hands from an explosion of a detonator. Ironically, it was reported that the live detonators were supplied at the last minute to add 'realism' to the exercise. The injured man was 2nd Lieutenant James Cottam. Another man, Private Ernest Tyers, was also injured in the accident, although less severely. They were both taken to hospital. A subscription was started for Mr Cottam, who was a butcher by trade, and it was reported that his fellow butchers were 'helping him out for the time being'. A month later, the subscription amounted to £422 6s 9d. Thankfully, these were the only injuries in the whole of the war period. The men were trained by professional soldiers and regular demonstrations were held in order to prepare them for any invasion.

By August 1941, the Rotherham Home Guard consisted of several battalions. All the battalions were included in a South Yorkshire demonstration, showing how the Home Guard should respond to a parachute attack. A reporter from the *Advertiser* was appointed to one of the battalions. He informed that the men were split into two; defenders and attackers:

Considerable initiative was shown by the attackers in their methods of disguise. It emphasised the fact that in a case of invasion the Home Guard must assume nothing at all but must make perfectly certain of the identity of people using the roads...For the first time I saw the terrifying spectacle of a bayonet charge on a strongly held position. The attackers could not have put more enthusiasm into their charge had the defenders of the position been cold blooded Nazis.

The day was considered a great success. Combined training exercises were regularly held in the town, which involved the regular army, the police and the National Fire Service, as well as the Home Guard and other civil defence services. These exercises were crucial in ensuring that good lines of communication were in place to protect Rotherham in the event of an enemy attack, and, as a consequence, they became very exciting. Another such exercise was reported in the *Advertiser* on 13 December 1941. Lieutenant Colonel M.C. Martyn DSO was in charge of the defending troops and Lieutenant Colonel H.E. Lowe headed the enemy troops. The task was for the 'enemy troops' to land by parachute and to cut off all communication with the rest of the country. They also had to secure military targets of importance and destroy power installations. The reporter noted that to obtain these results, spies would be employed. He commented, 'Their initiative and resourcefulness was exemplary.' Some of the 'enemy spies' overpowered three ARP wardens and one, dressed in an ARP uniform, managed to gain entrance into the headquarters, holding a 'bomb'. During this fascinating exercise, 'enemy troops' succeeded in getting to the centre of the town. There they rushed a Corporation Highway depot and commandeered a lorry, compelling the civilian driver to take them to the Town Hall, where a battle ensued between the spies, the police and the Home Guard. The reporter stated, 'While the action lasted it was good spirited stuff. Blank shots and fireworks exploded and as in other combats, blood was drawn.'

An hour's intensive bombing had to be improvised during the exercise, but it provided the National Fire Service and the Civil Defence with about sixteen incidents – all dealt with efficiently. As part of the demonstration, some empty cottages were set on fire. Rescue simulation was carried out swiftly and effectively by all the services. The umpires quickly called a halt to the battle when the Mayor's Parlour was captured, but it was said that 'an important military objective' remained undiscovered. The reporter pointed out that lessons were learned on both sides and everyone who took part in the exercise was to be congratulated. Perhaps the people witnessing the exercises caused some disruption, as when another event was announced to take place on 7 December 1942, civilians were asked to remain indoors. The military authorities asked for 'as little interference as possible'.

The same month, the Rotherham Home Guard celebrated their second anniversary with further demonstrations in Clifton Park. The operation started with the release of pigeons, to alert reserves once the 'enemy' had been sighted, and then the arrival of the reserves and the subsequent battle. These operations were usually well attended by the public, who saw the Home Guard at close quarters operating anti-aircraft weapons as well as a Northover projector (an anti-tank gun). There were bayonet charges through smoke screens in Clifton Park and the afternoon was rounded off with a concert by the 60th Battalion Home Guard Band. Mr E. Dunn MP praised the efforts of the troops and told them the whole community was indebted to them. Further demonstrations were given by the Home Guard in other districts, including an attack on a machine-gun nest at Maltby, an attack on North Stavely Cottages, and an attack using real ammunition in Ravenfield Park.

In June 1942, the Rotherham Home Guard were asked to develop an Ack-Ack battery by Major George Bromley Garnett, the chair and managing director of Garnett Bros of Rotherham and the newly appointed Commanding Officer since 23 May 1942. He told the assembled crowd that a recruiting station had been opened in the centre of town and that he would speak to local industries and collieries, asking for recruits. The men required for the

One exercise included bomb throwing by the Home Guard.

battery needed to be fit and strong, although no previous artillery experience was necessary as training was given. Major Garnett told the crowds that officers would be appointed from local men, who would be working on the guns as well as in the plotting room. However, he stressed that many more volunteers were needed. These Ack-Ack batteries were crucial, not only for the defence of Rotherham but of Britain as a whole. Enemy raiders would be spotted by observers, who would inform the plotting rooms of how many planes were headed towards Rotherham. This information was invaluable to the defending spitfires which would be employed in shooting them down.

On Sunday, 16 May 1943, the third anniversary of the Home Guard, the battalions paraded in the grounds of Wentworth Woodhouse, the seat of Earl Fitzwilliam. The event was watched by Lord Scarborough, who wore the uniform of a Major General. He was described as a 'veteran soldier who for most of his life had been attached to the Territorial Army.' The celebration, which included 3,000 officers and men, lasted all day and despite the fact that there was a transport strike, it was very well attended by civilians. The morning began with men drawn up on the large lawn at the front of the enormous estate. Then a service was held by Canon Baker the Deputy Assistant Chaplain General. Major General P.J. Shears told his men that since taking command, they had put up with a certain amount of disorganisation 'in the interests of the nation'. They had also changed 'from a mobile to a static policy', and had done 'cheerfully and happily all that was required'. He told them it was the duty of the Home Guard to forge links with the other services in order to defend their homes. The day progressed with the anti-tank weapons firing competition, which was won by the 61st Battalion. Various demonstrations of guns, from the Browning and Bren guns to a bayonet attack on a small but well-defended post, were given.

On 6 September 1944, the end of the war was in sight and it was decided that the threat of enemy invasion was no longer as urgent. The Home Guard's compulsory training and drills were to be discontinued and, on 27 October, orders were issued for the Home Guard to 'stand down' by the end of December. On Sunday 3 December, the people of Rotherham watched the Home Guard's 'stand down' parade, the battalions marching through the town following four and a half years of valiant service. Although there had been some ridicule in the early days of the war, when men were mustered holding broom handles and pitchforks, these men had proved their worth by defending our towns and cities. The five Rotherham battalions assembled and marched to Frederick Street in front of cheering crowds, where the 1,976 men saluted their Commanding Officer, Lieutenant Colonel Landon. They then proceeded to the Regal cinema to hear a service solemnised by the Bishop of Sheffield and the vicar of Rotherham. After speeches by all the parties, the battalions split into their own sections and were saluted by their own commanders as they marched off to band music. Lieutenant Colonel Landon spoke for all when he said:

Photos: "Rotherham Advertiser."

Col. J. W. B. Landon, D.S.O., J.P. (Rotherham Sector Commander), at the saluting base with the Mayor of Rotherham (Councillor H. Lake, J.P.), the Deputy Mayor (Councillor Mrs. F. L. Green, J.P.), and the Town Clerk (Sir Charles des Forges) at the "stand down" parade of the Home Guard

Lieutenant Colonel W.J.B. Landon, taking the salute at the Home Guard 'stand down' parade.

61st Battalion of the Rotherham Home Guard.

On taking leave of the Home Guard in the Rotherham sector I would like to express not only my regret at this farewell but my heartfelt thanks to all who have contributed to making the Home Guard in the sector an efficient fighting force...I pay tribute to the unselfishness of the womenfolk over the last four and a half years for permitting their men to devote their leisure time to the Home Guard.

He also paid tribute to the civil defence services and the Women's Auxiliary Service before continuing:

Let all of us now eased of one of our voluntary burdens concentrate in his or her own way on the prosecution of the war to its successful conclusion. Let us keep alive in the battalion areas the fine spirit of comradeship on which must have its inevitable influence on promoting good citizenship and the understanding of each others problems for the good of all.

There is no doubt that the people of Rotherham owe much to this body of men. Many had jobs which they undertook during the day, attending exercises for the Home Guard at evenings and weekends. The jobs in the town brought many changes to the way people worked during wartime. Men and women could be fined for not attending work and there was much criticism, as there had been in the last war, for the shirkers within the different industries.

# 20

# WAR WORK

For security reasons, very little was printed about industries during the Second World War. Even in local reports of bombing raids on Rotherham, it was referred to as a 'North Midland town'. Only after the war were the air raids acknowledged. As in the First World War, it was soon realised that more munitions factories and workers would be needed to produce shells and tanks. Recruitment for the factories began on 30 November 1940. The Ministry of Work offered free training courses in order to increase munitions production, and they were to be held at the Rotherham College of Technology, as well as other colleges across the country. The intention was to train men between the ages of twenty-five and sixty-five in machine operation. The request for volunteers was initially aimed at men who would be 'a vanguard' in the workplace. These men would soon be joined by women and boys. There were three types of training given: one at a Government Training Centre, which was a three to five months course with 'practical and theoretical instruction'; one that provided training in machine operating over an eight-week period; and the third type, a 'hands on' course with experienced workers at the specific site of employment. A further appeal was made in January 1942 for 'men and more men, women and more women', needed to 'enable us to hit back and hit hard at Hitler and his gang.'

Although the need for munitions workers was great, like in the First World War, it was not long before complaints were made about the 'slackers' in the factories. A letter was received by the editor of the *Advertiser* in June 1941 from a man working in munitions. He described some of his lazy comrades, claiming, 'Some young men think they are indispensable and are in key positions holding up jobs and keeping others from working.' According to him, these people acted as if the war was 'an easy way of getting money for nothing'. He said that in peace time, no firm would be able to carry on like that before going out of business. He continued:

We men of Rotherham should, for our countries sake, try and be worthy of what our men have gone through at Dunkirk, Greece and Crete and try to do our bit to get the munitions they need. Not sit down for hours in work time saying what should be done. Let us do a bit ourselves. I am only a labourer in the works but I did three years and seven months in the last war in France.

A bombed house
at Masbrough
after a raid on
29 August 1940.

He signed himself as WORKMAN. The following week, a steel works manager, Mr A. Thomas, wrote to the newspaper agreeing with this letter. He said that many of the workers had been recruited from the Labour Exchanges and were forced to work in the munitions. Although they were paid union rates, he said they would 'grouse and idle their time away playing cards'. He stated, 'These men don't care that fighting men are being slaughtered because they are short of the means of defence.'

The situation regarding the 'slackers' got so bad in February 1942 that a National Service officer was appointed to deal with the many cases. This officer would visit the person in question, find out what the problem was and try to find a solution. One case reported in the *Advertiser* was of 'a determined young man' aged seventeen, who had ignored three written warnings over his bad timekeeping and days taken off from the munitions factory. His family had tried their utmost to get him to work and his sister had often accompanied him to the works' gate. But he frequently went inside and clocked on, only to leave again straight away. The young man told his father that he didn't like working afternoons as it was 'too late to go to the pictures or play billiards after work'. His father told the National Service officer that he had thrashed his son until the boy had promised that he would change, but he had not kept his word. The officer had no success with the boy, who was brought in front of the magistrates on Thursday, 5 February 1942, charged with 'leaving his employment early to go to the cinema'. His father attended the court and told the bench that he didn't know what to do with his son. The magistrate, Alderman Dickenson, added that he 'didn't know either'. The father only knew his son had skipped work because the boy had no wages. The son told the court that he had got in with bad company and been led astray. The defendant told the court that he was 'addicted to playing billiards and couldn't keep out of billiard halls'. The bench warned him that he must, and his father suggested to the court that a change of employment could help his son; a job at a colliery, where 'an eye could be kept on him', was the father's proposition. The magistrate adjourned the case for a month, in which time it was hoped the son would establish himself at a colliery or return to work at his present job and make more effort. He was warned that any further breaches in his working hours would result in a further court hearing and prison.

Like in the previous war, vehicles were brought to the town in order to boost the sale of war savings bonds and increase the manufacture of munitions. The Regal cinema promoted a scheme, starting Sunday 3 October and finishing 7 October 1942, to buy a tank. Three tanks, accompanied by two armoured cars, visited Rotherham and toured the district in order to raise money and increase production of tanks and shells. The parade of vehicles included 'a Waltzing Matilda's tank, which was an early tank shaped like a duck. These were later replaced by the more efficient 'Valentine' tanks, two of which were included in the parade. It was reported that the vehicles were expected to arrive in Rotherham at 12.30, 'near the pumping station on Fitzwilliam Road'. The Mayor, Alderman G.C. Ball, and Alderman W. Dobbie welcomed the crew of the tank and accepted an invitation to complete the journey in the tank. The crowds lined the roads and there were loud cheers and waving flags. Led by a battalion of Home Guard, the procession went to the Regal cinema car park on Corporation Road, where the tanks were given a civic welcome by the Mayor. Standing on one of the tanks the Mayor talked about the need 'for Rotherham people to do their bit'. The officer in charge of the parade, Lieutenant P.G.L Crook, told the assembled crowd that the army was waiting for the people to give them the tools for war. He hoped that the visit of the tanks would show the people of the town what was needed to win the war. The MP Alderman Dobbie MP told the crowd that the Lieutenant and his men had seen service in France and Libya. He pointed out that they had 'tested the Italians but it was a fiercer and sterner job to tackle the forces of slavery represented by Hitler and to do that there must be more and still more tanks.' He added:

It is not a question of can we win the war. We must not lose and there is a terrible responsibility on the civil population of this country to see that the men who are entrusted with the life of the nation have the materials for the job.

The tanks were on show in Clifton Park from 2 a.m. on all three days. On the Sunday morning, the armoured vehicles toured through Rotherham, going out as far as the Brecks and Wickersley. In the afternoon, they toured Masbrough, Kimberworth and Wortley Road. On Monday they were at Greasbrough. The column reassembled on Tuesday morning at 10 a.m., once again at the Regal car park, and the Mayor cheered them on their way to Wakefield, which was the next part of the schedule.

One of the most well-known slogans to come out of the Second World War was 'careless talk costs lives', and a case emphasising this sentiment was heard in August 1942. A munitions worker from Conisbrough was brought into the Rotherham Police Court on Tuesday 25 August, charged with 'unlawfully recording information about munitions' and 'unlawfully communicating such information to another person'. His defence, Mr R.C. Linney, told the court that the defendant had written in his notebook some measurements connected with his work and that he had shown these measurements to a factory inspector in a public house on 25 July. The inspector had reported the matter to the police, who arrested the young man. The defendant made a statement saying that he had only recorded the measurements for his

The Mayor standing on a tanks and addressing the crowd.

own personal use at the munitions factory. Mr Linney pointed out that it was 'more a case of him wanting to show someone the interest he was taking in his work than any other more subversive reasons,' and the police were satisfied that it was simply a case of foolishness. The works' foreman stated that the young man was a hard worker and the court took this view into account, dismissing the charges. The magistrate stressed that this case should be a warning to everyone responsible for safety and security during wartime.

Such was the interest in the production of munitions that the workers of an unnamed factory received a Russian Trade Delegation on Wednesday, 14 January 1942. In June 1941, Hitler had invaded Russia and on 1 October, at a council meeting, the Mayor of Rotherham signed a book with an inscription for the people of Russia, which was sent to a city named Rostov situated, like Rotherham, on the River Don. The inscription read:

> We the people of Rotherham send warmest greetings in this our common struggle against Fascism to the people of the USSR. Especially to those of the Rostov on Don whose industries are the same as ours. We pledge with you our undying love of freedom and resolve that we will not rest until Victory is won.

The Russian people were so warmed by this inscription, it was announced that a delegation would come to Rotherham from the steel mills of Russia. The delegates received a very friendly welcome by the workforce, who had decorated the works with hammer and sickles and signs saying, 'Give it to Joe' and 'Good Old Joe' (for the leader of the Russian people, Joseph Stalin). One member of the group, Madame Klavdia Nikolayeva, shook hands enthusiastically with the workers, and it was reported that Mr L. Soloviev of the Kirov works in Leningrad smiled as he passed the Home Guard escort at the entrance to the works. Some of the workers appeared to be concerned that their hands were too grubby to shake hands with the delegates, but they were seized enthusiastically by two other members of the delegation, Madame A. Semeonoff and Mr N.I. Rotov. A message written in Russian stated, 'These workers greet you with these words: To strengthen the union with the USSR in war and peace.' Also there were an artist's impressions of Churchill and Stalin standing side by side. Accompanied by two interpreters, Madame Nikolayeva thanked the workers, saying to them:

> We have been very touched by your welcome as well as by the many signs and tokens of the regard in which you hold us. We regard it as an honour, not for ourselves alone but for the workers of Russia. You all understand what the situation demands and we are quite sure that what is essential is the coalition between the Soviet Union and Great Britain, so that together with our united forces we will present a front which will forever destroy and crush Hitler. The greater the production of munitions the better armed will be the Red Army and the British Army.

One of the Rotherham employees, Mr Francis, spoke in Russian to rousing cheers. He told them, 'Work, work, work and then Victory.' It was reported that the delegation had some tea before returning back to London.

During the Second World War, men could be sent, or 'directed', towards a job in any of the essential industries, according to requirements. Little choice was given to them and, as a consequence, many chose not to work, even though any infringement of working hours would have to be reported. In December 1942, the Rotherham magistrates stated that they were puzzled at the attitude of people brought before the court charged with disobeying a National Service directive. One man had been sent to work in an RAF aerodrome in Lincolnshire and, after staying only three hours, decided that the job was not for him and went home. A labour officer from the station told the court that the man could earn between £6 10s and £7 10s a week, have access to hot and cold water and enjoy the centrally heated accommodation. The solicitor employed to defend him, Mr C.D. Burgess, said the worker had complained that he would have to carry all his belongings with him as there was no locker at the workplace. There was also no provision for drying clothes and apparently the food was bad too. The magistrate, Mr W. Brooks, told him, 'I cannot understand this generation at all. Possibly even your relatives are risking their lives and you are not backing them up to give them the things they require.' Fining the worker £5 and 3 guineas in costs, the magistrate warned that failure to obey the next directive would lead to a prison sentence.

The several collieries around Rotherham were in full production during the war years, when coal was needed for transport, industry and domestic use. Thousands of tons were needed each week and mining was designated a reserved occupation. The 'Observer's Observation' section of the *Advertiser* revealed, in January 1942, that because of absenteeism, 'The country is 300,000 tons of coal a week short in the target figure.' They appealed to the 'shirkers' to be more patriotic, reminding them that they were bringing shame on a worthwhile industry. The matter had been sparked off by two miners appearing at the West Riding Police Court from the Dinnington Main colliery. They were described as 'two of the worst cases of absenteeism the bench had tried.' One man had been absent on ninety-seven occasions from 123 shifts and the other had worked only eleven shifts out of 123. The magistrate, frustrated by the limited power of the law in such cases, stated that if he could, he would have them enforcedly enlisted into His Majesties Forces.

The following month magistrates were becoming more forceful on people who refused to do essential war work. A miner was sent to prison with hard labour for 'failing to obey a National Service direction'. The twenty-eight-year-old man from Monk Street, Rotherham had been employed at Rotherham Main colliery for two years. He complained that he had been suffering from illnesses caused by dust and heat at the mine and he criticised the meagre wages (£3 a week). He had been warned several times by the Pit Production Committee, and on 10 and 19 December 1941, directions were served on him, instructing him to go back to work. In January 1942, the magistrates were told that he still had not been attending work. He told the court that he had appealed to the National Service officer for permission to leave the colliery and had asked to be sent to another colliery, or put on some other form of essential work. He wrote, 'If I am made to stop here I will resort to former tactics of going to sleep on the job.' He was hauled before the magistrate on Thursday 26 February. The prosecution stated that he had been given every consideration, but he made all sorts of complaints about his work. From September 1941 to February 1942, he had been absent from his work 26 per cent of the time; over a six week period, he had been absent a third of that time. The magistrate, Mr W. Brooks, told him, in no uncertain terms, 'You know the nation is going through a very serious crisis. If everyone took your attitude you would probably have someone here who would make you work.' He was then sentenced to three months' hard labour on all three counts, to run concurrently.

In June 1943, a youth had his Protection Certificate taken off him when he refused to work down 'any pit'. The young man, aged nineteen, had worked at the Rotherham Main colliery previously but had been dismissed because of misconduct. The magistrates were told that the Maltby colliery was the only one which would employ him, but he refused the employment, declaring, 'I come from a stubborn family. It was born in me.' However, he said that he would rather go in the forces than undertake pit work and the magistrates agreed. The chairman told him, 'If you will go in the forces and be honest I will adjourn the case and make sure that the authorities make it possible for you to join the armed forces.'

The magistrates were placed in a very difficult position when in June 1942, a seventeen-year-old Rawmarsh youth had been sent to prison for three months for refusing to work in a coal mine. Many of the populace felt that sending him to prison for three months for a first offence was too much. To make matters worse, the boy, named H. Mitchell, had been sent to Armley Gaol on 5 March, but became ill and was taken to Rotherham Hospital on 6 May, where he died on 14 May from an acute form of sleeping sickness. Mr W. Dobbie, MP for Rotherham, had asked the Home Secretary for an enquiry to be held into the circumstances of his death. A letter from the Association Employer Union expressed concern that the boy's sentence was too hard for a seventeen-year-old. Alderman S. Hall stated that the boy had refused to work and that there was no justification for saying this was a harsh sentence.

Despite the refusal from some people to work in any industry, the majority of the town's population worked very hard indeed. It was, therefore, quickly realised by Rotherham Corporation that, as in the previous war, a works canteen should be opened. A canteen, which was initially called a 'feeding centre for workers', was opened at the Mission Hall, Westgate on Tuesday, 24 January 1941, to serve hot meals for the workers at a very low

The Mayor, Alderman G.C. Ball, eating a meal with some of the workers at the British Restaurant on Westgate.

cost. These feeding centres opened to ensure that no one would be unable to feed themselves on the limited rations available. Cutting down on food waste was another objective. Winston Churchill disliked the term 'feeding centres' and the name was quickly changed to the more patriotic 'British Restaurants'. The Mayor, Alderman G.C. Ball, performed a ceremonial opening at 1 p.m., where he announced that a cook and four kitchen maids were engaged to provide good hot dinners between 11.30 a.m. and 2 p.m. for up to 200 people. The *Advertiser* reported, 'A bowl of soup and bread will cost 2d, meat and two vegetables 6d, a portion of pudding 2d and a cup of tea 1d. It will therefore be possible for a satisfying three course meal to be had for 10d.'

The restaurant was a great success and many of the townspeople attended, even those who were not employed. Over the first two days it was announced that they had served 500 meals. On Thursday, the numbers were swelled by the addition of 200 schoolchildren and a total of 790 meals were served. The following Tuesday, 750 meals were served. Such was the success, that a further canteen was opened in St John's schoolroom on Station Road on Monday, 10 March 1941. A third canteen was expected to open in the Eastwood area soon afterwards. The WVS, which helped at these centres, was praised for the work undertaken by the Mayor, Councillor Dickenson, in October 1941. He suggested that the restaurants might run more efficiently if the management of the kitchen was taken over by a committee elected for that purpose. It was agreed that a committee would be formed during the November council meeting and that a regular report should be heard. The following December, there were three food centres and the first report was read out at a meeting:

The March quarter [which was not a full one] there were served 34,800 meals with an expenditure of £1,137 and a deficiency of £336.

The June quarter showed there were 74,300 meals supplied to the restaurants, 8,600 meals sent to the works and 29,700 meals sent to schools making a total of 112,600 and an expenditure of £3,467 and a surplus of £358.

The September quarter had 71,000 meals served in the restaurants 13,000 sent to the works and 94,700 sent to the schools making a total of 178,700 meals which gave an expenditure of £4,739 and a surplus of £32.

So over the whole period there had been a surplus of £54. The Mayor pointed out that, whilst the scheme had not been set up to make a profit, it was hoped that a loss would be avoided. Another 'British Restaurant', at Rawmarsh, opened in September 1942. Alderman Dobbie MP told the assembled crowd that he hoped these community restaurants would continue after the war. The restaurant, which was opened in Green Lane, was described as 'a large airy structure fitted with the most modern appliances in order to provide low cost meals in comfortable surrounding.' The chairman of the council, Mr A. Jeffs, said that if the restaurant was a success, then yet another might open at Parkgate soon.

It was with some surprise when, the following year, it was announced that the WVS would cease their involvement with the British Restaurant on 31 October 1942. It was to be taken over by the Rotherham Corporation Catering Committee. For more than two years the women of the WVS had given their time unstintingly to serving meals, so there was great consternation at the announcement. Mrs I. Habershon, the WVS centre organiser, paid tribute to the way in which the volunteers had 'laid the foundation stone' for the restaurants. The Town Clerk sent a letter of tribute, which was read out at the annual meeting. It read, 'I should like to thank the WVS for the devoted service rendered particularly in the initiation of a scheme which has proved so successful in Rotherham.'

The decision, which Mrs Habershon described as 'a smack in the eye', was not to interfere with the duty expected from members of the WVS. She pointed out that, even though the service had been taken from them, there were still many tasks that the members could get involved in, such as knitting for the men in the forces, organising sleeping and feeding stations and providing the mobile canteens. At a town council meeting the following month, the reason for the 'sacking' of the WVS was explained by Councillor Barlow. He told his colleagues that problems had arisen with the hiring and firing of the paid staff. These decisions had come under the jurisdiction of the WVS, a voluntary service, which had caused conflict. Nevertheless, the British Restaurants continued in the town, although by March 1945 they were operating at a loss, and so a decision was made to approach the Ministry for permission to close some of the restaurants. This was agreed.

The majority of people engaged in war work in Rotherham worked industriously and efficiently; only those who broke the law or were reported as 'slackers' were listed in the local newspapers. Those workers who patriotically toiled throughout the war were rarely mentioned. But once again, as in the First World War, people who objected to working in war industries on religious grounds, quickly came to the attention of the local authorities.

Anyone wishing to register as a Conscientious Objectors (CO) had to state their case at tribunals held at Leeds. They were treated with slightly more dignity than those in the previous war, but the questioning was still quite severe. One CO, a gas meter inspector of Brecks Lane, Rotherham, making his statement to Judge Stewart in April 1940, listed several religious activities that prevented him from doing war work. The judge told him that the reasons were not sufficient and the CO replied that, in his opinion, war was 'evil' and he would not take part in it. One of the tribunal questioned, 'Are you going to allow Hitler to crush Christianity?' to which the CO replied, 'Hitler won't be converted by fighting Germany.' The judge interjected, 'No but he might be prevented from continuing his evil work.' In the end, the judge allowed him to take up a position in forestry.

Another CO, a twenty-five-year-old colliery-surface worker, told the tribunal, 'Hitlerism should be dealt with by prayer.' He said that he 'didn't want to lose the war nor to have Hitlerism spread to England,' and that he was 'willing to help the country in any civil capacity'. When the judge asked him how he would do this, he replied 'by prayer'. The judge said, 'I should think Hitler and his people would be very glad if they could get hold of enough people to make the approach that way.' The man was registered on the provision that he took on work underground at the colliery, to which he agreed.

Criticism on the stand taken by COs was taken up by the Rotherham Trades Council and Labour Party in a meeting at the Cross Keys on Tuesday, 23 July 1940. It seems that a letter had been received from Transport House, regarding the downing of tools by some men in the union who objected to a CO being sent there to work. One of the members said, 'A man who won't put on a uniform in the present need and serve his country should be drowned.' Another member, Mrs Sampson, defended the CO stance. She thought that the true CO was a very brave person:

> The present government has acted fairly towards the 'conchies' by setting up tribunals for them and I do not think that they should be victimised in any way. This boiling over of the war spirit will eventually die down and conscientious objectors will command respect.

Two Jehovah's Witnesses were sent to prison in July 1942 for failing to report for fire-watching duties and land work. The father and his son, who both lived on Doncaster Road, were sentenced by the Rotherham magistrates on Thursday, 16 July 1942. The father was sentenced to three months for failing to report for fire duty and the son was sentenced to six months for being registered as a CO but failing to undertake full time land work. Notice had been served to the father by the Fire Service Staff Officer on 8 May, requiring him to report for fire-watching duties on the night of 14 May. He did not attend, but instead sent a letter explaining that he was an ordained minister and, therefore, should be absolved from such duties. The prosecution maintained that even if he was a minister, the Secretary of State had authorised that ministers were still to undertake such duties at their local church. The prosecution, Mr S.C. Redhead, stated:

> When it is a question of performing military service Parliament has recognised that a man might have a genuine conscientious objection to do such duty and has laid down procedure of such objection to be stated. Fire watching is purely for the protection of property and human life. Parliament has recognised no right to object to it on

conscientious grounds. Therefore the defendant has failed to carry out his duties and there is no defence open to him.

The man told the bench that his 'beliefs and spreading the word of Jehovah' took up all his time and that, to him, this was 'more important than any earthly human organisation'. The magistrate asked him why, if he believed that fire watching was a good service, he was not prepared to perform this duty. The man told him that he was performing a higher service. Nevertheless, he was sent to prison for three months.

The case against the younger man was based on the fact that, even though he was a healthy and quite capable of working, he claimed that his religious beliefs prevented him from undertaking the tasks required of him. The young man had made an application to the North Eastern tribunal. He was registered as a CO on the proviso that he took up full time land work. The CO was not satisfied though, and on 14 April he made an appeal, which was turned down. On 1 May, he was told to report to Beverley but he refused to go. An appointment was made for him with the National Service officer on 15 June. He told the officer that he was not going to engage in any work related to the present emergency. He declared in court that he had 'laid aside all ambition in order to do service for the Lord Jehovah.' The magistrate reminded him he was getting food which other people had worked to provide and yet he was not prepared to do anything in return. The young man replied that to undertake land work would be a violation of the sacred agreement he had made with God. The magistrate sentenced him to six months' prison with hard labour.

On Thursday, 4 May 1944, the first female Jehovah's Witness was sent to prison for failing to take up her post as a bus conductress. The woman, who lived on Belmont Street, Rotherham, told the magistrates that she wanted to continue her 'God given task' and would 'not take up any form of service'. Mr Donald Dunn, who was prosecuting the woman, stated that, in appreciation of the fact that she did not wish to work in munitions, she had been offered, and had refused, work as a bus conductress. She told the National Service officer that she had 'made a covenant to do God's work only'. When asked by the bench how she spent her days, she told them she visited people's houses and talked to them about God. The magistrate gave her a fortnight to reconsider, but she said it did not matter how long he gave her, that her mind was made up. The bench had no option but to send her to prison for a month. It was reported that she was smiling as she left the court.

These were just some of the issues facing workers of the town during the war years. One of the greatest struggles endured by Rotherham people was rationing. Despite the cheap meals on offer at the British Restaurants, for many people the problem of rationing was remembered long after the war ended.

# 21

# RATIONING AND THE BLACK MARKET

uring wartime, the blockade on shipping meant that food rationing had to be introduced. Rationing started in Rotherham on Monday, 8 January 1940, when the population of the town was supplied with ration books. A family had to be registered with a shopkeeper and only they were allowed to remove the coupons. The listed civilian allowances per week were: 4oz butter, 12oz sugar, 4oz of uncooked bacon or ham or 3½oz of cooked meat. Understandably, householders had great difficulty in preparing nutritious meals with the amount of rations. There was lots of advice in the local newspaper on how to make rations go further. Regular recipes were printed and, in May 1941, a whole week's menu was planned. The week's lunch menu consisted of:

| | |
|---|---|
| Sunday | Steak and potato pie with mashed potatoes and spring greens<br>Sago pudding with stewed fruit |
| Monday | Curried vegetables with steamed potatoes and baked carrots<br>Brown Betty |
| Tuesday | Belgian soup with stuffed baked potatoes<br>Steamed batter pudding and jam |
| Wednesday | Vegetable casserole and baked potatoes<br>Honey apples |
| Thursday | Sausages and mashed potatoes with salad<br>Steamed apple pudding |
| Friday | Fish pudding and cauliflower<br>Chocolate pudding |
| Saturday | Oatmeal toad in the hole and bubble and squeak<br>Baked jam pudding |

A week's menu advising how to stretch the rations.

Cookery demonstrations were held at the Electricity House on Westgate, which took place daily from Monday, 8 December to Friday, 12 December 1941 from 11 a.m. – 3 p.m. To encourage the householder to attend, there was free admission and free recipe books given out. All these initiatives helped to make small amounts of rationed food go further.

Almost as soon as the war started, the people of the nation were asked to 'Dig for Victory'. This was a government initiative to urge people to supplement their meagre diet by growing their own fruit and vegetables. Many gardens had Anderson Shelters and families were unable to grow their own produce. It had been agreed by the town council in February 1940 that 9 acres of land, owned by the Corporation, would be made available for cultivation. Any person who wished to have a plot of land could register with the Allotment Society and be allotted a section for their own use. Chief librarian Mr F.J. Boardman had shown a lot of interest in the scheme and it was agreed that the Central Library, on Howard Street, would produce information for the plot holders. Horticultural books would also be available.

Several of the society members put forward their names so that people could contact them for practical help with the allotments. They were listed as:

> Mr A G W Measures, 209 Rother View Road, Canklow
> Mr Tom Sharp, the Post Office, College Road
> Mr J A Coley, 5 Shakespeare Road
> Mr A Kettell, 16 Whybourne Grove
> Mr Joe Thompson, 3 Gordon Terrace
> Mr J H Nicholson, 4 North Place
> Mr L E Flint, 9 Broom Avenue
> Mr W H Heald, 126 Henley Grove Road
> Mr A Yorke, 13 Herbert Street

Further pieces of land were found by the council and added to the list of allotments available in the town. In November 1940, it was announced that part of Herringthorpe playing field would be dug up to provide 100 allotments. People were urged to use their plots to full potential and all crops that were not needed were to be shared out. The driving force behind this scheme was the Society of Friends, along with the National Allotments Society, which offered seeds, seed potatoes and fertilisers at cheap rates to allotment holders. Such schemes were essential, as it was estimated that just one allotment cultivated successfully could save a ton of shipping space.

In a July 1941 council meeting, Councillor Barker reported that the Herringthorpe Park Superintendent, Mr Goodall, assisted by a man and a boy, was working day and night driving a tractor and doing other work to cultivate crops. The 'Dig for Victory' campaign was so successful in Rotherham that an 'Exhibition of Vegetables' was arranged for 9 March 1942 at the Town Hall Assembly Rooms. The exhibition was opened by the Mayor, Councillor A.E. Barlow, and was part of a week-long program. These shows attracted experienced gardeners, but were also places where more inexperienced people could ask for advice about the best vegetables to grow. During the war, carrots were said to be the most versatile vegetable to

Harvest time on Herringthorpe Playing Field.

grow on allotments and regular menus were printed in the *Advertiser* for everything from carrot cake to carrot marmalade.

The ration book became one of the most important documents during the war and the buying or selling of rations books or coupons was illegal. Naturally, it was not long before such illegal transactions were being reported. A married woman of Rother View Road was brought into court in August 1944, charged with having a supposed 'lost' ration book still in her possession. A duplicate book had been issued to her when she claimed to have lost the original, but when the new ration books were issued she went to another depot and produced the duplicate book receiving a new ration book in its place. The references were checked and the offence discovered. The woman pleaded 'guilty' but did not appear in court. She was fined £1 for the offence and another £1 for making a false statement.

In August 1942, a woman was fined £5 for having a ration document that belonged to another person. The woman was the wife of a fairground proprietor who regularly travelled to Rotherham. She told the court that a small boy had come to the fair in a pitiable, starving condition and she gave him some food. In return he did a few small jobs for which she paid him £1. On Sunday 16 August, the boy brought her some coupons. She refused to take them, stating that she had enough of her own, but he told her that his mother was a cripple and begged her to accept them, which she did. Nevertheless, despite her charity, she was fined £5 for the offence.

The shopkeepers of the town also had to get used to rationing. Overpricing was now illegal and any breaches would be prosecuted. At the beginning of the war, 114 shops in Rotherham had been given leaflets outlining the food prices that they must charge. So it was a great surprise to everyone when the Rotherham Co-operative Society Ltd on Westgate was charged on three counts of overpricing. The manager, Mr Armitage, had to appear before the Rotherham Borough Court on Thursday, 21 March 1940, on charges of selling overpriced potatoes.

In January and February, a housewife, Mrs Blanche Stead, had purchased a hundredweight bag of King Edward potatoes, which under the Ministry of Food Order should have been 8*s* 9*d*. She was charged 10*s* 9*d*. Another housewife, Mrs Elizabeth Lee, was charged 1*s* instead of 9¼*d* for 8lbs of potatoes, and another woman, Mrs Evans, was charged 3*s* for 24lbs of potatoes when she should have been charged 2*s* 2¾*d*. The manager protested that at the time there was a shortage of potatoes, particularly in view of the fact that local farmers refused to open potato 'pies' (huge mounds of stored potatoes), in case they were destroyed by frost. The manager had been forced to get 3 tons of potatoes from Sheffield market and had adjusted the price accordingly. The magistrates warned him that profiteering in wartime was unacceptable and that overcharging was a serious matter to poor people, before fining him the maximum penalty of £100.

By January 1942, the Ministry of Food had requested solicitors to remind the magistrates of the new penalties for overpricing offences. The new powers would enable magistrates to impose fines of three times the cost of food sold, in addition to the fine ordered by the court. Under the new penalties, a greengrocer's assistant was fined £10 with £1 2*s* 6*d* costs for imposing a condition of sale where customers who wanted to buy rabbit 'would have to buy something else at the same time' or be refused service. The prosecutor, Mr T. Williams, maintained that the assistant had told a protesting customer, 'I don't care what you do.'

Another greengrocer, of Duncan Street, Brinsworth, was charged £4 for two charges of excess cost for oranges and onions. He was fined 15s costs. A third greengrocer was charged with asking 3s for a rabbit which should have cost 1s 8½d. She tried to defend her actions, stating that she had paid 13s for four rabbits from Sheffield market, but the magistrate was unmoved and ordered her to pay 15s costs. What made the situation more difficult was that many people of the town, now working full time in munitions, had more money than before and so were prepared to pay the higher prices. The 'Observer's Observations' column questioned, 'Do munitions workers push up the prices?' The reporter stated that exorbitant prices were being asked by local businesses for goods which were not rationed. He discussed 'youthful munitions workers with more money in their pockets than they know what to do with purchasing clothing and delectable fruits in front of poor individuals who have to think of the pennies whilst the newly rich, squandering quids, is left looking on.'

Rationing was not immediately brought to an end when it looked like hostilities were about to cease. In January 1945, the butchers of Rotherham, who must have been under pressure from irate householders, took out a piece in the *Advertiser* for the following announcement:

> The butchers of Rotherham regret that supplies of beef are so short that they appear negligible. The fact is the majority of supplies allocated to the Rotherham butchers consist of lamb, mutton and pork. Your sons on the battlefield require the shin beef, not us at home. Take pork and do not grumble, your butcher cannot alter it!

Thankfully for the population of the town, only two months later, in March 1945, rationing was eased. Pictures in the *Advertiser* showed men carrying 'thousands and thousands of bananas arriving in the town'. The reporter stated that out of all the bananas only one was ripe. It was given to 'a young lady who ate it whilst the men looked on enviously.' The remainder were taken to special 'ripening rooms' at Messrs H. Brook Ltd and Messrs Hobkinson & Sons Ltd, before being distributed to the under 18s at the weekend.

With restrictions on food and goods, there were people who tried to stockpile. Such a case came before the bench in July 1942. A hotel owner of Badsley Moor Lane was charged with 'acquiring articles of food in excess of the normal quantity between July 1st 1941 and March 22nd 1942.' She was also charged with obtaining an excess quantity of meat, bacon and ham during the week ending 27 April 1942, and for failing to furnish particulars for the above transactions on 13 May 1942. Town officials visited the Hotel on 29 May and found two large hams in the pantry, weighing 22½lbs and 17½lbs respectively. In the cellar they found the remains of two home-fed flitches of bacon weighing 82lbs, as well as large quantities of tinned food and excess amounts of pickles, salads, dried peas and cereals. There was also a large, unopened 10 stone drum of white flour, as well as an opened part-used one, and thirty-one 1lb packets of self raising flour. When asked who had supplied the extra goods, she refused to tell the officials. They said that her refusal constituted an offence and she replied, 'I am sorry but I can't disclose that.' Her solicitor told the court she had been given the meat by 'a person who thought he was doing her a good turn', and that the meat had been slaughtered legally. He pointed out that the hotel had very large premises and that, until recently, four other adults had also lived there. The extra commodities were acquired for the group of eight people. He also stressed that up to January of the previous year, the landlady's husband had a caterer's license and, therefore, was entitled to keep large supplies of goods. But since then he had decided that catering was not a feasible proposition during wartime and had made no effort to dispose of the supplies. Despite the defence, she was charged a total of £35 in fines.

A female greengrocer of Drummond Street was charged with obtaining milk from someone other than a registered retailer in August 1944. She claimed that the milk was delivered by a Sheffield man employed by the North Midlands Pure Milk Company, who was seen taking a crate of a dozen empty bottles out of her shop on 2 June 1944. The woman admitted to selling small amounts of milk from someone she was not registered with. The Ministry of Food had revoked the license of all retailers supplying milk to less than twenty-six customers when milk rationing was introduced on 29 January 1943. The woman could have appealed if she had felt it was unjust, but she did nothing about it and her eleven registered customers were transferred to another shop. The man supplying the milk told the Food Control official that he had given her the milk, which he had paid for out of his own pocket. He did admit to supplying her with milk on a previous occasion when her husband was home on leave though. The bench imposed fines of £1 for each offence.

One of the most-missed commodities during the war was fresh eggs. Although they could be bought in other forms, fresh eggs were in such demand during the war that people would literally pay any price to get hold of some. A case was brought to court on 19 April 1945, when the owner of a canal barge and a soldier were convicted of stealing three crates of eggs from the Ministry of Food. The eggs had been loaded onto the barge at Hull and three crates containing ninety eggs had been kept back. The men were jointly charged with stealing the eggs, selling them at excess prices and supplying them to people with whom they were not registered. The bargee had unloaded part of the consignmnet of eggs at their Sheffield destination on 5 April. It left on 10 April to go to the Holmes Lock, Rotherham, where the crew stayed the night. They went to a nearby public house, where they found customers and took them to the barge to exchange the stolen eggs for cash. A police sergeant was dispatched to the boat and the bargee told him, 'It's the first time I have touched anything and it is the last.' More eggs were found in a bowl on the barge as well as in an unopened crate. Both men made statements declaring that no documentation had been given when the eggs were loaded and that they had kept three crates back to sell. The bargee had been given 38s 6d by the soldier for his share of the eggs and he expressed his regret, telling the court that he had now lost his job. The soldier told the bench he would not have taken the eggs if he had got his pay from the army. He claimed that he thought anything left over after unloading belonged to the owner of the barge. Both men were fined a total of £28 for the offences, as well as £3 17s 6½d, which was sent to the Ministry of Food for the stolen eggs

During the war years, another black market supplied clothing and other such articles covered by ration books. Fines amounting to £200 were imposed on a husband and wife of Badsley Moor Lane on Thursday, 22 April 1943. The couple were charged with having sold articles of clothing without the surrender of coupons. The male defendant was a commercial traveller and his wife had a hairdressing business. It had come to the police authorities' attention that goods were being sold without coupons. A person from the Board of Trade, Miss Margaret Smith, and a member of the Rotherham Borough Police, Miss Constance Houghton, visited the hairdressers shop. They were taken into the domestic side where they purchased items for which twenty-two coupons should have been surrendered. They made a second visit two days later and bought some utility stockings, for which they paid 12*s* 6*d*. When she was visited by the police, the female defendant stated that she had had the stockings for some years, but it was pointed out to her that the stockings had the utility trademark (a wartime symbol) on the packet. The house was searched and more clothing was found. She told the police that the articles belonged to her husband, who brought them home, and she had nothing to do with it except to charge the amounts for the clothes that her husband instructed her to. The male defendant stated that he had picked up the clothes 'on his travels', but the prosecution, on behalf of the Board of Trade, stated that the husband was aware that many people, having used up their coupons, were prepared to pay heavy prices. Both the husband and wife pleaded 'not guilty'. The woman stated that the business, which was run under her maiden name, had been collecting drapery for eight years. The male defendant said he had not been at the shop at the time of the illegal transactions and therefore was not guilty. However, the magistrates found them both guilty and fined them £50 each on four counts. They were given a month to pay, with the threat of a three-month prison sentence if they refused. The magistrates ordered that all the clothing from the house be confiscated.

Again, as in the First World War, rationing caused terrible queues. The matter of queuing in the town was brought to the fore in May 1941, when everyone, it seems, was complaining about it. Shopkeepers were saying that queues were not only bad for business but lowered morale too. The authorities were concerned that women waiting in queues for hours were 'prone to spread dissatisfaction and sedition'. In a case reported to the Board of Trade in June 1941, a family of six had split up to take their place in different queues and each had got something, 'leading to accusations of gross selfishness'. The board explored ideas such as shops remaining open for longer and the rationing system being extended to cover products such as sweets and tobacco, but no decision was come to.

Another trader complained that if he put something in his shop window that attracted a crowd of people, he would then be charged with obstruction. He suggested that the police should tackle this issue. It was, therefore, resolved that the local authorities would 'take such measures as was necessary to prevent the assembling of queues.' But it was agreed at the next town council meeting that there was very little Rotherham Corporation could do about the matter. Some of the councillors felt that the queues had been brought on by the number of shopkeepers who only remained open while stocks lasted. Another believed it was the fault of, what he termed, 'professional queuers', who did not work and could go from one queue to another getting more than their fair share of food. He pointed out that women and men who worked could not stand in a queue all day and had to be grateful for what they could get. They discussed some recent incidents where shopkeepers had put signs on their door to say that butter or eggs would only be available during a certain time. This made the queuing situation worse. It was felt that the proper distribution of food throughout the country was the only way of solving the matter, and that this was something the National Food Controller should deal with it. There was no resolution to this problem; it only ceased when rationing ended and food was more readily available.

With the majority of men away fighting, it was women who were blamed for the large queues at home. During the Second World War, women took a far more active role in the defence of the town. They had more freedom than in the First World War and the town council was more open to employing them in positions that had been unthinkable in peace time.

# 22

# WOMEN'S WAR

In June 1939, the Mayoress appealed for women to join the ATS (Auxiliary Territorial Service). The campaign began as a joint initiative by the Ministry of Information and the Ministry of Labour. The offices in Westgate, which opened on Monday 28 July, showed photographs of the kind of work the ATS girls could do, and there was a uniform on show. The Mayoress announced that free uniforms would be supplied and stated:

> The army of women will be maintained by its capability, intelligence and integrity. Many Rotherham women and girls are already playing their part in the war effort but I would like more to come forward and offer their services to the country. In fact I consider Rotherham to be second to none in the land and those who can be spared best should be the first to go. Afterwards we can if necessary call on those with other responsibilities.

Councillor J. Rafferty toured the area around Westgate, using a microphone to encourage women to join up. It was reported that a steady stream of volunteers had been going to the offices during the week and, as a result, the 2nd West Riding Company Territorials was formed in June 1939. On Friday 23 June, the newly formed company was inspected by Lady Lawson Tancred in the Drill Hall. As the Chief Commandant of the Auxiliary Territorial Service, Lady Tancred told them it was the first time that women had been privileged to serve in the Territorial Army, pointing out that it was up to them to 'make a success of the job'. She said that the group of twenty-three women needed another thirty to bring the unit up to its required strength. The unit performed a squad drill headed by Mrs Ryder Briggs, to the satisfaction of the trainer, Sergeant Major Thurlow. Despite the will of Lady Tancred, the ATS women at that time were not going into battle. They were, however, used as army cooks, typists and clerks. She told them, 'British Tommies need to be well fed.' Many of the newly formed company attended a military camp over the next few months in order to get practical experience, and as time went on, the women of the ATS were employed as radar operators and on anti-aircraft batteries.

One ATS girl from Rotherham, who had been working in London, got to meet the King and Queen at Buckingham Palace in June 1941. Ellen Buchanan Thompson was working with other ATS girls at the time when the Houses of Parliament were damaged by heavy bombing. The courage and bravery of the girls resulted in the Queen requesting to see some of them at the Palace on Wednesday 4 June. Four of the girls attended. Ellen wrote an excited letter home to her parents, Mr and Mrs James G. Thompson of the Alders, Aldred Street, Rotherham:

> It was the most momentous incident of my life. The Queen chatted to each of us and she asked me of my experiences...Then the King came bounding in wearing an Air Force uniform. He is a wonderful man, full of vim and in high spirits and making fun of our new uniforms. He was not in the least shy but dominated the scene. He is so witty and English. He just 'took the cake'.

Miss Thompson was described as a teleprinter operator attached to the War Office. Strangely, before her letter arrived, her mother, Mrs Thompson, had attended a WVS garden fête in Rotherham and had her fortune told. She was informed that her 'daughter was in the services and would be honoured by Royalty'.

As the numbers of women from the ATS and the Women's Auxiliary Air Force (WAAF) increased in the town, it was decided, in March 1942, that a canteen would be provided solely for their use at the Eastwood Methodist Church schoolrooms. It was reported that the premises had an upstairs games room, which provided writing materials as well as games. The downstairs room was to be the canteen, providing snacks and hot drinks. The church workers had been concerned to recreate a homely atmosphere for these young women. A former Eastwood church minister, Revd J.M. Neilson, who had been invited to the opening, said it was not so much the provision of tea and cakes, but the offer of friendliness and hospitality that young people needed. The Mayor, who opened the canteen, hoped it would offer the hand of fellowship to strangers passing through the town. He expressed the wish that this new spirit of friendship would continue after the war was over.

During the Second World War, women once again demonstrated their suitability for munitions work. In April 1941, it was announced in the local press that women were wanted for war work. A film from the Ministry of Information was shown at the Talbot Lane Methodist Church on Wednesday 9 April, showing the kind of work that women could do in munitions. It was announced that wages would be paid whilst training and a settling-in allowance would be given to women who agreed to work in other districts where board and lodgings were provided. By February 1941, there were so many women working in the munitions factories that the Board of Education announced they would provide nurseries to help with childcare. That same month, a site had been established in Dalton and Thrybergh when the Rural District Council discussed the problem once again. Some of the councillors were against women working and felt that only single women should be employed. The clerk pointed out that many married women were already working in munitions at that time and leaving children in the care of grandmothers and neighbours; some were even left with fourteen-year-old siblings. Government funding was available to provide these nurseries for working mothers, and so the clerk urged the council to ensure that this service was available to eligible families.

The following month, the opening of a new nursery in Maltby was announced. It could 'accommodate 22 toddlers and 18 babies'. Other suitable sites were being sought to provide such nurseries, which were open twenty-four hours a day to enable women to work shifts. By 5 October 1942, three more nurseries had been opened, on Arnold Road, Thames Street and Erskine Road. Alderman W. Dobbie MP opened these nurseries and spoke of the many Rotherham mothers who had patriotically undertaken government training in order to take their place in wartime industry. Alderman Buxton stated:

> The country very urgently needs the services of mothers who are fit to go into the workshops and it is hoped that as a result of nursery provision mothers will respond to the call for their services. The children whilst at the nurseries are in the care of skilled staff many of whom are hospital trained nurses.

Alderman Dobbie expressed hope that this excellent nursery provision would continue after the war. He said that thousands of women were needed for war work and it was the duty of local representatives to provide free places for children to be cared to allow this to happen.

Work in munitions was hard and repetitive, and female munitions workers were praised at the end of the war in April 1945. A gathering had been arranged in order to thank the groups of women who had spent the war working in the three gun shops of Messrs Steel, Peech and Tozer. Councillor F. Davies was invited to the tea and concert for these workers at the Co-operative Café in Rotherham, as an appreciation of the women's war effort. Although their work was no longer necessary, Councillor Davies spoke about the camaraderie amongst the women who had 'put their backs into the production work'. Mr Spafford, a member of the advisory board for the firm, stated emphatically that the women had worked 'during blitzes and black-outs' and had 'never failed at their machines'. Mr Norburn, the manager, said the women had been trained at the Rotherham Technical College and were so highly skilled that Steel, Peech and Tozer had never been behind on any contract. They had 'undertaken work which many other firms believed that women could not do.' He continued, 'With the end of the war in sight many of the women are now employed elsewhere and others have returned back to domestic work.'

Women were not all used in munitions. Upon the announcement of the war, 250 Rotherham women volunteered their services to the WVS. As well as working in the British Restaurants, the WVS were utilised in the many salvage schemes throughout the war. These started in September 1941. People of Yorkshire were asked to comb their homes and attics for newspapers, metal, bones, rags, old books and newspapers, that could be recycled to reduce imports of raw materials. The WVS was in charge of the collection of essential materials, which were then picked up by council lorries and transported to a central point. The scheme was very successful. In the first year, Mr Pickles, the clerk to the Rural District Council, informed the board that the total salvage collection to date amounted to £2,519. In April 1942, surveys were undertaken in the districts to assess what unnecessary railings and metal gates could be used for scrap. The public were asked to 'prepare for the same sacrifice and inconvenience – small in comparison with the sacrifice of our Fighting Forces – that have already been made in hundreds of towns.'

Later that month, it was announced that during January 1942, the total collection of waste paper in the town had been 143 tons 8 cwts. The lists of local firms' own salvage collections were printed in the local newspaper, as firms would vie with each other to beat the targets. That month, the total amount of 15 tons 18 cwts had been collected by the WVS and Rotherham Corporation; Messrs J.J. Habershon Ltd had gathered 6 tons 4 cwts, and three other firms had contributed over a ton each. Other collectors that contributed to this figure were scouts, schools and the *Rotherham Advertiser* itself.

Practically nothing was wasted in wartime, and in October 1943 the WVS was involved in the 'Shirts off to Berlin' campaign. The Ministry of Information told readers of the *Advertiser* that old shirts or any old rags, if properly salvaged, may end up as a map, a bombing chart, part of a soldier's uniform, a sailor's blanket or the padding for the seat of a tank. Housewives were advised to:

> Salvage every scrap of cloth
> Save even old household cloths and dusters remembering oily rags are needed as well as clean ones
> Keep them all with old sacking and string for salvage collection

By November 1943, a review of the work that the WVS had been engaged in during the war was outlined. It seems that the woman of Rotherham had been very busy. Mrs I. Habershon JP, who was the centre organiser for the WVS, thanked the women for their efforts and stated that although many of its members were on standby until an emergency occurred they were 'not resting on their laurels'. She announced a demonstration to take place later that month in the Assembly Rooms, to show the work of the WVS.

The women of the WVS organised knitting and sewing clubs, mobile canteens, a Food Advisory Bureau, war savings, housewives' services, clothing exchanges, basic training lectures, make do and mend classes, salvage schemes, emergency car pools and vitamin distribution. Regular garden parties were held throughout 1943, raising money for rest centres, furniture for troops situated in the districts and sewing and knitting clubs making items for soldiers at the front. Almost £1,000 had been raised that year from 1 January to the end of October, allowing the WVS to make donations to the Red Cross Prisoners' Comfort Fund, the Merchant Navy Fund, Lady Cripps' Aid to China Fund and Mrs Churchill's Aid to Russia Fund. There was also a Toy Exchange scheme. This scheme collected toys for those children who were underprivileged during wartime. Mrs Habershon told the members that her own aunt, aged eighty-five, had made a bed with a doll in it from bits and pieces around the house. She paid tribute to the work done on the domestic front in Rotherham. For the first time, she said, women were taking their place in the wartime activities of the town. There were at that time thirty-four rest centres in the town and the districts and sixteen emergency meal centres, all in readiness and staffed by the women of the WVS. It seems that the reason for the success of these schemes was the enthusiasm and efficiency of the organiser, Mrs Habershon, and the approach of the housewives of Rotherham and districts, with their 'it all depends on me' attitude. After the war, the work of the WVS continued and in 1956, Queen Elizabeth II became its patron. In 1966 the WVS was given the honour of having 'Royal' added in its title.

Many Rotherham women decided that they would undertake war work in the Land Army. The Land Army had been formed during the First World War to replace the millions of men no longer working on the land. In September 1939, it was announced that the very first land girl, Miss Jean Worrall of Doncaster Road, had completed her fortnight's training and was ready for service. The *Advertiser* reported that another girl, Miss Lewis of Wentworth, who had almost completed her training, was also expected to be ready to start her service soon. Both girls had been taught by a Mrs Landon, who recruited the girls before training them. Mrs Landon told reporters that both girls would soon be placed on farms. For her training, Miss Worrall had been sent to a relative's farm in Devonshire. Although working on important war work, Land Army girls had to pay their own way and she told reporters that Miss Worrall would pay board and lodging to the farmer, which was estimated to be around 15s a week, although some farmers were charging only 10s. Both girls would shortly have their uniform of green jerseys and brown breeches supplied, and she announced that another fifty recruits were undertaking training for the South Yorkshire area. Miss Worrall told the reporter that during her training, she had milked cows, sterilised milking equipment, hoed turnips, cleaned out the cow house, driven sheep to market and learned how to ride a horse. By the end of the war, Britain was less dependent on overseas supplies for food, thanks to the effort of these Land Army girls. The service was not completely abandoned until 1950, when food supplies improved.

Around this time a discussion took place in the council chamber about whether woman could be employed as police officers. On Wednesday, 2 July 1941, one of the councillors, Mrs Green, asked the Watch Committee to reconsider their previous decision not to use women in such a capacity. She pointed out that female police officers could be much more effective when working with woman and children than male officers. It seems that Alderman Hall had already been having discussions about this matter with the Chief Constable, who assured him that many women could be used as clerical and administration workers within the police force. However, he was unsure as to whether they could be used on patrol, and so referred the matter back to the Watch Committee for a decision to be made the following week. It would seem that Rotherham Watch Committee was hesitant; it was not until May 1944 that female police officers were appointed, following a communication from the Home Secretary, Mr Herbert Morrison. It has to be said that the decision finally taken by the Watch Committee was not a popular one and it was certainly not unanimous. However, the recommendation was ratified and 'women in blue' were soon to be seen on the streets of the town.

Despite the fears of the Watch Committee, it seems that women were considered very capable of driving, and four women were appointed as mail-van drivers in September 1941. Although it seems derisible now, the scheme was said to be one of the first initiatives of its kind in the country. The postmaster had little option and had been forced to appoint female drivers when almost 100 of his workers had joined the forces. Of the pre-war staff of thirty-five clerks, only five were still working and temporary female clerks took their turn at the public counter.

The question of women drivers had been discussed at a council meeting on Wednesday, 13 August 1941, when it was decided that a female chauffeur could be appointed for the official cars. The same month, Alderman Caine questioned whether suitably trained women might be able to drive single-deck vehicles. It was pointed out to him that this was more of a possibility as women were now driving heavy vehicles in the army. In November 1941, it was reported that Rotherham had the first female trackless bus drivers in Britain. Within a week, three fully trained women were regularly driving buses during the blackout. The girls, named as Mary Bacon, aged twenty-seven of 118 Coleridge Road, Winifred Mary Jennison, aged twenty-five of 14 Broom Grove and Winifred May Hallam also twenty-five of 5 Fisher Street, had all passed the driving test with flying colours. They had previously been employed as conductresses and had gone on to study to take their driving tests. The official handing over of their driving certificates was undertaken on Thursday, 13 November 1941 at the Transport Department, by Major F.S. Eastwood, the deputy transport manager. The manager, Mr Sykes, praised the girls and said that they were undertaking a very important service. If there were no buses to take the munitions workers to their place of work then essential war work could not have been done.

Despite the fact that women were proving their worth, it was not only the town councillors who were hesitant to give women more control. Heated discussions took place at the Rotherham Borough Court on Thursday, 8 January 1942, following an application made for the transfer of a public house license to the widow of a former licensee. The Chief Constable would only sanction the application providing that men would be on hand 'to assist if possible'. The licensee, Mrs Elizabeth A. Tyrrell of the Foljambe Arms, Eastwood, objected when the Chief Constable said the pub was in a 'rough district'. Mrs Tyrrell told the bench that she disagreed with the remarks made by the Chief Constable and that she was quite capable of turning anyone out of the pub who misbehaved. Mr E. Twigg, who appeared for Mrs Tyrrell, informed him:

Women are doing magnificent work for the country and are taking part in its defence. It rather non-plusses me to think that a woman who has spent her life in the management of various hotels can not manage one in 1942. Two sons aged 36 and 39 will assist Mrs Tyrrell in the conduct of the business and the staff have been at that house for many years.

Still hesitant, the court ordered that a temporary license was granted to her. Along with Mrs Tyrrell, Ada Hutchinson of the Cutlers Arms, Westgate, and Emily Cooper of the Horse and Tiger Inn, Thorpe Hesley, both gained temporary licenses. These small victories for women resulted in the license of the Cinema House on Doncastergate being transferred to Barbara E. Simpson, but only, once again, on the understanding that male assistance would be on hand if required.

Women proved their worth once again during the Second World War, taking on more and more responsibility, despite the doubts of male councillors. The misogynistic attitudes of some were echoed by the Police Courts, which expressed a view that women should be confined to the domestic sphere. Some believed that working women were responsible for the rise of what became known as juvenile delinquency.

# 23

# JUVENILE DELINQUENCY

In March 1941, a huge rise in juvenile crime in the town was noted. Magistrates put forward several theories to explain it; missing fathers and mothers, who were out at work leaving young people unattended, was identified as a key reason. One unnamed young man, aged fourteen, went on a mini crime spree, starting at an approved school in Northumberland and ending in Rotherham. The boy had been caught stealing 30s from the till of a shop on Effingham Street. He had stolen from the shop previously and was caught and taken into custody when he foolishly returned to the premises. He told the police he had run away from the approved school on 11 February 1941, where he had been sent after absconding several times from reform school. He had stolen from shops in Newcastle and Barnsley, and with the proceeds had bought himself a suit, shoes and a shirt. He also admitted stealing a watch from Mexborough.

The magistrates tried to put themselves in the mind set of these young people, in order to discover the reasons for their petty crimes. When this boy was asked why he had committed the offences, he could give no reason. Detective Inspector Thompson told the court that the boy had twice been birched and on one occasion, when Leeds police were trying to arrest him, he struggled so much that he had to be handcuffed. Sent back to the approved school, he escaped again and was brought before the Rotherham magistrates a week later. Once again, he was escorted back to the approved school, after being kept in a police cell until his escort arrived.

The same month, a case of theft was heard in the Rotherham courthouse. This involved three girls, aged ten, eleven and twelve years of age. The eleven-year-old girl had two charges of stealing money and goods brought against her and the other two were also charged with stealing goods. The twelve-year-old girl was also thought to have been involved in the theft of money. When asked what they had spent the money on, the girls admitted that it had been spent on sweets, chips and chocolate. The eleven-year-old girl appeared to be the ringleader, although she denied this. The ten year old was dismissed on a promise of good behaviour and the older two were put on probation and ordered to pay 7s 6d costs. The *Advertiser* reported on the careful way young people were dealt with in the Juvenile Courts:

All young people who are brought to the court are treated with great care in accordance with the Children and Young Persons Act of 1938.

No uniforms are in evidence as the police wear civilian clothing.

The magistrates themselves are usually a man and a woman who question the children carefully and gently.

The children are kept with their parents in a room outside the courtroom until they are needed to appear before the magistrates.

The probation officer, Miss Butterworth, was asked why she thought there had been such a rise in juvenile delinquency during the war years. She told the magistrates that, in her opinion, it was to do with absent fathers – the family member who exerted the most control. She also suggested that the numbers of juvenile delinquents would diminish if parents co-operated with her, instead of viewing her with suspicion and behaving defensively.

On 15 March 1941, a further case was brought in front of the magistrates. An eleven-year-old boy had killed a puppy by throwing a stone at it. His mother was in court and she told the magistrates that he was fond of dogs and that his father had told him if he did such a thing again he would 'have him sent away'. The magistrate remonstrated with her, stating that it would have been better for the boy's father to have punished him at the time instead of bringing the case before the bench. He said, 'No one seems to think about corporal punishment these days.' The boy was fined £1 and ordered to pay 5s for the cost of the puppy.

Another incorrigible case, reported in the *Advertiser* the same week, was of a boy aged fifteen who had led a steady life of crime. He had been living with a man who had convictions for indecent acts with young boys. The boy admitted to stealing 12s from him. When it was reported to the police, they found him about to board a train to Scotland. He was arrested and £22 was found on him. He also admitted to breaking into Aston Church on two occasions and stealing from the offertory box. The magistrate said the boy had chosen to pursue a life of crime and that they had no option but to send him to an approved school. But the magistrate was in for a shock when the clerk informed him that all approved and reform schools of the West Riding were full. Unbelievably, the boy was detained in Armley Jail until an appropriate place could be found for him.

By the beginning of May 1942, the question of what to do with juvenile criminals was pressing. Rotherham magistrates instructed the clerk to write to the Home Office to ask that more approved schools be established. Councillor Brook and Councillor Moorhouse had that same week tried a case of a twelve-year-old boy, who on Wednesday 30 April was brought up on a charge of stealing a bicycle. As there was no accommodation for him, they had been forced to return him home. The magistrates pointed out that there was another boy who had been waiting for a place at an approved school since March, who was also still at home with his parents. The magistrates, in their frustration with the lack of reform schools, ordered young people to be birched in August 1942.

A ten-year-old boy, who had appeared before Councillor Brooke on Wednesday 5 August, had stolen a 10s note from a shop on Badsley Moor Lane. He admitted to another theft committed less than a month previously, when the magistrate had warned he would be birched if he appeared in court again. He was ordered to have four strokes of the birch.

A letter to the editor of the *Advertiser* stated that there were 'thousands of readers who had clenched their teeth' after reading about this case, but pointed out that the magistrates had little option. The boy had been warned previously and the writer believed the birching would 'have more effect than sending him to an approved school'.

When yet another boy aged fifteen, who admitted to stealing six bicycles since 22 May 1942, was ordered to go to an approved school, one of the court officials had to remind the magistrate that there were no places available. Councillor Brook told him that the situation placed the magistrates in a very difficult position; the youths would either have to be sent home or go to prison. The boy's father promised to keep the boy at home until a remand home could be found for him. The magistrate told the father that if the boy appeared there again, he would be sent to prison, and remarked:

> I don't mind if there is criticism or not. The time has come when somebody has to put this right. It seems to me the magistrates' position is a ridiculous one. We come and try to carry out our duties but we cannot do anything and we might as well not come to court. There ought to be places provided: it is a short sighted policy somewhere.

The following month, three young boys had to be sent home as there was no room for them anywhere else. The magistrate, Mrs E. Slack, told the Borough Court, 'We are now at our wits end to know how to deal with this wave of juvenile crime in the Borough. Parents are working in many cases and children seem to be allowed to do just what they like.' After warning the boys, who had all been accused of theft, that they would be birched if they appeared before the court again, they were sent home to their parents.

The Rotherham and District Christian Council blamed the increase of delinquency on the fact that young people were working in local industries and, consequently, had more money, which they spent on alcohol. They condemned the sale of alcohol to young people in a resolution made at their meeting in the Doncaster Road Congregational Church on Thursday, 19 March 1942. They had 'grave concerns' about young people being exposed to 'the pernicious evils of drink'. They made the statement, 'We humbly request that those responsible for selling alcohol to these young people to diminish the temptations and as far as possible to respect the temperance principles of our young folk.'

The Rotherham Education Committee blamed the indulgent parents of these delinquents, once again stating that many parents were working and, therefore, had less time to control their children. At a meeting on Wednesday, 5 August 1942, the town council discussed the fact that parents who had been brought before the courts were very aware of the kind of control needed for their children, but refused to exert it. Councillor Davies said juvenile delinquency was not just an issue for Rotherham; it was a nationwide problem and very little could be done if parents refused to co-operate. Councillor Barker spoke about the spate of vandalism in some of the cemeteries around the town, where flowers and ribbons had been stolen. He had heard cases of ribbons from wreaths being worn by girls in the town within a couple of hours of the burial.

In October 1942, yet another thirteen-year-old boy was brought before the Juvenile Court. He was reportedly 'out of control'. The boy had been before the bench in July on charges of theft and the magistrates at that time had wanted to send him to an approved school, but as before there were no places available for him. On Wednesday, 30 September 1942, the boy had twice visited a seventy-five-year-old pensioner along with two different twelve-year-old accomplices. On the first occasion, he had stolen 7s 3½d and on the second occasion a purse and 3s in cash. He had also sold the old man some tobacco, which the police believed he had stolen from local shops. Once again, the magistrates in this case did not know what to do with him; they were reluctant to send him to prison. The magistrate's clerk stated that at long last an approved school was being built by the West Riding County Council, but there would not be places available for a year. They discussed whether the boy was to be birched, but decided instead to adjourn the case for a fortnight in the hope that a place could be found somewhere for this boy. The problem of birching was raised once again when a new magistrate, Alderman Dickenson, was welcomed onto the bench on Thursday, 12 November 1942. He stated that it was:

> ...repugnant for any magistrate to inflict severe punishment on children but I assure you that in some of the cases coming before the juvenile courts the magistrates are absolutely at their wits end to know what to do with them. If the people who criticised really knew the true facts of the cases they would not be so severe in the condemnation of the justices. I want to assure the public that everyone coming before this court will have a fair and square deal.

The following year, there seems to have been more approved school accommodation available. Two nine-year-old boys were brought before the magistrates and both were sent to different approved schools. The boys, while still on probation, had broken into the re-winding room of a Rotherham cinema in August 1943 and stolen boxes containing seven films, with a total value of £13 5s. It seems that they stole for the fun of it, as several of the films were later found in the river, whilst others were found on a bus. One of the boys, whose parents had reportedly 'disappeared', was known to be the ring leader. His father had given him 10s and, in order to get rid of him, had sent him to his friend in Rotherham. On Monday, 8 August 1943, the boys were allowed out and stole the films from the cinema, breaking in through a ground-floor window. The films that had been in water were unusable and the cinema manager was forced to borrow films to be shown.

Finally, in the latter stages of the war, two boys aged ten and eight were brought before the bench on Wednesday, 29 August 1945, when the magistrates once again stated that they were 'at a loss as to what course to take'. The boys had been charged with setting fire to a stack belonging to farmer, Charles Osbourne, at the Eldon Road land settlement the previous week. Mr Osbourne told the bench that the first he knew of it was when he saw a man chasing the two boys and shouting to him 'your stacks are on fire and these two boys have done it.' He saw the stacks were in flames and called out the fire brigade. The stacks were uninsured and, as a consequence, there had been £30 to £40 worth of damage. Detective Inspector Thompson told the magistrate that since then, the ten-year-old boy had been seen driving a car out of the fire brigade car park on St Ann's Road, before getting out of the vehicle and running away. Councillor Brookes, the presiding magistrate, incredulously asked, 'Can he really drive a car?' 'Oh yes,' said the Inspector, 'he has 28 different charges brought against him.' Even his parents begged that he be sent away. The magistrate told the court that he had just that week written to the Home Office about establishing a special school for delinquent children. The boys were remanded in custody for a medical examination before a decision was made as to what to do with them.

Matters seemed to ease gradually as war conditions came to an end. On 3 August 1946, it was reported that there were fewer delinquents appearing before the magistrates. The court recorder felt that it might be the result of fathers returning back from the forces. However, this was an oversimplified view, as we know today that many single-parent families successfully manage their children's behaviour. Undoubtedly, the strains of working full time and looking after children did affect family life, but there was little research done at the time on the impact that warfare aggression and the American gangster films had on the minds of young people.

# 24

# THE BEGINNING OF THE END

Indications that the war might be coming to an end came about early in September 1944, when it was announced that blackout restrictions were to be eased in Rotherham. Reported to be one of the 'most welcome decisions of the war', the blackout ceased along with night and day fire watch duties, Home Guard duties and compulsory training. It was reported that, although duties were suspended, 'In the resumption of enemy attacks, instructions to resume full Fire Guard duties would be issued.' Ten months later, Rotherham welcomed arrangements to switch on street lighting along the main streets of the town. In July 1945, it was announced that a great 'switch on' was due to take place on Monday 16 July, to which no doubt a great crowd would have assembled. It was noted that for many young children it would have been exciting to watch, as many had never seen lights on the streets before.

Rotherham had been extremely lucky regarding air-raid casualties during the Second World War. Attacks on nearby Sheffield had been much more severe: a total of over 600 people killed and more than 40,000 homes damaged. In fact, there had only been two serious raids on Rotherham and, terrifying though they were, casualties were very low.

The very first air raid took place on Monday, 19 August 1940, when two people were killed. Several families also had to be re-housed due to bomb damage in the area of Armer Street. It seems that no warning was given for what was to happen. People were preparing to go to bed when the sound of an aeroplane and the whistling of a bomb were heard. Thankfully, the bombs fell on a limited area. However, a sixty-year-old watchman and another unnamed male victim were killed. Survivors found doors and windows of their houses blasted off, with plaster and soot everywhere. Many of the houses were uninhabitable and the families were taken to the first-aid post. On the following morning, 200 people were found at a feeding station and temporary accommodation was obtained for them. Some of the other bombed houses were not in such a bad state and the families elected to remain in them. It was reported that one of the bombs had made a crater 5ft wide and 5ft deep. This had fractured a gas main. Half a mile away, windows of shops and houses were damaged and it was reported, 'In the capricious nature of bombs it is noted that two out of three windows have been damaged and in other areas it is every alternative window which is damaged.'

But the spirit of local people was high as they joked with ARP workers in their shattered homes. Stories of the townspeople and how they survived the raid began to be told. One lucky

Bombed out houses on a street in Masbrough.

Cleaning up after an air raid on the British Oxygen works on Monday, 19 August 1940.

survivor was a deaf man, who had not heard the plane until his wife ran outside and dragged him back into the house, just before a close explosion was heard. Another man spoke of sitting in his chair in front of the fire, when he was suddenly blown across the room. Before he could get out of his chair, he was covered in plaster and soot falling on his head. A reporter who visited the scene the following morning spoke of damaged houses in which the wirelesses were still playing even though the furniture was overturned.

Most of the damage was to a row of cottages near to the explosion site. Police and ARP wardens attended promptly and fire-fighting squads turned out too, although they were not needed. Residents of the badly damaged properties had gone to live with relatives or friends and others had been re-housed. Those who chose to remain in their damaged properties made the best of it they could.

A few days later, in a second attack, bombs were dropped in the area of Ferham Road and one hit the railway line from Masbrough to the Holmes Station. German planes could be seen clearly in the skies over Rotherham on the night of Thursday 22 August and the early hours of Friday, 24 August 1940. Although the area was quite heavily populated, many of the bombs were dropped onto open country and the only casualties of this raid were three horses. Damage was caused to some farm outbuildings and many windows were shattered as a result of the blast. One of the enemy planes was seen to drop two bombs, but was quickly chased off by anti-aircraft guns. Another bomber came in low and dropped the bomb which killed the horses. A patrolling fighter plane spotted him in the searchlight and attacked. Machine guns were heard, but the watchers on the ground were unable to distinguish what was happening. Two more planes were seen, but they were also chased off by gun fire.

On Thursday, 29 August 1940, a more serious air raid took place during the early hours of the morning. Several people were injured, some of them quite seriously. Once again, the target was Masbrough, in the same area around Ferham Road, and the railway line at Holmes. The first bomb landed on an industrial office, where the caretaker, his wife and their fifteen-year-old son were sheltering in the strong room. All were uninjured, but they were forced to draw the attention of the AFS as they were unable to escape due to the debris around them.

The railway line itself was undamaged, but some windows had been broken in the signal box. A gas main had been fractured and caught fire, but was quickly brought under control by the fire service. The sense of humour which is often found in Yorkshire folk appeared to be undiminished. An elderly couple was found sat by their fireside, unfazed by the damage. When the police enquired if they were alright, the man told him, 'Ay but we shan't have to have our chimney swept. Hitler's swept it for us.'

Another woman whose house had been damaged wondered if she would have to pay rent that week as she had spent most of her time in the shelter. A bomb fell 3ft from a brick and concrete shelter, blowing off the heavy roof, but the seven people inside were fine, apart from bruises caused by flying bricks. A man sitting in his chair heard the bomb and dived under a table. The door flew off its hinges, but he was safe, as was a baby in its cot underneath the shattered window. A reporter from the *Advertiser* praised the co-ordination of the ARP and AFS, which shows that the practice drills had had a good effect. Damage had been inflicted on a nearby fish and chip shop and the owner had just sighed when he surveyed the damage. He told the reporter that he had never had such a shaking. The most destruction happened to a greyhound track. A man and two women had taken shelter in the club premises, but were unharmed. In a less populated section of the town, a crater 60ft in width and 15ft deep was caused by a bomb. The explosion threw up several pieces of Roman pottery, an indication that the area had a Roman encampment nearby.

The longest night of bombing occurred on Thursday, 12 December 1940, when the town was pounded for nine and a half hours. Householders heard anti-aircraft gunfire for all that time. Many incendiary bombs were dropped, but were dealt with quickly by householders before the emergency services could attend. More bombs were dropped on a cricket ground and a park, but they did no damage here at all. A house belonging to a medical man was set on fire, but the fire service had it under control very quickly. Several people escaped injury from shrapnel and a 'well known resident and officer of the Home Guard' escaped injury when a piece of jagged metal pierced the car he was driving. The enemy aircraft returned in daylight on Sunday 15 December and attacked so vigorously that many people believed that the town was under serial bombardment. Thankfully, in the morning it was found that no explosive bombs had been dropped on the town. The noise was mainly caused by the terrific anti-aircraft barrage against enemy aircraft intent on bombing the nearby town of Sheffield. It was later reported that an enemy plane had been shot down onto the city allotments. The air crew escaped by parachute and an immediate hunt for these men was organised. Two more German aircrew escaped from their aeroplanes and were hunted outside the city. Raiders returned over Rotherham on Tuesday afternoon, 17 December 1940, and a German plane was observed over the town, moving in a westerly direction. Three spitfires chased after the enemy plane, which was later rumoured to have been shot down.

The last air raid took place in daylight on 3 August 1942, a Bank Holiday. Many people of the town saw the Nazi aeroplane, with the swastika on its side, come out of the clouds and drop a stick of four bombs. One bomb exploded over the school playing field of the Municipal High School, whilst a second exploded in Clifton Park, near to a theatre erected for the 'Holidays from Home' scheme. As the event hadn't started, there were very few people in the park at the time. If the event had been in full swing, there would probably have been many more casualties. There was a near miss when a family, which was unable to reach their air-raid shelter, had stayed in the house. One of the bombs landed on the shelter, causing slight damage to it and the house. Anti-aircraft guns attacked the enemy plane, which was reported to have soon left the area. Only ten people were injured and one was from the Home Guard, Captain L. Sylvester. The others were civilians and amongst them were Alice Wilkinson aged twenty-six, James Storey aged seventeen, Vera Harper and James Pickering, both aged twenty.

In the town council of October 1944, when Peace Celebrations were anticipated, the costs were counted. It was announced that in Rotherham there had been 130 air-raid alerts sounded, although not all of those resulted in an air raid. In 1940, in what was thought to be the worst month, there were fifty-five alerts; in 1941 there were forty-nine. In September 1940 the alert only sounded twenty-two times, but in one night there were four air-raid warnings. The reality of it was that Rotherham had escaped relatively unscathed from the bombing. The Nazis had tended to concentrate on the more industrialised city of Sheffield.

Slowly, as the town returned to normal, more and more news was heard about the return of prisoners of war. It was reported that there was great joy for a Maltby family when they heard that driver John Coope was returning to his home at Cavendish Place, Maltby. He had gone to join his unit on 8 March 1940 and his mother had not seen him since. Mrs Collins was duly notified that her son had been captured after the evacuation at Dunkirk and was in a German prison camp. Exactly five years later, on 8 March 1945, she heard a rumour that the Russian Army had freed the prisoners from the camp. The story was verified by her daughter, Mrs Mary Harris, who had read a report on Tuesday 13 March that the freed former prisoners were waiting for transport home 'at a Black Sea port'. A reporter was sent to interview Mrs Collins and she told him she hoped that her son would be back for his birthday on 12 May, as she was having a birthday cake made for him. Flags and decorations were collected to welcome him home. Another Rotherham woman heard her husband announce on Russian radio that he had been released and was returning home to Byron Road, Maltby. In the broadcast, Corporal Cyril Jackson said to his wife, Catherine:

> Hello darling. This is a big surprise for you. I was released by the Russian Army two weeks ago and am now at Odessa on my way home. I would like to relate my experiences of how I was released. I was working in a hospital in a prison in Germany looking after sick and wounded men who had been left behind by the Germans. The able bodied had been marched away a few days before. I am very much looking forward to seeing you all. Love to everyone at home. Your loving husband Cyril

Another returning prisoner did not wait for release by the Russians, but escaped from a prison camp in Poland, where he had been held captive for four and a half years. Thirty-five-year-old Sergeant 'Jock' Wadsworth arrived back in the town on Easter Monday, 1945 to find a real Yorkshire welcome waiting for him from his wife, friends and relations. He had been captured at St Valerie in 1940 and had been kept at a prison camp at Thorne in Poland ever since. On 23 January 1944, he and a friend from Leeds named Preston escaped. They went through Poland and found the Polish people to be very friendly. They witnessed the bomb damage inflicted in Warsaw, where few buildings were left unscathed. In Russia, they found great confidence in the Russian people, whose motto was 'Berlin or Bust'. Sergeant Wadsworth told a reporter, 'This is all the Russians are living for.' He would not speak of his time in the prison camp, but he talked about the arrogance of his captors, who slowly diminished in number as Britain held out and when America joined the war. By the time of his escape, the morale of the German people was very low. Although he refused to elaborate, he told the reporter that the prisoners had their own way of hearing the news, and when it was announced that the D-Day landings had taken place, there had been great rejoicing amongst the prisoners.

The nation as a whole was determined to celebrate peace. It was announced that Victory over Europe celebrations were to take place in Rotherham on Tuesday, 8 May 1945, the day after the military surrender of Germany. Flags and bunting were gathered and the events were reported in the *Advertiser* of 12 May 1945. Effigies of Hitler had been burnt and strung up around the town and even the torrential rain that hit the town early afternoon could not dampen the spirits of the people. The parish church was lit up as dusk arrived and illuminations were seen at the Old Town Hall, which attracted many people. Flags of many countries were also on display at the Town Hall, including China, Australia, New Zealand, Russia, Holland and Belgium. A huge 'V' for Victory was lit up from the College of Technology, casting its light over College Square. Music was played on outside

Dvr. J. Coope.

Driver Coope, who had been released from a prison of war camp by the Russian Army.

speakers in All Saints Square on Tuesday and couples danced around the buses and cars on the street. A reporter standing on the clock tower observed 'thousands of people attending the service of Thanksgiving held by the Bishop of Sheffield.' He said, 'The numbers were so high that many spilled over to an outside service relayed by speakers placed in the square.' Hearty singing of hymns was heard until 9 p.m., when a transmission of the sound of Big Ben, preceding the King's speech, was broadcast. Hats were removed and heads bowed as the people of Rotherham listened to His Majesty's speech to his people. The King spoke to the nation from the war-torn Buckingham Palace, giving thanks for the end of hostilities but warning that Japan had yet to be defeated. Music was then transmitted from the BBC and dancing in the square went on until midnight. On Wednesday night, illuminated trolley buses parked in the square and dance music was played once again.

An effigy of Hitler strung up during the VE celebrations.

Celebrating crowds in All Saints Square, where dancing went on until midnight.

Peace Celebration in Clifton Park.

Just one of the hundreds of street parties which were held in May 1945.

Victory peals were rung from St Stephen's Church, Eastwood by a band of ringers led by Mr A.W. Measures, on Tuesday 8 May and again on the morning of Wednesday 9 May. Other peals were heard across the district, including Kimberworth, Masbrough and Greasbrough. On Sunday 13 May, another Thanksgiving church service was to be held, followed by a civic parade in the afternoon at Clifton Park. The procession started at the fairground on Main Street at 2.30 p.m., and a salute was taken at the cenotaph. Another service of Thanksgiving was held in the park and Alderman S. Hall extended the gratitude of the town to the civil defence services and to the hundreds of munitions workers who had been invited. A special film of the week's ceremonies was made by the Regal cinema and was shown throughout the week. The reporter from the *Advertiser* announced that the newspaper had been invited to hundreds of street parties for children and had to turn them down. Almost every street in the town held their own street party, the children and adults no doubt very thankful for the war being over.

More celebrations were held again for VJ day (Victory over Japan) on Wednesday, 15 August 1945, following a midnight announcement. More street parties were held and flags and bunting appeared once again, flooding the town with colour. The *Advertiser* listed some of the treats which had been organised to celebrate the victory. These included bonfires, donkey rides and a victory party on a barge. The reporter commented that the women of the town had done a great job in feeding the children. At a time when rationing was still being endured, no one was stinting themselves with the refreshments.

Messages from families whose sons had been in the war were chalked on walls and doorways of homes to greet the returning soldiers. It was reported that 'more fires were seen in the town than previously and more fireworks were also in evidence.' The church was illuminated once more and the 'Victory' sign on the College of Technology reappeared. The parish church bells were rung in the morning and evening and the doors of most churches were thrown open during the day for private prayer. Once again, there was an open-air service of Thanksgiving in Clifton Park, where the Mayor, Councillor H. Lake, spoke of the terrible price for peace that the world had to pay, in the form of the atom bomb. Prayers were said and the service finished with a rendition of 'Jerusalem'. The King's speech was once again relayed. He gratefully thanked the nation for 'the great task that has been accomplished'. He also requested that Sunday 19 August be Thanksgiving Day and it was arranged that dignitaries of the town would parade from the Town Hall to the church for a service. The crowds assembled in All Saints Square, where, after a short delay, the illuminated trolley bus arrived and groups of people danced to the music it provided.

This was the story of the impact of war on a South Yorkshire town. No doubt as people counted the cost in 1945, they were reminded of the hundreds of dead soldiers who would not return to the town of their birth. There was a great sense of community in the town. Living through the war years was difficult on many levels, with food shortages, fear of air raids and the outbreak of juvenile delinquency, which continued to be a menace during later years. The majority of local people spent their time living as best as they could, whilst others turned to crime and the black market. Yet, there is no doubt that through the columns of

Children of the town at the VJ celebrations.

*Right*: A VJ barge party for almost 300 adults and children.

*Below left*: The children, more interested in the camera than the refreshments on the barge.

Some of the hundreds of people who attended the open-air service of Thanksgiving in Clifton Park in August 1945.

the *Rotherham Advertiser*, the townspeople pulled together to survive the war and joyfully return to peace.

This book has barely touched upon the thousands of stories of how Rotherham people survived the war and the accounts of the returning heroes. Many of these stories remain unrecorded, and it is imperative that they are captured before they escape from living memory. This has been my own small attempt to share some of them and to relive, however briefly, the experiences of some of the townsfolk.